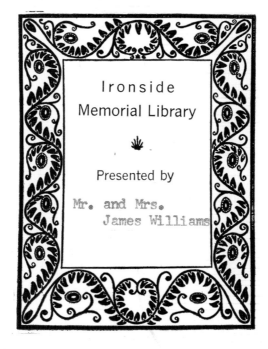

THE WORLD OF MISSION

THE
WORLD OF MISSION

by

BENGT SUNDKLER

*Professor of Church History
and Missions at Uppsala University
formerly Bishop in Bukoba, Tanzania*

WM. B. EERDMANS PUBLISHING COMPANY
GRAND RAPIDS, MICHIGAN 49502

25742

CONTENTS

*The Revised Standard Version of the Bible
has been followed in quotations*

FOREWORD

THE great surveys of the history of Christian missions by modern writers such as K. S. Latourette and S. C. Neill provide an invaluable framework for the understanding of the growth of the Church throughout the centuries. This book approaches "the world of mission" from a slightly different angle. The historical account has been reduced to a brief section centring on the problem of missions and politics. Otherwise the main emphasis is on the *ecological* aspect: the milieu in which the Church has to live, and the interchange between Church and milieu.

This book on the Christian mission represents an attempt to come to terms with the specific problems posed by the study of missions. In most other theological subjects the teacher has a body of relatively well-known parallels and associations on which to draw. Thus, to take only one example, general church history can, and indeed must, be linked with the geography, political history, history of literature and art history of Western Europe. This support is largely lacking in connexion with the study of missions. The Western student of missions is faced with the difficult task of mastering such unfamiliar backgrounds as the religions and cultures of the Orient and Africa. But the task is unavoidable for anyone who would study missions with a full measure of understanding.

This book concentrates on three main problems, or groups of problems: first, the biblical basis and theology of mission; secondly, a historical review, concentrating on the problem of Church and State, or missions and politics; and finally, a section in which the young churches are

7

viewed against the background of their respective religio-historical and social milieus.

This approach has inevitably led to a revision of traditional priorities. For instance, we are not particularly concerned to describe the missionary societies of the eighteenth and nineteenth centuries; there are more important things in the history of missions. Nor have we followed the traditional missionary grand tour, from country to country in Asia and Africa. There are far too many countries to visit, and their number is steadily increasing! We have instead tried to stress that we are here dealing with missions and churches in two main types of mileu: in the "animist" tribal milieu, and in the milieu of the great religions of Asia. In the former case we occasionally meet with tribal and folk churches which are relatively dominant; in the latter, Christians are often no more than a tiny minority. This comparison and contrast is by no means without its special significance.

An approach of this kind has furthermore made the omission of many intrinsically interesting problems inevitable. Thus it has not proved possible to carry out a planned comparison between the problems confronting the Christian mission in the West and those facing missions in the Orient and Africa. The current problem of the relationship between mission and 'Inter-Church Aid' is another which we have had to leave practically untouched.

BENGT SUNDKLER

PART ONE

KING AND PEOPLE

CHAPTER I

ALL NATIONS—ONE PEOPLE

The Old Testament

THE HISTORY OF MISSIONS BEGINS WITH ABRAHAM. The Lord said to Abraham:

> Go from your country and your kindred and your father's house to the land that I will show you. And I will make of you a great nation, and I will bless you, and make your name great, so that you will be a blessing. I will bless those who bless you, and him who curses you I will curse; and in you all the families of the earth will be blessed (Gen. 12: 1–3)

It is true that the covenant with Abraham had been preceded by God's covenant with Noah, Gen. 9: 8–17. Some have even claimed that it is Noah's covenant which is the real foundation of the Christian mission. And that covenant, sealed with the sign of God's "bow in the cloud", is indeed an important expression of the universal purpose of the Old Testament.

> When the bow is in the clouds, I will look upon it and remember the everlasting covenant between God and every living creature of all flesh that is upon the earth.

But the story of Noah's covenant is followed in the Bible by an event which is painted as nothing less than catastrophe—the confusion of Babel. Men in their conceit had determined to build a city, and a tower reaching to the heavens. But the Lord came down and confused their language, so that they were no longer able to understand one another's speech. Then He "scattered them abroad from there over the face of the earth . . .".

The multiplicity of languages has been one of the basic problems facing missions ever since. Mission is translation, in its widest meaning: interpretation into new thought-forms. But mission implies, too, a task of translation in a more specific sense: the translation of the message of salvation into more than a thousand languages. According to the teaching of the Bible, the vast variety of the languages of man is not only beauty and richness: it is also a curse. It is the task of mission to break the curse and replace it by understanding and unity. When Abraham left his home in faith, knowing nothing of the future, he took the first decisive step along this road.

The covenants of Noah and Abraham are important elements in the Bible's interpretation of the history of salvation; in fact the call of Abraham and the election of Israel are of primary importance for this view. Without this perspective—in the history of salvation—it is impossible rightly to understand the place of the Old Testament in the history of missions. "The missionary thought of the Old Testament" is not something which can be confined to the stories of Ruth and Naaman (non-Israelites admitted to the Israelite family); nor have we sounded its depths when we have followed Jonah on his adventurous journey to Nineveh.

It is the theology and the history of salvation contained in the Bible that make it a unity—that hold together and yet arch over all its many books, from the first chapter of Genesis to the last chapter of Revelation. There we may see a double "line of salvation" on the two principles of *election* and *substitution*: a minority is elected, chosen, to bear, by a process of substitution, blessing to the masses. This is perhaps best shown by a diagram.

Mankind, created by God but fallen into sin (A), is represented after the call of Abraham by the chosen people Israel (B). But the process of election continues; the chosen are now only a fragment of the people. When the people as a whole (the tribe of Judah) no longer measure up to their calling, they must in their turn be represented by "the faithful remnant" (C). Finally this remnant is reduced to one man, who takes upon himself the burden of Israel. Isaiah calls him "the suffering servant". In him Daniel sees "a son of man". This Solitary was chosen to represent mankind on the Cross—to save the nation; to save the nations; to save *all men*. Here takes place the great renewal, the great transformation. From this point the line of salvation changes direction. Instead of a progressive reduction, leading from the people to the remnant, from the remnant to the Solitary, there bursts from the Cross a progressive expansion—to the Apostles (D) who bore out the message of salvation of the missionary Church; from them to the new people of God, the *ecclesia* (E); and through the Church to the company of the redeemed of mankind in the Kingdom of God (F).

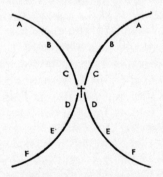

This "diagram of salvation" shows how the missionary thought of the Old Testament coincides with that of the Bible as a whole. Without the Old Testament background it is unlikely that we shall understand the universalism of the New Testament, and it is well that we should pay it proper attention.

The catastrophe of Babel's tower marks the end of the first chapter in the history of mankind. Its original universal purpose and its cosmopolitan scope became drastically reduced. The perspective of salvation became foreshortened and narrowed into a way of substitution. The blessing had to be concentrated upon one people—a people chosen by God for His very own.

The election made Israel the people of God, and His property. It separated them from other nations. Even the word meaning "nation", *goy*, *goyim*, differs from the word used of Israel, which is *'am*. As the property of Yahewh they are *'am qadosh*, a people of holiness.

The call of the patriarch Abraham and the election of Israel to be the people of God also meant that Israel came to be isolated, a "peculiar people" among men. But this could never be absolute; the lines of communication between the chosen people and the Gentiles could never be entirely broken: ". . . in you all the families of the earth will be blessed." This fundamental passage in fact contains the two great contradictory themes in the Bible's history of missions. We may perhaps call them particularism and universalism. But there is a hint in Gen. 12 that the contradiction can be resolved. Deutero-Isaiah (Isa. 40–55) brings this line to its fulfilment in a universalism which crowns the Old Testament view of the nation and the nations, Isa. 49: 5–6, 12–13. This is not a universalism liberated from its focus in the chosen people; it goes almost without saying that the people of God stand at its centre. Here, however, we must draw a clear distinction between mission and universalism. The "universalist" vision of Deutero-Isaiah aims neither at proselytism in the Jewish sense nor at mission in the modern sense. The very existence of Israel, bearing witness to Yahweh as God and King of Israel, confirms at the same time that He is God and King of the whole world. The fate of the world depends on the role played by Israel, and the witness of Israel among the nations. As Blauw has said, "The chosen people, by living for the Lord, live for mankind."

This theme is further illustrated by the "coronation" psalms (Ps. 96–101 and 110).

> The LORD reigns; let the earth rejoice;
> let the many coastlands be glad! (Ps. 97: 1)

The festive congregation in the temple at Jerusalem, singing to the Lord, sang also as a confession of faith—the faith of the chosen people and their protest against the idols of the world around them. At the New Year festival in Babylon there was celebrated the coronation of the god Marduk; the people shouted, "Marduk has become king," and at the same time shouted defiance to the whole of the Near East. Nowhere were the claims of Babylon rejected so summarily as by the singing congregation of Jerusalem. Confessing their faith in Yahweh, they made their implicit protest: "Marduk is *not* king." None but Yahweh has the right to be called king, for he is "a great King above all gods," Ps. 53: 3. "For thou, O Lord, art most high over all the earth; thou art exalted far above all gods," Ps. 97: 9.

Deutero-Isaiah had the same confidence:

> How beautiful upon the mountains
> are the feet of him who brings good tidings,
> who publishes peace, who brings good tidings of good,
> who publishes salvation,
> who says to Zion, "Your God reigns." (Isa. 52: 7)

The conflict between particularism and universalism in Israel was in the last resort resolved in the idea of Israel and the Jerusalem temple as standing at the focus of the world and of the nations. With the temple at the centre, universalism could be seen as something centripetal. For universalism can be either centrifugal or centripetal—centrifugal universalism actualized by a messenger, who crosses frontiers and passes on his news to those who are afar off; centripetal by a magnetic force, drawing distant peoples in, to the place or the person who stands at the centre. In the Old Testament, the temple is the centre of centripetal movement: the Gentiles must come to Zion, to the holy mountain at the centre of the world. To turn once more to Deutero-Isaiah:

> Lo, these shall come from afar,
> and lo, these from the north and from the west,
> and these from the land of Syene. (Isa. 49: 12)

But there is more involved than merely a journey to Zion. The centripetal universalism of the earlier part of the Book of Isaiah includes the picture of a sacramental banquet, to be held at the end of time:

> On this mountain the LORD of hosts will make for all peoples a feast of fat things, a feast of wine on the lees, of fat things full of marrow, of wine on the lees well refined. (Isa. 25: 6)

At the centre of this eschatological vision—this vision of the future—there stands the Messiah, both as the suffering servant of Isaiah and the son of man of Daniel. But the Messiah is not a missionary, going out to win adherents. The accent is placed entirely on God's initiative, on the new creation which will take place when Zion is raised up once more in the last days.

Another similar vision of the last days is found in Zechariah, a prophet whose universalism is centripetal like that of Isaiah. Zechariah's vision is more tangible; he sets out the role of the chosen people in these words:

> In those days ten men from the nations of every tongue shall take hold of the robe of a Jew, saying, "Let us go with you, for we have heard that God is with you." (Zech. 8: 23)

This view implies that, although the Gentiles serve strange gods and must thus be regarded as the enemies of Israel and Yahweh, they nevertheless have their place in the divine plan of salvation. There is another line, running alongside the line of election, which began with Abraham and ended at the Cross. This second line began with the universal covenant of Noah; it embraced all living creatures. Even the Gentiles are subject to the lordship of the God of Israel, since he is God of the whole world. He is their Creator, and he draws their line in, to meet the line of salvation and blessing along which move the chosen people.

> All the nations thou hast made shall come
> and bow down before thee, O Lord,
> and shall glorify thy name. (Ps. 86: 9)

So we see that there are two aspects of universalism in the Old Testament: one is the line of election and blessing, and stretches from Abraham to the Messiah; the other is the line of the Gentiles. The Christian faith claims that these meet at the Cross.

CHAPTER 2

ONE KING—ALL PEOPLES

The New Testament

THE MOTIFS WHICH WE HAVE NOTED AS PLAYING SUCH a large part in the Old Testament recur in the missionary outlook of the New Testament. Indeed, the understanding of the missionary sayings of the New Testament depends in large measure on the recognition of the organic unity of the Bible, and these sayings must in every case be viewed against the background of the Old Testament world of ideas. We may begin with a verse which is seldom quoted in missionary contexts, Matt. 5: 14, the saying about the city on the hill. Gerhard von Rad has shown that these words do not refer to simply any city on any hill, but to "the city of God on the hill of the world". They provide a characteristic expression of Israelite-Jewish universalism—a view which we also find in another closely related saying of Jesus:

> I tell you, many will come from east and west and sit at table with Abraham, Isaac, and Jacob in the kingdom of heaven, while the sons of the kingdom will be thrown into the outer darkness; there men will weep and gnash their teeth. (Matt. 8: 11–12)

This has to do with that same vision we have previously met with in Isaiah: the actual words are based on a passage in chapter two:

> It shall come to pass in the latter days
>> that the mountain of the house of the LORD
> shall be established as the highest of the mountains,
>> and shall be raised above the hills;

> and all the nations shall flow to it,
> > and many peoples shall come, and say:
> "Come, let us go up to the mountain of the LORD,
> > to the house of the God of Jacob;
> that he may teach us his ways
> > and that we may walk in his paths."
> For out of Zion shall go forth the law,
> and the word of the LORD from Jerusalem. (Isa. 2: 2–3)

The centripetal tendency here is plain. The subject is the eschatological pilgrimage of a whole nation to Mount Zion—a pilgrimage which leads, according to the Matthean vision, to sacramental participation in a great banquet. The link between mission and Eucharist—"my blood of the covenant, which is poured out for many for the forgiveness of sins", Matt. 26: 28—is set in the wider context of the history of salvation. A related passage which may be mentioned at this stage, is the description of the cleansing of the temple in John 2: 13–17. This text corresponds typologically to those texts in the Old Testament in which Yahweh is described as renewing the world from his throne in the temple. Jesus' symbolical action in cleansing the Court of the Gentiles was a declaration that He had prepared a place for a new humanity, the new people of God. But this characteristically takes place at the very heart of affairs, in the temple itself. Jesus, the Saviour of the world, stands at the centre; toward Him stream the peoples and the nations: that is what is meant by centripetal motion. It is true that some of His Jewish contemporaries asked whether He was contemplating going out to the Jewish *diaspora* (John 7: 35). But He had His place; and that place was Jerusalem. There He was to die on the Cross—for all men; there He was to be lifted up—again, on the Cross. And being lifted up, He would draw all men to Himself (John 12: 32). The Risen Lord told His disciples "not to depart from Jerusalem, but to wait for the promise of the Father", Acts 1: 4. All lines converge on the centre, where stands Jesus, the Son of David, the Son of Man. It is there He acts; it is there He dies for the sake of the world, that He might draw all men to Himself. On the Cross, Christ unites the two Covenants: the line of Abraham with its theme of election and the universal line of Noah both point forward to the same Cross.

The universality of this Cross is emphasized in the 'missionary commandment', Matt. 28: 18–20. Christ is King: He who was lifted up on the Cross comes as the Risen Lord, with His universal message and His command. This text, too, can be better understood in the light of one of the most famous passages in the whole of the Old Testament:

> I saw in the night visions, and behold,
>   with the clouds of heaven
>   there came one like a son of man,
> and he came to the Ancient of Days
>   and was presented before him.
> And to him was given dominion
>   and glory and kingdom,
> that all peoples, nations and languages
>   should serve him;
> his dominion is an everlasting dominion,
>   which shall not pass away,
> and his kingdom one
>   that shall not be destroyed. (Dan. 7: 13–14)

The Matthean tradition sees the prophecy of Daniel as having been fulfilled in the Risen Lord. The last words of St. Matthew's Gospel are in fact a Christological re-expression of the text from Daniel. But both are connected with the ancient Near Eastern coronation ritual of exaltation, presentation and enthronement. In this way is completed the line which begins with the coronation hymns of the Psalter, with their universal perspective, and which ends in the proclamation of the universal rule of the King. For the "missionary commandment" is mightier than a commandment: it is a proclamation of the Kingship of Christ over the peoples. "The Lord is now King" was proclaimed by the solemn assembly of the Old Covenant in the temple. "Christ is now King" answers the missionary Church in all ages, among all peoples, in every tongue.

This claim—that Christ is King—can however be defined still more closely. The claim was first made at a moment in the history of the world when the Romans had no king but Caesar, and when the Jews had no king of their own (Herod was of course a foreigner). At that moment Jesus came before Pontius Pilate, the representative of the kingdoms of this world, and confessed that He was a king, though His kingdom was not of this world. Christ the King applies to Himself both the idea of the Son of Man in Dan. 7: 14 and that of the Suffering Servant of Yahweh in Deutero-Isaiah. There is a close and important connexion between these two concepts and mission. It is said of the Son of Man in Daniel that "all peoples, nations, and languages [shall] serve him," Dan. 7: 14. And the Servant was set to be "a light to the nations, that . . . salvation may reach to the end of the earth", Isa. 49: 6. Christ the King, by identifying Himself with the Son of Man, and with the Servant, proclaims the universality of His commission. The Cross and Resurrection usher in a new epoch in the history of salvation. We have seen that in the Old Testament there had taken place a "progressive reduction"—from mankind to the people of Israel to the "remnant" to the Solitary, the King-Messiah. Now the history of salvation proceeds in a "progressive expansion", from the Solitary to the many: from the Cross to the Apostles to the Church to mankind. For the aeon of the Spirit has come. The Risen Lord, who commanded His Apostles "not to depart from Jerusalem", Acts 1: 4, now shows them their future commission, in all its world-wide significance:

> But you shall receive power when the Holy Spirit has come upon you; and you shall be my witnesses in Jerusalem and in all Judea and Samaria and to the end of the earth. (Acts 1: 8)

This is not to say that there is no tension between universalism and particularism in the New Testament. Indeed, the existence of this tension must be recognized, if we would understand the place of the "missionary commandment" in the context of the Gospel. On the one hand Jesus is seen as a particularist, concentrating on His own people; on the other, as consciously universalist, a King whose rule extends over the whole world. This tension seems to be present in Matthew. We have Matt. 28: 19, with its command to "Go . . . and make disciples of all nations," and we have the clearly limited instruction to "Go nowhere among the Gentiles, and enter no town of the Samaritans," Matt. 10: 5. How are we to understand this apparent contradiction?

Scholars have long argued as to the solution. Nineteenth-century scholars, conservatives and liberals alike, were largely agreed that Jesus' own view of His commission underwent a certain measure of development. Liberals, from David Strauss to Johannes Weiss, considered that there had taken place an evolution, from the narrow rejection of the Gentiles in Matt. 10 to a more generous attitude on the part of Jesus. Conservatives such as Martin Kähler (a theologian whose influence on German Evangelical missiology, and particularly on Gustav Warneck, was considerable) stressed that only the Risen Lord, being Lord of the whole world, could issue such orders to His disciples. Gustav Warneck supported this view, claiming that the Risen Lord, as He appears in Matt. 28, is the "universal missionary": in other words, that Jesus was clearly a universalist.

Harnack and the modern liberals reversed this judgment. In their view Matt. 28: 18 was a late gloss, without evidential value. Only Matt. 10 consists of genuine sayings of Jesus. The conclusion, inevitably, was that Jesus was a particularist, and that He had no conception of the Gentile situation. The edge of Harnack's criticism was however blunted somewhat by the emphasis he laid on Jesus' mercy towards publicans and Samaritans. But although Harnack believed that research had shown Jesus not to have possessed a transcendent extensive universalism, he did not hesitate to speak of Jesus' "intensive universalism". F. Spitta, a contemporary of Harnack, read in his New Testament that Jesus actually crossed the boundaries of Israel towards Tyre and Sidon. Therefore Jesus must have been "the first missionary", and the founder of the Christian mission. Another interesting contribution came from Albert Schweitzer, whose very first theological publication was a study of Matt. 10 and the particularism of Jesus. Not surprisingly, Schweitzer's solution was along the lines of eschatology. Matt. 10, he claimed, must be viewed in an eschatological light. Jesus was a particularist because the end of all things was at hand. And such universalism as He represented was likewise eschatological. Not until the final messianic age dawns will the Gentiles recognize the Risen Lord. His final conclusion was that Jesus thought like a universalist, but acted like a particularist.

However, it is possible—and indeed highly likely—that this particular debate has missed the mark altogether. The alternative, "universalism or particularism", is essentially a modern alternative, taking no account whatever of the biblical outlook on life. Furthermore it overlooks the central Old Testament perspective of the place of Israel and Zion at the centre of the world. We have seen something of the way in which central New Testament concepts—the Son of Man, the Church, the Wedding Feast—can be understood only against their appropriate Old Testament backgrounds; and we have taken due note of the fact that the tendency of these latter was clearly centripetal. It is this tendency that resolves the tension between particularism and universalism, since it is a demonstration of the simple fact that anyone seeking to influence the whole world must start at the centre before he can reach the periphery. That is why the universal message of salvation is so firmly grounded in the particular biblical history of salvation—that which was accomplished in and through the people of Israel. It is precisely in His particularism that Jesus' universalism is best seen, and, it may be added, it is precisely His sacrifice of Himself on the Cross, at the heart of the world and of human history, that sets the seal on His universal kingly rule. The commandment of the Risen Lord was followed by His promise of perpetual fellowship; and the charge to His disciples to stay in Jerusalem was also accompanied by a promise, "the promise of the Father", Acts 1: 4. Such was the disciples' foretaste of Pentecost.

The coming of the Holy Spirit marked the first completed stage in the course of the Church, God's new pilgrim people. It is entirely appropriate to the biblical line of salvation that the descent of the Dove should have taken place in Jerusalem, at the heart of the world. There was reopened a perspective towards the nations, and many of their tongues were heard on that day. For language has its given place in the economy of salvation: the catastrophe of Babel (Gen. 11) was finally repaired at Pentecost (Acts 2). The confusion of languages and discord among nations has in principle been overcome by the new unity of the Spirit, given in the Church. The Spirit and mission are inseparable in the new aeon which dawned at Pentecost— an insight stressed repeatedly in the Fourth Gospel, where we find a saying of Jesus which sums up the whole of the history of salvation, and this is bound up with the gift of the Spirit.

> Jesus said to them again, "Peace be with you. As the Father has sent me, even so send I you." And when he had said this, he breathed on them, and said to them, "Receive the Holy Spirit." (John 20: 21)

The eschatological emphasis of these themes is still more in evidence in the last book of the Bible, with its "great multitude which no man could number, from every

nation, from all tribes and peoples and tongues", Rev.
7: 9. Here, too, is the link between martyrdom and mission. Here is the crown and climax of the line which began
in the first book of the Bible, continued through Babel and
then, via Pentecost, is fulfilled before the throne of God.
The path leads from the Tower, through Tongues, to the
Throne. It is the assurance of this, and the vision of the
Crown, which has given the missionary Church strength
and courage to witness "before the Gentiles and kings and
the sons of Israel" (Acts 9: 15) to the unsearchable riches
of Christ.

From Jerusalem the horizon widens, in accordance with
the words of the Risen Lord: "you shall be my witnesses in
Jerusalem and in all Judaea and Samaria and to the end
of the earth" (Acts 1: 8). The crux was the transition from
Jewish to Gentile, from Israel to the Hellenistic world
round about. This is the problem with which the Acts of
the Apostles—our first history of missions—deals. The
Jerusalem church turned naturally to the circumcised in
Judaea first of all. At the same time it probably modelled
its missionary strategy on the words of commission
addressed by Jesus to the twelve in Matt. 10. The witnesses went out two by two, without gold or silver or
copper in their belts; without a pack; nor had they two
tunics, nor sandals, nor a staff. They were the new pilgrim
people of God, on the march with the news of the coming
of the Messiah.

The first of those who broke through the Israelite ethnic
barrier, and crossed the border into Samaria, was the
Apostle Philip. But he went one step further. Led by the
Spirit, he taught and baptized the Ethiopian courtier, a
representative of Africa, Acts 8: 5, 26–39. Peter was forced
to come to terms with the problem of Jew and Gentile in
connexion with the case of a Roman proselyte, the cen-
turion Cornelius. The solution, it is recorded, came to him
in a vision; it is formulated in words, the significance of

which can scarcely be overestimated for the future of the
young Church:

> Truly I perceive that God shows no partiality, but in every
> nation any one who fears him and does what is right is
> acceptable to him. (Acts 10: 34f.)

The consequences were drawn in Antioch, where the
early Christians preached to Greek-speaking refugees from
Cyprus and Cyrene. The barrier of the law had been
broken. The Gentile mission was a fact. This development
was officially sanctioned by the Council of Jerusalem in
A.D. 49. The exclusive Judaizing party in the Jerusalem
church was not allowed to have the last word. The circumstances surrounding this decision are far from clear; the
picture which emerges is highly complex. There were
"Jewish" groups in the Gentile congregations who refused
to accept Paul as a genuine Apostle, and who rejected his
interpretation of the faith; these demanded that all Christians should be subject to the Torah. Nevertheless the decree promulgated by the Apostles stated that "it has
seemed good to the Holy Spirit and to us" to demand no
more from the uncircumcised than that they should ab-
stain from meat sacrificed to idols. The sign of membership in the Church, the new Israel, was no longer circumcision, but baptism and faith.

Peter became the Apostle of the Jewish *diaspora*. Paul,
on the other hand, had been commissioned as the Apostle
of the Gentiles, and was recognized as such by the other
Apostles. Yet at no time did he forget Jerusalem and
Jewish culture. It was natural for him to keep in touch
with the Jerusalem congregation. One of his concerns was
to help the "saints" in Jerusalem by means of a collection
from the young missionary churches. In this connexion
Paul clearly stresses the central role of the Jerusalem congregation in the Church: the Gentile Christians have been
permitted to share in the spiritual benefits mediated
through Jerusalem, and it is therefore only seemly that

they should be prepared to place their material resources at the disposal of the saints in Jerusalem, 2 Cor. 8–9. It has been pointed out by the Danish scholar Johannes Munck that the Apostle, on his way to deliver the gift to Jerusalem, travelled with an unusually large company, and that these were possibly representatives of Gentile Christian communities, on pilgrimage to the Holy City of Israel. And when Paul, in his letter to the church in Rome, describes the extent of his work as a missionary, he takes as his starting point, not Antioch, but Jerusalem: "... from Jerusalem and as far round as Illyricum I have fully preached the gospel of Christ", Rom. 15: 19.

Paul was also passionately concerned with the twofold problem posed by Israel's rejection of the Messiah. The fact that Paul was "the Apostle of the Gentiles" must be viewed against the background of the role of Israel; not until this is done can the radically new aspects, and the greatness, of Paul's interpretation be understood. The words of Rom. 9: 3–5 indeed come from Paul's heart:

> For I could wish that I myself were accursed and cut off from Christ for the sake of my brethren, my kinsmen by race. They are Israelites, and to them belong the sonship, the glory, the covenants, the giving of the law, the worship, and the promises; to them belong the patriarchs, and of their race, according to the flesh, is the Christ. God who is over all be blessed for ever. Amen.

Here Paul reaches a solution which attempts to do justice both to the Gentile mission and to the mission to the Jews. Israel was not given its place in the history of salvation merely for its own sake, but also for the sake of the Gentiles; and in the New Covenant, the Church has not been brought into being for its own sake only, but also for the sake of Israel—to inspire and prompt the Jewish people to believe that Jesus is the Messiah. This emphasis—that the conversion of the Gentiles is to prompt the Jews to believe —is something radically new and original in the thought of Paul.

27

In the second chapter of the letter to the Ephesians, the Apostle shows how the reconciliation accomplished by Christ has brought to an end the differences between Jew and Gentile. "For he is our peace, who has made us both" —Jew and Gentile—"one, and has broken down the dividing wall of hostility" (v. 14). This new unity was of the essence of the Church, the new people of God, who had in fact taken over Israel's place as the hidden centre of history and of the world. The key to the Apostle's tireless missionary labour was his consciousness of having been called and commissioned, stemming from his experience on the Damascus Road, Acts 9. He knew himself to be an Apostle of Jesus Christ, set apart (*aphorismenos*) for the preaching of the Gospel of God, Rom. 1: 1. The words of the Acts of the Apostles, that he was "a chosen instrument" to carry the name of the Lord "before the Gentiles and kings and the sons of Israel" provide an appropriate summary of his work. Paul the Apostle knew, too, that he was an eye-witness (for he had seen the Lord), and therefore a reliable instrument for the transmission of the Apostolic tradition. His message never varied: Jesus Christ, crucified and risen. However, his approach to "the Gentiles and kings" was not altogether identical with his approach to the children of Israel. The basic religious question, the cry of the heart, was different. The problem of the Jew was guilt, the consequence of the transgression of the law. The Gentile's problem was the fear of death. But both received substantially the same answer. He who "cancelled the bond which stood against us with its legal demands", Col. 2: 14, is the same Christ through whom "the perishable puts on the imperishable, and the mortal puts on immortality. . . . O death, where is thy victory? O death, where is thy sting?" 1 Cor. 15: 54–55.

"From Jerusalem and as far round as Illyricum I have fully preached the gospel of Christ," wrote Paul in Rom. 15: 19. The claim was comprehensive, perhaps, but it gives us some idea of the missionary strategy of the

Apostle of the Gentiles. We may note some of the lines of that strategy.

1. First a negative definition: Paul would not build on another's foundation. His ambition, he wrote, was "to preach the gospel, not where Christ has already been named, lest I build on another man's foundation", Rom. 15: 20. He did not feel called to preach in those places in which others had already made a start, and in which the Church already had its representatives. There was one exception, however: Rome. But Rome was no little provincial city; it was the capital of the *oikoumene*. And, further, Rome was important to Paul as the base for his projected mission to the West, to Spain. Thus for Paul, the ellipse of the known world, round the Mediterranean, had the two foci of Rome and Jerusalem.

2. Once Paul had founded a church in the capital of a country or a province, he regarded the Gospel as having in principle been preached in that country. It was now the concern of the congregation to take the message of the Gospel out to the rest of the district. The breadth of the Apostle's confidence in the evangelistic capabilities of the young churches has been stressed in two twentieth-century missionary classics, Johannes Warneck's *Paulus in Lichte der heutigen Heidenmission* (1913) and Roland Allen's *Missionary Methods: St. Paul's or ours?* (1912).

3. The Apostle, who had himself grown up in a port, was well aware of the importance of international trading centres as missionary bases, particularly for the Jewish *diaspora*. At the same time it must be remembered that these considerations were of minor importance compared with the central role of Jerusalem. On Cyprus, in Pisidia, Galatia, Macedonia and Achaia he founded a church—or a number of churches—which could serve as centres of missionary strategy. He was not concerned with mission in country areas: his programme was based on the cities— Ephesus, Corinth, Athens, Thessalonica, Rome.

4. This enabled him to attain another goal. He came to

29

the great centres of Hellenistic religion: Paphos in Pamphylia, with its famous temple of Aphrodite; Corinth, the home of many religions, but also a centre for the worship of Aphrodite; Ephesus, the city to which worshippers of Artemis came on pilgrimage from all over the ancient world; Athens, with its Acropolis and its mystery religions; and Rome, with its Pantheon and its cults. Thus the Apostle of Jesus Christ came to the greatest cult centres of the Hellenistic world, and there confronted these cults with the message of Jesus Christ, crucified and risen.

5. As a Jew, it was only natural that Paul should make his way first of all to the centres of the Jewish dispersion. Of the Roman Empire's 40–60 million inhabitants, some $4\frac{1}{2}$ million were Jews of the *diaspora*. Paul was particularly concerned to come into contact with one particular category among the people of the synagogue: the "God-fearers"—those who, though not circumcised, worshipped Yahweh, observed the Sabbath and avoided certain kinds of food. Among these the Apostle encountered a far greater openness than among the narrow proselyte groups. The majority of "God-fearers" were women, and it is characteristic that Paul's first convert in Europe was a woman. She was one of the "God-fearers": Lydia, a seller of purple goods, who was converted and baptized in Philippi, where she provided lodgings for Paul, Acts 16: 14. However, we have seen from our sketch of Paul's attitude to the Jews that his efforts to establish contact with Jewish groups were not dictated simply by considerations of strategy. Of immeasurably greater importance was the theological conviction that in every place the Gospel should be preached to the Jews first of all.

6. The Apostle's labours ended in martyrdom. Paul and the other Apostles were well aware that mission and martyrdom belong together in the strategy of God. In the course of his labours the Apostle experienced that measure of "the sufferings of Christ" which he had to undergo. "Now I rejoice in my sufferings for your sake, and in my

flesh I complete what is lacking in Christ's afflictions for the sake of his body, that is, the church," Col. 1: 24. Paul calls himself an atoning sacrifice for the world, and there is not the slightest doubt that his martyrdom, and that of Peter, in Rome, was of vital significance for the mission of the young Church.

Paul's mission is characterized by the line from the cross of Christ to the kingly rule of Christ. This is expressed powerfully in Phil. 2: 5–11, in which Paul interprets the connexion between Christ's death on the cross and the message of the Christian mission, that Christ is Lord. Here as elsewhere in Paul's missionary thought, it is the eschatological element which places the message in its right perspective. Similarly it is Paul's eschatology which explains the restless eagerness with which he attempted to pass on the message to the greatest number of people in the shortest possible time. (According to Cullmann, the obscure saying in 2 Thess. 2: 5–7 refers to the role of mission in the last days: "what is restraining him" is the world mission and "he who now restrains it" is the Apostle Paul himself.) Paul's view of mission is Christocentric and universalist throughout: "So we are ambassadors for Christ, God making his appeal through us. We beseech you on behalf of Christ, be reconciled to God," 2 Cor. 5: 20. The message which is to be passed on to the world is a message of reconciliation; Christ the King, who sends out His ambassadors, is at one and the same time the content, and the guarantor, of the message; in fact he is fundamentally the Bearer of the message: He is Himself the Missionary for the world.

CHAPTER 3

THE DIALOGUE OF THE CHURCH
WITH JUDAISM

FOR PAUL, THE FOUNDATIONS OF THE HISTORY OF
salvation were the promises which God had made to
Israel. Dealing with the question of the place and the role
of Israel in mission, Paul writes that "the gifts and the call
of God are irrevocable" Rom. 11: 29. We have seen how
Paul the Jew, the Apostle of the Gentiles, wrestled with
this fundamental problem of the Christian mission. And
the question of the Jews has never ceased to exercise his
Church. It is no part of our purpose in this chapter to deal
with the whole of the problem of Christian missions to the
Jews; we shall instead, after having provided some basic
data, restrict our account to a bare outline of the actual
debate.

The situation of "missions to the Jews" has changed considerably since the Second World War. Indeed, the term
"missions to the Jews" seems to be on the verge of dis-
appearing. Instead we talk about the Church's "dialogue
with Judaism", or about the Church's "approach", contact and confrontation with Judaism. But the history of
Christian missions to the Jewish people, as we have already
seen, stretches back to the early days of the Church.

In medieval Europe, Jews lived in closed ghettoes, and
the methods used by the Church to reach them could be
both insensitive and unmerciful. The mendicant orders,
and particularly the Dominicans, were greatly concerned
that the Jews should be converted, and introduced the
study of Hebrew to that end. In 1521, Martin Luther

attacked the Church of Rome for its persecution of the Jews, but the ageing Luther polemized against what he felt to be the Jews' exclusiveness and pride. It was Halle Pietism and Herrnhutism which first seriously concerned itself with missions to the Jews, at least in Germany. In Britain, the London Society for the Propagation of Christianity among the Jews was formed as a result of the Evangelical Awakening in 1809. And to take another example, in Sweden the Society for Mission to Israel was started in 1875. The Anglican-Prussian Bishopric of Jerusalem, founded in 1841, was an interesting initiative. Samuel Gobat, who had earlier been a missionary in Abyssinia, was raised to the Episcopate of the Church of England in 1846, and was largely responsible, thanks to his contribution in the field of education, for laying the real foundations of the Anglican Diocese (the Anglican Bishop in Jerusalem became Archbishop in 1950). In 1817 the New Testament was first published in Hebrew; this translation was greatly improved sixty years later by F. Delitzch. And in 1930 the various international organizations for missions to the Jews were combined to form the International Missionary Council's Committee on Christian approach to the Jews. The greatest contributions of this Committee have been made on the North American continent, which has at present a Jewish population of some six millions— half of the entire Jewish community of the world. Attempts have been made to inspire local Christian churches to a positive and constructive approach to their Jewish neighbours ("the parish approach").

The emergence of modern Zionism created an entirely new situation in Judaism as a whole. Th. Herzl and Ch. Weizmann were largely responsible for the demand for a Jewish State of Israel, and in 1917 the Balfour Declaration promised the Jews that they would in time be given a national home in Israel. The foundation, in 1948, of the State of Israel, with its two million inhabitants, is one of the most remarkable of all modern political phenomena.

About 20–30 per cent of the population of Israel regard themselves as orthodox Jews, and a similar percentage as having no religious affiliations; the rest come in between. In Israel there are some 250 Jewish Christians and perhaps double that number of "secret Jewish Christians". Daniel Zion, who was formerly Chief Rabbi of Bulgaria, aroused a storm of protest in Israel when in 1952 he confessed that he had become a Christian; for twenty years he had been reading his New Testament, until in 1950 the Spirit of God had revealed to him that Jesus was Israel's Messiah. The reactions of the orthodox Jews were violent, and directed in no small measure against Christian missions. "More than four hundred messengers of Satan (*schlichey hasatan*), missionaries, among them baptized Jews, traitors to their own national heritage, have swept over our country like a swarm of grasshoppers. . . ." But reactions of this kind are unusual. The recent change of attitude on the part of the Christians, together with the avowed religious neutrality ("smiling tolerance", it has been called) of the State of Israel, have brought about a lessening of tension and led to limited contact. The Swedish Theological Institute in Jerusalem is one of the centres in which that contact is at present being widened.

A number of Christian-Jewish friendship organizations have been formed, mainly as a bulwark against the threat of anti-Semitism; in America, the first of these dates from 1928. In Israel, attempts have been made since 1959 to bring about some measure of "religious co-operation" between Christians and Jews. It is claimed that there are great socio-political problems—war, famine and the like—which can best be tackled on a co-operative basis; furthermore, the Scriptures of the two religions agree on such matters as these.

The concept of revelation is one which Judaism and Christianity to a large extent share: both are equally aware that God is the God of history. As Pascal put it, "Not the God of the philosophers, but the God of Abraham, Isaac and Jacob." Thus the Church's dialogue with Israel and Judaism keeps alive the question of the nature of the revelation of the Messiah.

But the problem which troubled Paul has been seen in a new way in our own day. The reason for this is the dreadful fact, which cannot and must not be overlooked, that during the Second World War the Nazis exterminated six million of Europe's seven million Jews. This has caused a number of prominent modern theologians to call in question the right of the Christian Church to carry on missions to the Jews. Dr. Reinhold Niebuhr, as one of America's leading theologians, has recently advanced three reasons against such missions. The first of these is the fact of the persecutions. The second is that Christian missions to the Jews are, and always have been, futile: their results have been negligible. And thirdly and most important, because in his view Judaism and Christianity are so much alike theologically, and because he considers that the Jew finds God more easily in the context of his own spiritual heritage. There can therefore be no reason for exposing the Jew to the feelings of guilt which must inevitably follow, should he be converted to Christianity. The Jew, as a member of a religious minority, looks upon Christianity as the symbol of a powerful majority culture—quite apart from the intrinsic merits of Christianity as a religion.

A similar conclusion has been reached by the great European theologian, Karl Barth. His contention is that Israel is one: the people of the Covenant, before and after the coming of Christ, are but two forms of one and the same inseparable fellowship. Christ, in the unity of His Person, is both the crucified Messiah of Israel and the Lord of the Church. Thus Israel, as the chosen people of God, is also potentially a Church for the world. The continued existence of the synagogue alongside the church is "a practically intolerable wound in the body of Christ". In practical terms, Barth seems to favour a *rapprochement*, or even a "reunion" between the two Israels. Similar opinions have been expressed from within the Roman Catholic Church, where the motto is "not missions to the Jews, but reunion"; the Roman Catholic Church also publishes a bulletin "for the furtherance of friendship between the old and the new people of God according to the meaning of both Testaments".

Niebuhr's view of the two equally defensible ways of salvation is echoed by Jewish theologians. Thus Martin Buber has said, "God's doors are open to both. The Jew has no need to become a Christian, and the Christian has no need to become a Jew in order to come to God." And H. J. Schoeps adds, "Jesus Christ is the turning point for the peoples of all ages; for all, that is, except Israel." In point of fact, Jews, Christians and Muslims all trace their religious descent back to a common forefather, Abraham, the father of faith. In his letter to the Galatians (3: 39), Paul writes, "And if you are Christ's, then you are Abraham's offspring, heirs according to promise." We are united more deeply and more intimately than we can conceive. As Ch. Wardi has said, "We are all Israelites."

The criticisms advanced by Niebuhr and the other theologians are not restricted to missions to the Jews. Their consequences are such as to challenge the world mission of the Church in every sphere. The Church of Christ can never abandon her missionary claim, if she would be true to her calling. The words "Jesus is Lord" imply that He is a Messiah for Israel—the seed of Abraham —just as much as for the Greeks and for us all. The fact of her election and her commission makes it impossible for the Church, the new Israel, ever to abandon the attempt to carry the message of Jesus the Messiah to the people of the promise.

However, contact with the synagogue does intensify our view of the Church in the world. In face of that contact we discover that the Church, too, is part of the *diaspora*, spread throughout the world, influenced, it is true, by the cultures and surroundings in which she has to work and witness, but essentially a different kind of fellowship from these. She is a "colony of heaven" (Phil. 3: 20, Moffatt's translation), and hence a fellowship in the midst of all the colonial systems of this world; but at the same time she is called to proclaim to all these the good news that Christ is King—both of the Church and of the world.

CHAPTER 4

CHRIST IS KING

A Theology of Mission in Outline

CHRIST IS KING—SUCH IS THE MESSAGE AND THE claim of the Christian mission. This is a vital theme for modern missionary theology, with its foundation in biblical theology. The view of the missionary obligation of the Church has been deeply influenced, both by modern biblical research, in which eschatology is given a large place, and by the apocalyptic events of the present world situation. There are three conclusions which may be drawn from this. First, that Christ is the King who will return; secondly, that Christ is King of the Church; and thirdly, that Christ is King of the world.

Christ is the King who will return

In our day missionary thought has become more and more conditioned by the idea of the end of all things. The international missionary conference in Whitby, Canada, in 1947 expressed the missionary task of the Church in the words "expectant evangelism". It is vital that the biblical history of salvation should be taken seriously, since on this view mission is the most important thing that can take place in the interim period between the Resurrection and the Second Coming of Christ. Mission makes sense of this interim period. Its task is to prepare the way for the return of the King, convinced that He has already won the victory, once and for all.

This view implies that all human programmes and all human expectations are called in question. It is also a

38

conscious criticism of the "established church" principle in the missionary enterprise, and of a too-optimistic "folk church" ideal on the mission field. This calls for a few words in explanation. Unrealistic attempts have in the past been made to transplant our Western ideas of "national churches" or "folk churches" from Europe to Africa and Asia. But the biblical revelation of the history of salvation shows the missions that they are not called to build churches in the style of fortified castles or European manor-houses, but as porches—giving access to the Temple of the Lord. Or, to put it somewhat differently, to found a church on the mission field is to establish a colony of the Kingdom of God.

The people of Christ are revolutionaries in a totalitarian world, a company of pilgrims on their way to the New Jerusalem. In 1 Peter 2: 11 they are called *paroikoi*, strangers and foreigners, homeless wanderers in the world. This view of the nature of the Church has been expressed in dynamic terms in the idea of "the Apostolate of the Church", which has been a central theme in ecumenical missionary discussion since the 1950's. The Church is *sent* —sent into the world with the Gospel of Jesus Christ. But it is a vital necessity that the Church should make it perfectly plain what is meant by the word "Gospel". If we turn to the New Testament we find that this is far more than merely a Greek term; more even than a theological concept. To be sure, terms and concepts are necessary— but they cannot convert the world. The Gospel which can save the world is not an idea; nor is it a thing; it is a Person —the Person of Jesus Christ. The early Church confessed its faith in Christ as Lord, and it was this confession which formed the basis of her missionary message. Thus the Gospel of Christ—that Christ is risen and will return, that He is Lord and King—sums up the proclamation of the missionary Church, in word and deed, in all generations.

But at the same time it is actually Christ Himself who is the missionary. It is His Holy Spirit who draws men to

Himself, and then sends them out as His messengers. Such is the twofold secret of mission: the call of Christ, the power by which He draws men to Himself, and the commission of Christ, by which He sends men to the ends of the earth and to the end of time.

The practical implications of this view are far-reaching. It means that the Church must be constantly prepared to review its methods and its results, and to rethink its strategy, in this light. There can be no ready-made solution. The Church must consider every case on its own merits, and in every case determine what is the most important factor, to which all else must give place. This view makes missions far more mobile and flexible than ever before. Institutions and organizations are not the most important things. The Church—the new pilgrim people of God—is a group, a dynamic group, bearing its message to the world; if it is less than this it does not deserve the name of Church. The life of the whole Church has a missionary dimension. As Emil Brunner has said, "The Church exists by mission, as fire exists by burning." And on the deepest level every Christian is a missionary.

Christ is the King of the Church

Mission, based as it is on biblical theology and conscious of the end, is well aware that its calling is to build up the Church. But this Church is a porch to the Temple of the Lord, a colony of the Kingdom of God. This realization is necessary for the understanding of the much-discussed problem of the establishment of the indigenous church. It is common knowledge that the Protestant missions have for a century past regarded the establishment of self-governing, self-supporting and self-propagating churches as one of its most important concerns. It may be of value at this stage to summarize the discussion which has attended this problem.

The "three-self" programme was formulated in the mid-nineteenth century by Henry Venn of the Church of

England and the American Congregationalist Rufus Anderson, and was later taken up by the German theologian and missiologist Gustav Warneck. Since then, the object of Evangelical missions has commonly been expressed in terms of this three-point plan. Self-government, or autonomy, implies, as far as the missionary Church is concerned, that the indigenous church should as soon as possible be placed under its own ordained leadership and have its own ordained ministry. Self-support implies that the church must as soon as possible become independent of the financial support provided by Western missionary societies and rely instead upon the economic resources of its own people and its own country. The question of "stewardship" has assumed important proportions in such contexts as these. And finally, self-propagation implies that it is the task—the essential task—of the young church to carry the Gospel out to its own surroundings, to the people of its country as a whole, and even beyond its national frontiers.

The "three-self" formula was valuable as an instrument of church construction on the mission field. And it would not be too much to say that the nineteenth-century missionary debate—from the simplest of village congregations to the highest organs of the churches—constantly circled around one or other of these questions. Its programme as such was highly stimulating. But it gave rise to problems, particularly in the matter of the relationship of the three parts to one another. It was claimed on a number of occasions that the Western "mother-church" or missionary society was only in a position to "grant" independence to such young churches as had become financially self-supporting. Five-year plans and ten-year plans were drawn up, the object of which was to calculate the rate at which the financial support of the Western missions might be withdrawn, and the young church's contribution increased. This was a symbolic expression of the idea that the Western missions stood in a "John the Baptist" relationship to the young churches: the mission must decrease in order that the Church might increase. Henry Venn looked forward to the "euthanasia" of the missions when they had completed their task; the missions should aim at a process of "devolution"—i.e. the transfer at the earliest possible date of the responsibility for practical government to the administrative body of the young church in question. The main topic of conversation in mission-church debates was usually *when* this was likely to be able to take place. It is perhaps not surprising that this did little to improve relations between the two parties.

It is interesting to note that there was often a close relationship between the "independence" debate in the Church and the quest for political independence in the country concerned. Dramatic changes in the political life of the country often helped to bring Church independence more rapidly than might otherwise have been the case. This is seen in the case of a number of churches founded by German missionaries. Their leaders were twice interned, during the two World Wars, and it became possible to speak of "orphaned missions". Thus the Lutheran Chhota Nagpur Church in Central India, which had been founded by the Gossner mission, gained its autonomy soon after the First World War. This type of situation has been even more pronounced during and after the Second World War, especially in Tanganyika. Further examples of the same tendency—rapid autonomy forced on by political crises—are to be seen in the Protestant Churches of the Congo.

Among the positive measures undertaken in order to speed up the process of autonomy was improved education, and in particular theological education. New constitutions were drawn up in order to regularize the relation between mission and Church, and these as a rule presupposed that missionary conferences and missionary councils were as soon as possible to be replaced by synods under indigenous control. Africans and Asians became the Presidents or Bishops of the new churches. The Whitby conference of 1947 called the new relationship between mission and Church "partnership in obedience". This development was consolidated during the 1950's. Asian, African and Latin American church leaders, meeting at Willingen (Germany) in 1952, expressed their convictions in these words: "We are convinced that missionary work should be done through the Church. We should cease to speak of missions and churches and avoid this dichotomy not only in our thinking but also in our actions. We should now speak of the mission of the Church."

Recent experience has however shown that the most important factor in the life of the young Church is not autonomy but "Christonomy": not independence, but Christ-dependence. The Christian mission is far more than an organ for the foundation and creation of churches. It is not concerned to create static religious societies, closed ghettoes in the midst of a non-Christian world. The Church must continually be crossing its own frontiers; it must be a point of contact between the Gospel and the non-Christian world, and a centre for the evangelization of that world. The Church is sent into the world; the Church is the people of God on the march. It is thus only reasonable to speak of the Church as being synonymous with mission. In fact the Church *is* mission. And because Christ is the King of the Church, it can never cease to labour for Christian unity: "One Lord, one faith, one baptism, one God and Father of all . . ." Eph. 4: 5. It is not without significance that during this century it has been the young churches who have stressed, time and time again, that the unity of the Church is the greatest of all Christian concerns. And the existential wrestling with the problem experienced by the churches of India, Ceylon, and East and West Africa has been an immeasurable source of inspiration for ecumenical discussion in the West. The integration of the International Missionary Council and the World Council of Churches in 1961 was a most important expression of the dynamic view, that mission and ecumenics are essentially one and the same. This is one of the great steps forward of recent years.

Christ is the King of the World

Christ is the Saviour of the world, and the propitiation for the sins of the whole world (cf. 1 John 2: 2). Thus Christ is a matter of concern for the world, and the Church and the world are in the last resort subject to one and the same Lord. Oscar Cullmann has likened this situation to two concentric circles, the Church forming the inner circle, the world the outer circle. According to the Scriptures, both together form that kingdom over which the King exercises His authority. Therefore the difference between the Church and the world is not that the Church belongs to Christ while the world belongs to some other "authority". Both in fact belong to Christ. Nevertheless there is a fundamental difference between the two: the Church knows and recognizes Christ, and is called to make Him known; the world, on the other hand, does not know Him—whether this be taken to imply that the world does not *yet* know Christ, or that the world *no longer* knows Him. The Kingly power of Christ is revealed in the Church and recognized in the Church; in the world, the power of Christ, though latent, is hidden.

The authority of Christ as King has consequences for the social responsibility of the Church, and for her encounter with the non-Christian religions. We shall deal with these in turn.

The Social Responsibility of the Church

The history of mission shows that there is a close relationship between the bearing of witness to Christ and social action. If the authority of Christ the King is to be recognized in, say, present-day India, the Gospel, which is the concern of all men and of the whole man, must also be demonstrated in social service. This connexion has not infrequently been interpreted to mean that the Church's

44

social contribution can serve as some form of preparation for the *real* work of missions. Thus medical and educational work have been looked upon as preparation for preaching, or "direct" witness to Christ. Consequently, missions have all too often been regarded as an attempt on the part of the Church to "save" the world—to attract non-Christians from the world into the Church. In such cases "the Church" has usually meant the mission station.

But the connexion between proclamation and service must be thought out afresh, and given a radically new orientation. In the first place, because the recognition that Christ is Lord both over the Church and the world forbids such an over-simplified argument: we simply cannot draw a hard and fast line between the spheres of religion and the world; nor can we define "mission" as that part of the Church's work which attempts to conquer the secular sphere by removing men and women from its influence. Is it not rather so, that the world is the latent Kingdom of Christ, in which the Church is called to make Christ known? The lordship of Christ is the lordship of Love, and His claim on the world is conditioned by the claims and the challenge of Love, with all its profound social consequences. The Lord of this world is also the bread of life, and the claims of Love are best seen in the drama of the broken bread. It is thus that Christ in His Love comes to the world, and the Church is called to follow her Lord along this path. The Church is called to witness to her Lord in a world which Christ desires to win by Love. It is Christ who calls His Church to serve all men, and the whole man, in a love which knows no other justification than the fact of loving. This is a realistic view, and implies that the need of the world, and the Church's possibilities of helping, are realistically evaluated. We must remember that Christ suffered and died outside the walls of the city—outside the walls, in the Johannesburg locations, in the slums of Calcutta, where Christ is identified with His brethren, where He once more gives Himself to

45

the world in the liturgy of Love. And it is in small and great situations, with concrete application and with the stamina of Divine Love, that His call to His faithful people can be made real.

But the social responsibility of the Church may equally well be turned in another direction. At the East Asia Christian Conference, meeting at Kuala Lumpur in 1959, the Christians of Asia claimed that democracy could not become a living reality in Asia if it were not based on Christian principles. Social responsibility was on this occasion crystallized in the work of developing the political and social resources of the Asian countries. Thus obedience to the Lord of the world implies a deep concern—which is both social and prophetic—for the social and political problems of the new states. It is in situations such as these that the cumulative experience of the churches, mediated through the World Council, has been applied to the field of social witness. J. H. Oldham spoke of "the responsible society"—an idea wholly in line with the experience of Asian church leaders. The discussion continues, in Africa, Asia, Latin America, and even, perhaps, in the West.

Christ and the Religions of the World

Christ is Lord, not only over the Church, but over men of other faiths. Christ has died and been uplifted for Hindus and Buddhists, as well as for Christians. He is the Saviour of the world, and the propitiation for the sins of the whole world. Such is the missionary message and the claim of Christianity when confronted by the faith of Islam, Hindu mysticism or the serious asceticism of Buddhism. It is with this message that the Church is called to make Christ known, and it is through this message that the Christ is called to bring men of other faiths to their rightful Lord.

On this point, it would seem that mission must take account of a danger which is greater now than a genera-

46

tion ago. It is probably true to say that the areas of contact between the Church (or the mission) and the non-Christian religions are more circumscribed now than they were a mere thirty years ago. Too few missionaries are given the opportunity of getting to know the non-Christian religions, and of taking an active part in the real missionary task of confrontation between the Gospel and the religions. This is a serious matter. The demands of love are such, that before witness can be borne to the Lordship of Christ over men of other faiths, the messenger must know—and know intimately—the people concerned. Knowledge of the social and religious milieu in which the service of Christ is to be fulfilled is an absolute necessity, quite apart from the interpretation the missionary places on the relationship between the Gospel and the religions. This has been made abundantly clear in the experience of the young churches. If it be true that Christ is Lord over men of other faiths, and the Answer to their questions raised by the religions, then to bear witness to Him requires close knowledge of the situation of those religions. For the Final Answer cannot be accepted as a real answer until it becomes the answer to a real question and a real desire, the answer to the concrete questions asked by real men and women.

This situation of witness implies the further problem of how other religions are to be interpreted, and how contact is to be made with their several worlds. This has been a theological problem in every age of the Church, and it may be worth pausing at this point to take a closer look at the question of the Gospel and the religions. In the last resort the answer depends on certain basic theological assumptions, sometimes conscious and explicit, sometimes unconscious, but no less important for that. Many different approaches are recorded. We shall consider only four of them here: four characteristic ways of looking at the problem—the Catholic, Lutheran, Liberal and Barthian solutions.

47

This approach is first seen in the work of Clement of Alexandria (d. *c.* 215). Clement, taking up a line of thought begun in the Logos theology of St. John's Gospel, and in the Apologists, taught that the Christ-Logos, "the true light that enlightens every man" (John 1: 9) is represented in the world of the religions by scattered or disseminated *logoi*, "*logoi spermatikoi*". These lesser lights anticipate the coming of the true Light.

Thomas Aquinas (d. 1274), the seminal theologian of the Church of Rome, developed this view into a system in which the natural religion of mankind is seen as a *praeparatio evangelica*, a forecourt of the Temple. The fundamental theological thesis, that grace does not annul, but fulfils, nature, made it possible to hold a generous view of the religions, and resulted in extensive accommodation in practice. Nature, as it exists in the empirical religions, was fulfilled and consecrated by being adopted into the Church's scheme and brought within the sphere of Divine grace.

A modern exponent of the Catholic missionary attitude was the Belgian Jesuit, Pierre Charles (d. 1954), who expressed the Catholic view in a thought-provoking way. His basic assumption was that there must of necessity be concord between the Creator and the Redeemer. God's creative activity cannot be limited to a time "in the beginning"; He has not ceased to create. His creative activity in all ages harmonizes with his plan of salvation. It is true that sin has disturbed the order of God's creation; but sin has not been able to make that order wholly evil. Human nature is not displeasing to God merely because it is human. In the purpose of God the Church must be universal. Therefore there is room in the Church for everything she is able to accept: in other words, for everything which does not explicitly contradict the Divine nature. Herein lies the purpose of creation, not only of the separate gifts given to men, but also of social institutions, art, customs, language, systems of faith, religious rites: all this finds its due place as the raw material from which the Church is built. Divine Providence has been at work in all ages, among all peoples, and though it has met with opposition from the sin of men, its labours have not been entirely fruitless. To condemn or reject this work is tantamount to dishonouring God. Clearly, the practical consequence of such a view must be a spirit of tolerance. Superstition is not condemned out of hand as *Unglaube*, the diametrical opposite of faith; instead the watchword is "fulfilment". The non-Christian religions are only to be conquered by being fulfilled, though they are at the same time corrected and purified; they blossom and bear fruit in their own true goal, the Alpha and Omega of all creation and all reality.

This is the line followed by all Catholic missionary theology, and substantially that of a great part of the Anglican Church since B. F. Westcott. It is thus characteristic that the theology of Pierre Charles should have profoundly affected the missionary theory and practice of the Church of England in recent years, though his view of the Church has there been modified, and reinterpreted in dynamic terms, as a growing organism.

The Lutheran Approach

Luther's own attitude to the non-Christian religions must be seen against the background of his age, of his relations with the theology of the Church of Rome and—most important—of his evangelical rediscovery.

The only non-Christian religions with which Luther had any acquaintance were Judaism and Islam, the latter being particularly topical. But he had also come across non-Christian piety in his studies in the field of Greek and Roman literature. The expansion of the world in an age of exploration, and the greater knowledge of non-Christian religions which came as a result, belong to a later age than that of Luther.

Luther's attitude to Roman Catholic theology was twofold. On the one hand he was careful to perpetuate what

D

he considered to be fundamental Christian truths; but on the other he attacked the Roman interpretation energetically whenever he suspected it of advocating "salvation by works". The same may be said of his attitude to the non-Christian religions. Thus Luther is able to speak of a general knowledge of God, and to develop the mediaeval doctrine that natural law consists in the knowledge of the sovereign will of God, and that all men are to some extent acquainted with that law. In this way Luther made possible a theological interpretation of the religions, but an interpretation, it would be well to note, which depends in the last resort on his evangelical view of Christianity.

All men know that God exists, and that He is a God of law. But not all men stand in a right relationship of trust toward God. Many rely on their own ideas instead, worshipping the creation instead of the Creator. Such is the paradoxical situation in which the adherents of the non-Christian religions stand: they know that God exists; but they do not know who He is.

It is characteristic of Luther's view that faith in God and trust in God belong together. In the Greater Catechism he wrote, in his exposition of the first commandment, "For these two, faith and love, belong together. That on which your heart relies, I say, is in reality your God. . . . To have a God means to have something in which your heart can trust unreservedly."

This perfect confidence, and hence this true knowledge of God, are not granted to man merely for the asking. Men rely on their own notions of the Divine, and worship creation instead of the Creator. True faith, and knowledge of God as He is, are accomplished by the work of the Holy Spirit, and come through the enlightenment given by the Gospel. Alongside the general revelation must be placed the special revelation, the revelation given in Christ, and mediated by Him in and through the Gospel. The content of the special revelation is the knowledge of the identity and nature of God.

Revelation in Christ fulfils general revelation, and puts natural law in its proper place. In Christ there is revealed the true nature of God as grace and mercy; and in fellowship with Him we are enabled to make proper use of the law. The law exists, not to enable us to build up a form of righteousness on the precarious foundation of our own vanity and accomplishments, but to help us to live in the world in service of our neighbour.

Regin Prenter, a modern Danish Luther specialist, has interpreted Luther's attitude to the non-Christian religions as being evidence of a "paradoxical" view of religion. Prenter characterizes the non-Christian religions as "truth off the rails". They contain a certain measure of truth, in that they are fully aware that God exists, but they are "off the rails" in that, although they know that God exists, their views of His identity and nature are mistaken.

The Liberal Approach

The Liberal position is one of cultural openness and positivism. Among the factors giving rise to this approach may perhaps be mentioned a closer acquaintance with the history of religions, an interest in the development of the individual personality, and in general a positive view of progress. Traditional theological categories, such as "natural religion" and "general revelation" were re-interpreted and deprived of their eschatological elements in order to leave room for the findings of "comparative religion" or "the science of religion". The religions tended to be interpreted as manifestations of a deep-seated human instinct. At the same time the evolutionism of the late nineteenth century, in its religious application, regarded Christianity as the end and goal of all religious development. In Great Britain, this view was popularized by Max Müller and Monier Monier-Williams, and was taken up by a number of prominent missionaries, among whom J. N. Farquhar (1861–1929) is worthy of particular

mention. In Germany, E. Troeltsch became the spokesman of the religio-historical school of missionary thought.
Much of his best work was done on the question of the ab-
soluteness of religion, viewed as a separate and distinct
category within the thought and the spiritual life of man.

Characteristic of the Liberal position, particularly in the
English-speaking world, was an active concern in social
matters. W. Rauschenbusch's *Social Gospel* of the 1920's
may be regarded as a late and extreme expression of this
particular tendency.

On the ecumenical front there has in recent years been
continual discussion between representatives of the Liberal
position and those who have held to a more traditional
missionary theology. The 1928 Jerusalem conference of
the I.M.C. may be taken as an example of such discussion.
On this occasion the Liberal argument, that there are to
be found "values" in the non-Christian religions, was subjected to severe criticism, not least by Continental theologians. The most fully developed statement of the Liberal
approach is perhaps that of the American theologian, W.
Hocking, in his much-discussed book *Rethinking Missions*
(1932).

The relation between the Gospel and the religions is a
problem which presses hard upon theologians in the young
churches. The Liberal approach has prompted some of
them to undertake bold ventures of speculation. As an
example we may point to the work of the Indian laymen
G. V. Job, P. Chenchiah and V. Chakkarai, and in particular to their joint book *Rethinking Christianity in India*
(1938).

The Barthian Approach

The brunt of Karl Barth's polemic has been borne by
Liberal Protestantism, whose religio-historical approach
placed historical Christianity on a par with other religions. This led to the revelation in Christ being allowed
only relative validity, since in the history of religions

Christ is viewed against the background of religions generally. "Liberal Protestantism did not see the religion of revelation: it saw the revelation of religion," and it therefore fell into "the heresy of religionism". In Barth's view, religion is an attempt on the part of godless man to re-establish contact (*re-ligere*) with God, without recognizing the fact of the Fall, without taking sin seriously, and without allowing the necessity of salvation in Christ. Religion is therefore *Unglaube*, the opposite of faith, and the revelation of God in Christ is such as to abolish religion altogether. Everything necessary to man's salvation is given in Christ. But since Christ is an active participant in the work of creation (Col. 1: 16), He is also in the last resort the subject of the religions. Men of other faiths—Muslims, Hindus, Buddhists—who are to be approached with the Word concerning Christ, have themselves been created by Christ. From this point of view Christianity as a historical phenomenon and as a religion is subject to the same conditions as other religions: like them, Christianity is subject to the judgment of the revelation of Christ and His Cross. Liberal Protestantism judged Christ against the background of the religions; theology judges the religions, Christianity not excepted, by the measure of Christ.

Barth's contribution has led to a re-evaluation on the part of Evangelical missionary theologians: the distinction that must be drawn is not between Christianity and the religions but between the Gospel, Christianity and the religions. But they are one and all subject to the judgment of the Cross, and all stand related to reality, as it has been made known in the revelation of Christ. According to Barth there is one criterion, and only one, which divides Christianity from its noble parallels, such as Amida Buddhism or India's religion of *bhakti*. That is the name of Jesus, the Gospel of the living Christ. The idea of "points of contact" between the Gospel and the world of the religions Barth rejects sharply—mercilessly, even. Incidentally, it was this question which led to the celebrated conflict between Barth and Emil Brunner. The crux was the question of anthropology—a subject in which Barth has little interest. Barth's categorical *Nein!* (1934) was written in answer to Brunner's attempt to recognize and explain the extent of the knowledge of God in the religions, outside the revelation of Christ.

A number of missionary scholars have, under the influence of "dialectical theology", advocated an "Evangelical science of religion", as distinct from the general comparative history of religion. This trend is to be seen in the work of the German scholars Althaus, Frick, Hartenstein, Holstein and Rosencranz, who have stressed the need for a study of religion in which the ostensible objectivity of the history of religions is abandoned; instead, they claim, the religions must be viewed and understood in the light of the Gospel itself. Of particular importance for the Evangelical mission in our day has been the fact that the Dutch scholar Hendrik Kraemer, in his influential book *The Christian Message in a Non-Christian World* (1938), appears to have accepted Barth's view of the impossibility of "points of contact", thereby going a long way toward accepting Brunner's overall view of the relationship between the Gospel and the religions.

One positive result of Kraemer's work has been to help liberate missions from naïvety in their attempts at adaptation: for the belief that it was possible to disengage an idea here, and a concept there, from the complex world of the religions, and use them to help build the Church, can scarcely be regarded as other than naïve. Kraemer, like Karl Hartenstein before him, stressed that a religion must be viewed as a whole, focussed on its given centre. Cultural elements and religious phenomena must therefore undergo a radical change of meaning when they are separated from this centre and pressed into the service of Christ. Kraemer further claims that points of contact in the religions can serve only an antithetical purpose in the context of the Christian message (though this is of course not to say that they can only be evaluated negatively). The only genuine point of contact is to be found in the attitude of the missionary: it is the missionary who brings about "communication" between the Gospel and the religio-sociological milieu. But it must be remembered that Kraemer is consistently dialectical in his dialectical theology, and that he has succeeded in combining his radical emphasis on the revelation in Christ with a desire (and an ability) to understand the heritage and forms of expressions of other religions. He has of course been a missionary himself: from 1922 to 1935 he was in the service of the Netherlands' Bible Society in Indonesia.

In his most recent books Kraemer has made a number of valuable and stimulating contributions to the discussion of the "problem of communication"—a question which has been closely studied at the Ecumenical Institute at Bossey. Another scholar who has recognized, on the basis of practical missionary experience, the difficulties and opportunities attending the communication of the Christian message in the present cultural situation, is H. R. Weber.

It was perhaps only to be expected that Kraemer's *The Christian Message*—the most important work of missionary theology this century—should have been interpreted in some quarters as advocating the breaking off of the dialogue with the religions. Such was, however, very far indeed from being Kraemer's intention. The heated debate between Kraemer and the Norwegian missionary, K. L. Reichelt, at Tambaram only served to confirm that impression, at least in Asia. Not until the 1950's was the debate taken up once more, this time with a new emphasis. Asian theologians and churchmen—D. G. Moses and P. D. Devanandan in India, D. T. Niles and S. Kulandran in Ceylon—have expressed their views on a matter which is of the essence of the situation. It is characteristic that they should have begun with the problem of anthropology, with the concrete religious needs and aspirations of Asian men and women, and attempted to view these in the light of the Gospel, in order to confront Asian religion with universal Christianity. The International Missionary Council and the World Council of Churches have tried to meet this most pressing of all missionary needs by setting up a number of research centres at strategic points in Asia: Kyoto, Hong Kong and Bangalore. From these centres scholars are able to watch developments in the world of the Asian religions, and are enabled by this means to gain a deeper understanding of the encounter between the Gospel and the religions.

The Commission to Translate

The missionary task is to proclaim Christ as King, and to make Him known to the nations. This implies that the Gospel must be translated, in word and deed. But an observation such as this can be applied in a virtually unlimited number of ways. A whole theology of mission can in fact be built on the thesis that mission is translation. The overall task of the missionary Church is to interpret and translate, in its preaching, teaching and works of love, the will of God to salvation, as it is revealed in the eternal mission, the Father's sending of the Son. This commission to translate may be summarized under six heads.

1. Mission is translation. "As the Father has sent me, even so I send you," John 20: 21. This we have seen to be one of the fundamental missionary texts of the New Testament. In reality there is but *one* mission, from which all other missions are derived: the first mission, from eternity, the Father's *missio* (sending) of His Son.

In order that men might know who God is, He translated His will to salvation, by sending His Son into the world of men. The eternal Christ emptied Himself of His glory, and accepted our human condition, with all its limitations. He humbled Himself, and identified Himself with us. In order that we might know who God is, God sent the Logos, the Word, and the Word spoke the language of our poverty.

2. Translation is a risk, but a risk which must be taken. A Swedish author has written that "translation is an impossibility. To re-express the work of an English, a French or a Hottentot author in Swedish terms is in the last resort impossible. But translations are needed, and that is why some people must spend their time in the attempt to achieve the impossible." Such is the measure of difficulty attending all translation, and the missionary task of interpretation is no exception. In point of fact, it is highly improbable that the contents of the biblical message, expressed in Greek or Hebrew, will ever come fully home to a Zulu, a Tamil or a Swede. St. Augustine was one of the first to realize the existence of this problem; he pointed out the difficulties attending the "christianization" of the Latin language. Two persons meet, and in the course of conversation both use the word *salus*; the Christian means "salvation from evil", the non-Christian still uses the word in its classical sense of "good health". The situation has not improved since St. Augustine's day.

It is not self-evident that the missonary task of translation will ever be possible. But should success come, it will be due less to the missionary than to the work of the Holy Spirit. He who proceeds from the Father and the Son builds a bridge of understanding between man and man, and between nation and nation; He alone makes it possible for an African or a Swede to receive the message of the Gospel. The Spirit builds, in new lands, a Church speaking new languages.

God Himself took the risk of translation when He became incarnate, when He translated the Word into our stumbling language—and misunderstanding is inevitable. The offer of salvation becomes a stumbling-block. His translation—His offer of self-giving and self-effacing love —led direct to a cross. But the cross of risk and suffering is inscribed anew upon every translation as soon as an attempt is made to express the message in new terms.

But the risk must be taken. Otherwise there can be no communication.

3. Strangers and translators.

(a) The Church is a stranger to the people and their culture. We may recall our sketch of the biblical theology of mission, and say that she is a porch of the heavenly temple, or "a colony of heaven". She has not grown up of herself, by virtue of her own natural resources: she is sent by others, a link in a chain of mission, a succession of servants stretching back to the Father's sending of His Son. She is sent by others, from other lands, incorporated as a link in the long, holy chain created by the Holy Spirit in and through the tradition and history of the Church. Sent from Jerusalem and Antioch to Greece, Italy, Gaul and Ireland; from the country of the Franks and Saxons and Angles to the country of the Swedes and Goths; from Sweden to Zululand; from Sweden to Minnesota, and from Minnesota and Kansas to Tanganyika and Hong Kong. The Church in Africa is not a spontaneous growth; she has been sent by others, planted like some exotic shrub by the emissaries or missionaries of other churches.

(b) But the "strangeness" of the Church is even more fundamental. The message of Jesus Christ as Lord and Saviour is a message of repentance, conversion, change and newness of life. This means making a radical break with the past: "the old has passed away. Behold, the new has come," 2 Cor. 5: 17. It follows that in order to be able to translate at all, the would-be translator must know his original text, through and through. In order to preach the Gospel in Zulu you have to know the Gospel, and not merely Zulu!

(c) The converse holds good, too: the translator must know not merely the Gospel; he must know Zulu, Zulus and Zululand. The apostolic impulse to make Christ known compels the missionary to a responsible and thorough study of his future milieu, with all its cultural, religio-historical, social and other aspects. This particular aspect of missionary work needs to be stressed today, more than ever. The present generation of theologians have stressed, and rightly so, the foreignness of the Church in the world, but now it is true to say that the "Apostolate of the Church" requires that the emissary of Christ must go "the second mile" with men of other faiths. The missionary is no longer able to shut himself up in his "mission station". He must go to meet them with whom he would speak; he must seek them where they are, listen to their troubles, speak their language and serve them in boundless human solidarity. The missionary must even be prepared to face situations in which solidarity compels him to recognize that other religions are attracting him. His proclamation of Christ as King is never more relevant than in such situations as these.

4. When the Gospel is carried forth and translated into new languages and new cultures, new aspects of the given Message are revealed. When the Word, as once given, is proclaimed in new situations, among new peoples, new tribes and new languages, the missionary catches a glimpse of new facets of the given Word, the Message takes on new dimensions. It may be a new meaning, some richer and deeper interpretation, never before seen, and perhaps waiting to be revealed in that particular situation.

5. The spiritual heritage of the Church Universal is projected on to previously existing patterns, in Africa or Asia. The result of this projection is a combination of old and new, and can never be wholly identical with the tradition as known in the sending church. There have been cases of missionaries breaking down the patterns they have found. That is why it is a matter of vital concern in Africa or Asia what kind of mission comes to build the Church there. It may be a narrow, ignorant and therefore despotic mission; or it may be a mission with breadth and depth, capable of exercising a liberating influence, and of arousing creative forms in the life of the people.

6. Choice and interpretation must be a matter for the young church itself to decide. When the missionary church receives beliefs and customs through the mission, it acts

selectively. Some things it rejects; others it chooses as being fit for incorporation in the new pattern which it is in process of drawing up. This choice and this interpretation is the responsibility of the church, not of the mission. The task of the mission is not to direct, but to stimulate. The church's own African or Asian leaders carry out creative work on the basis of the material placed at their disposal.

We must not attempt to force them into our time-worn patterns; we must, on the other hand, show interest in, and sympathy for, let us say, the African's own cultural heritage; and we must be prepared to learn from him. It is as important that missionaries should be prepared to listen, as that they should be prepared to teach. As Arthur Cripps, a missionary in Southern Rhodesia, has well said, "We came to teach; we stayed to learn."

The question of the attitude of the missionary church to its own national heritage is however highly complex. On the one hand we find that most Christian converts of the first and second generations tend to reject their national heritage, its form, its colour and its rhythm. They have often shown too great a readiness to invest the forms and customs introduced by the first missionaries with an aura of sanctity. But on the other hand the best of these converts soon show signs of a healthy impatience with the exotic Westernness of the traditions brought by the missionaries. These are the men and women on whom the burden of translation ought to lie heaviest. It is in this situation that the need of solid theological education is most felt: an education which leaves room for a constructive confrontation between Christian theology and the traditional heritage.

It is possible, in a free Africa, India or Indonesia, to accept the manifold variety of God's creation; it is equally possible to give that variety full expression in the various forms of worship and the devotional life. But at the same time the leaders of the Church will emphasize that the task of the Church in a politically independent Africa is not primarily to be an African Church, but to be the Church of Christ in Africa.

The Missionary—a Translator

We have seen that the biblical theology of mission, with its eschatological dimension, implies that mission is the concern of the whole of the Church of Christ. But at the same time the Church has always observed the practice of setting apart and sending out men and women for special service. Christ the King sends out His ambassadors. Commissioned and sent by the Lord of the Church, the *missionary* goes out into the world with the Gospel, and his task is that of translating the message of salvation in Jesus Christ. However, the word "missionary" has been somewhat of a problem. The great age of expansion in the history of the Christian mission came simultaneously with the period of Western imperialism; the growing nationalism of Asia and Africa, reacting as it did against all forms of colonization, often connected the words "mission" and "missionary" with Western imperialism and its patriarchal attitude. The expression "native helpers" was still being used in missionary statistics, well on into the twentieth century, to describe the local leaders of the young churches. The implication is clear: they were looked upon as the missionary's assistants. It was taken for granted that it was the Western missionary who provided the initiative and stood at the head of affairs. The "missionary council" or "missionary conference" on the "mission field" was the final authority in all matters concerning the growth of the young church.

In recent years, a Copernican revolution has taken place. The first stages could be seen during the period between the two World Wars, and a decisive statement of policy was made by the international missionary movement at the Tambaram conference of 1938. But the actual revolution has really been precipitated by developments since the Second World War. The Church—the young

61

church in the Congo, in Kerala, in Korea and elsewhere —has now come to occupy the central position, the point of departure and penetration for mission. Leadership is now in the hands of the young churches' own people, and the task of the missionary has changed accordingly. It must be reshaped with reference to the new national leadership of the church concerned.

The distinction once drawn between "the Christian West" and the non-Christian East is now totally irrelevant. The whole world is now a mission field, and we all have our place on the missionary map. The missionary is no longer merely the one who crosses geographical or cultural boundaries; instead he stands on the boundary between belief and non-belief, and there bears witness to Jesus Christ. Of course the missionary commission is still valid "to the end of the earth", and the missionary must still go, a stranger, to other peoples and other tongues; but he goes as the representative of a supernational fellowship, whose message he must interpret and translate as faithfully as possible. It must not be supposed, therefore, that the coming of autonomy to the churches of Asia and Africa has rendered the missionary obsolete and unnecessary. His presence in the young church serves as a necessary reminder of the supranationality of the Church of Christ, and as a symbol of the Catholicity of the Church. There, too, he can be a witness of Christ: a bridge-builder between church and church, nation and nation, man and man.

The stranger, in order to bear witness, must attempt to translate his message. And mission, viewed from one angle, is the translation, in word and deed, of Christ's message of salvation. This commission cannot be carried out unless the person concerned be prepared to penetrate deep into a new world, a new language and a new culture, in a serious attempt to identify himself with those to whom he is sent. An identification of this nature can take place on one of two levels. It may take place on the level of social fellowship: that is, in an attempt to understand and appreciate, as far as is humanly possible, the cultural patterns of the people or tribe concerned. But this is insufficient for the missionary, who is sooner or later forced to identify himself with his people on a deeper level, *in Christ*. The missionary and his people work together and bear responsibility together: soon they are compelled to confess their sins together and pray together for forgiveness. It is at this level that the barriers of race, nationality and prejudice are broken down. Throughout the whole of the history of the Church *missio* and *passio* have been found together—necessarily so. The nature of the One who took upon Himself the form of a servant is most truly revealed in the Cross (Phil. 2: 7). It is at that same Cross that the King's emissary learns what it is to be a missionary.

The development and growth of the young church makes new demands of the foreign missionary. He may have to relinquish his front seat, and slip into the background, as an adviser to the church's own national leaders, as an instructor in a theological college, teacher training college or medical school, as an expert in many fields, as a consultant in the use of mass media—the Press, literature, radio, TV. The list might be extended almost indefinitely. But whatever shape his work may take, he must come as a friend, as a trusted fellow-worker, and perhaps as a pastor of souls. This is a question of identification on the deepest level. The world missionary movement has not forgotten how, at the 1910 World Missionary Conference in Edinburgh, the young Indian, V. S. Azariah (later Bishop of Dornakal, d. 1945), turned to the leaders of the Western missions, saying, "You have given your goods to feed the poor. You have given your bodies to be burned. We also ask for *love*. Give us FRIENDS!"

The time has perhaps come for the white missionary to make a similar appeal to the Church leaders of Asia and Africa. But whoever may take the initiative, the fact remains: that the result of the missionary's labours depends in no small measure upon that personal fellowship which springs from common obedience to our Lord Jesus Christ.

In the 1950's it was proposed that the problematical word "missionary" should be removed, and replaced by "fraternal worker". This vague term, not without some measure of condescension, was to be applied primarily to those "short service" workers; short service having come to replace the earlier ideal of life-long missionary work, particularly since the Second World War.

The conditions under which the missionary works, and his possibilities for service, are very much affected by political climate. This is a topic to which we shall have frequent occasion to return in our historical section. The Western missionary's chance of making any contribution at all in the Communist countries of Asia has virtually disappeared. Other missionaries working in autonomous Asian churches found there to be "no room for whites" (the exaggeration was deliberate).[1]

In India the problem was rather similar. Permits of residence were issued to missionaries only if it could be proved that there was no Indian able to carry out that particular duty. Under this heading India was prepared to accept, for example, medical or agricultural "experts". But the Westerner wanting to enter India in the service of the Gospel is liable to find his way barred.

In recent years, and particularly since the Second World War, the churches of the West have come to recognize the necessity of *interchange* between East and West. This has in some cases led to practical results, in that leaders of the young churches have been invited to come and spend some time in parish or administrative work in the West. The presence of African clergymen or Asian theologians in the churches of the West is thoroughly stimulating, and a necessary expression of the universal mission of the Church Universal.

[1] Cf. G. Schultz, *Kein Platz Mehr für Weisse* (1956).

It is important that we should remember that "missionaries" do not have to be Westerners. The term is one which applies to every Christian messenger, irrespective of nationality or race. Apolo Kivebulaya of Uganda (d. 1928), the Apostle of the Pygmies of Central Africa, and many others of the same people, members of the Anglican Church in Uganda, may serve to remind us that in this century Africans are acting as missionaries to other tribes and peoples. The National Missionary Society of India, founded in 1905, was a mission of Indians to Indians. The Church of Samoa in Oceania has sent out many missionaries to the islands of the Pacific. The Samoans, with their fragile canoes, have long been bold sailors; now their instinct is filled with a new spirit, as they sail into unknown waters bearing the Christian message.

The churches of Asia, gathered recently for conference, drew up an inventory of their missionary enterprise. The result was striking: these young churches supported about two hundred missionaries in various parts of Asia. We may give some examples, as indication of what is happening in the world of mission.

From the Church of South India: missionaries to Thailand and Malaysia.

From the Mar Thoma Church: *ashrams* have been founded in various parts of India (outside Malabar) with *c.* 130 Indian missionary workers; one family to Katmandu in Nepal.

From the United Church of North India: to East Africa.

From West Pakistan: evangelistic teams to Kashmir.

From the Methodist Church in India: missionaries to Burma.

From the Karen Church of North Burma: missionaries to South Burma and Thailand.

From the Presbyterian Church of Korea: to Thailand.

From the United Church of the Philippines: five missionaries to Thailand; three to Indonesia; three to Iran; one to Korea; two to Honolulu and two to the United States.

From the Methodist Church of the Philippines: one to Okinawa; four to Malaya and Sarawak.

From the United Church of Japan (*Kyodan*): to Okinawa and Formosa; one family to Indonesia.

From Anglican Churches in East Asia: comprehensive exchange of Asian workers between Anglican Churches in the area; particularly to Malaysia and Hong Kong.

From ten Indonesian Churches: to other parts of the Indonesian archipelago.

From the Y.M.C.A. in Asia: exchange of personnel with other strategic points in the Asian Y.M.C.A. network.

PART TWO

CHURCH AND EMPIRE

The King's messengers are sent to proclaim a kingdom which is not of this world. The proclamation of the Gospel and the foundation of churches points towards a reality beyond the bounds of this world. But the Apostle, although he reminded his Gentile Christian congregation that they were not "*of* the world", knew very well that they were "*in* the world". The missionary Church, wherever she may be called to work and witness, is continually being confronted with the intractable material of national group interests and the power-political constellations of international affairs.

The relations of the Christian mission to kings, states and colonial politics are of greater importance in the history of missions than is often realized. This relationship is much more than incidental framework within which missions have full freedom of movement: it exercises direct influence on the conditions under which the Church lives and works. The importance and centrality of this influence is such, that we have felt it necessary in this section of the book to treat the history of the Christian mission as the history of the confrontation of missions and politics.

CHAPTER 5

THE EMPIRE AND THE APOSTLES

THE CHURCH GREW UP WITHIN THE BOUNDARIES OF the Roman Empire. "In those days a decree went out from Caesar Augustus"—that taxes should be paid, that men should serve in the imperial army, that roads should be built. The Empire built roads but men of faith travelled on them. The *Pax Romana*, the Roman peace, was established from the Tiber to the Thames. Despite the variety of languages, religions and philosophies, the Empire was held together by the Hellenistic Roman culture, its law, and its official cultus of the classical pantheon. The pillars of this culture were the upper classes; the aristocratic foundations of ancient Roman society were deep: the blessings of classical civilization were enjoyed only by a privileged urban minority.

For the country people, Pan was of more consequence than Zeus. The old fertility religion had retained its vitality, and its hold on popular piety. It was at the sacred groves, springs and trees—in Gaul, Spain, Italy and elsewhere—that the rhythm of the turning year was more clearly felt. This was part of the *mos maiorum*, the custom of the ancients, and it was on this that the people's *pietas* was based. Myths and sacred actions from the world of the fertility religions penetrated the Oriental mystery religions, which at this time enjoyed great and growing popularity in the Empire: Cybele's baptism of blood, sacral prostitution and the sacrifice of children in the worship of Baal and Astarte. Eastern deities—Isis and Mithras, Cybele and Attis—came to the cities of the West, where they proclaimed their various answers to moribund Antiquity's preoccupation with the beyond, and its longing for salvation and immortality.

But the mystery cults, then as now, were the prerogative of the upper classes: secret societies to which only birth and money could gain admittance. They had little or nothing to give the lower classes; least of all to those rapidly expanding groups in the urban population who were called the "inner proletariat", the masses of slaves in the slums, and the common people, the *humiliores*. Despite certain tendencies towards emancipation among the upper classes, women were still under-privileged; so were children. Classical Antiquity was a man's world, and educated its children more by force than by love.

The political development of Ancient Rome culminated, during the time of Augustus, in the cult of the emperor. On the new imperial coins Augustus carried the sceptre of the King of heaven, wore the halo of the sun-god, and sat on a divine throne. The Emperor became a god, and remained so, at least so long as he was able to take such a politically convenient myth seriously.

The claims of Caesar reached even as far as Palestine. The carpenter's son from Nazareth called for a *denarius*, and saw on it the image and superscription of Caesar. This was the symbol both of the power and the culture of the Roman Empire. It was probably an image of the Emperor Tiberius, and the superscription described him as the worshipful son of the worshipful god. The carpenter's son said, "Render to Caesar the things that are Caesar's . . ." (Matt. 22: 21). No one could object to that. And as long as no one did object, there need be no fears for the future of the *Pax Romana*. But the Prophet in Judah went further, adding the revolutionary clause, ". . . and to God the things that are God's." His followers were later to stand before kings, judges and tribunals, and say, "We are Christians, and we cannot sacrifice to idols." In Carthage in North Africa, one of those who was accused during the

70

course of the Emperor Commodus' persecutions, Speratus, said, "I know nothing about the empire of this world; I serve the invisible God. I know my Lord, King of Kings and Emperor of all peoples." This was the good seed, which grew and bore fruit, thirtyfold, sixtyfold and a hundredfold in and through the Christian mission.

There is one Master Idea which can be discerned in the expansion of the Church in the Roman Empire. It was present in Paul's own missionary work: the goal of reaching the cities in the Mediterranean area, as far west as Spain, the boundary of the *oikoumene*: from these centres the Gospel could then be spread to the mass of the people. Paul's method of first making contact with groups (in his case of Jewish) exiles in the cities was followed by many other messengers in later centuries.

The strategic centres were Antioch, Alexandria, Edessa and Rome. At this time the work of evangelization was far from being directed from a common headquarters. Its nature was more spontaneous: in every centre it was kept up by a system of living cells—the *communautès rayonnantes* of which we speak today. In each place the Christian community consisted of a bishop (the heir of the Apostles and the Apostles' disciples), his clergy, the faithful and a steadily growing group of catechumens.

It was in Antioch that the disciples first received the name "Christians" (Acts 11: 26). It was from Antioch that Paul set out on his missionary journeys. An enthusiastic and well-loved Bishop of Antioch, Ignatius, welded together Church and mission. The martyr Bishop and his congregation, strengthened by the Eucharist ("the medicine of immortality"), set on foot an intensive missionary activity out into Asia Minor and the Orient. It is true that the city itself was one of the more tenacious strongholds of heathenism, well into the fourth century, but the Christian minority opposed it energetically. By the beginning of the fourth century Coele Syria (now El-Biqua) had no less than twenty-two Bishops, two of whom were appointed to exercise oversight over the country districts—proof that the new religion had left the towns and begun to take root in the country.

The missionary work of the Apostles Paul and John in Asia Minor was based on Antioch. According to Pliny, Christianity had reached Bithynia on the Black Sea by about A.D. 100. In Cappadocia, the evangelization of the country was begun by soldiers of the imperial legions. In Greece and Asia Minor archaeology has enabled scholars to trace something of the transition from pagan to Christian. It is common knowledge that the Parthenon in Athens was converted into a church, dedicated to the Mother of God, probably about 435. The rebuilding of the temple of the goddess Athena Polias took place at about the same time; it too became a church of the Mother of God. The church of St. George was built above the temple of the blacksmith Hephaistos. Frequently old temples were pressed into service as churches and given new names, thus preserving some semblance of connexion between the old and the new cults. In Asia Minor, on the other hand, the Hellenistic religion was less active, and has not left traces to the same extent on the missionary history of the period.

From Antioch, the first missionaries crossed the bounds of the Empire eastward, into the mighty kingdoms of Asia to the boundaries of the *oikoumene*, and even beyond. Ptolemy, the brilliant astronomer of Alexandria (d. A.D. 160) had drawn their map of the world. On it were three continents, Europe, Libya and "Asia". New perspectives opened; new doors; a new freedom—through this new astronomical map, with its world globe resting in the universe: five-sixths covered with water, the remainder habitable land.

The Jewish Christian commercial colony in Edessa (now Urfa in S.E. Turkey) became the centre of a rapidly expanding church, whose theologian was Bardesanes. Bardesanes gave Christianity a new and original expression:

in the Syriac language, in theological statements and in hymns, coloured by Gnostic ideas. Christ was praised as "Son of the sun and the moon, and the first-born brother of the stars". Bardesanes the theologian and hymn-writer was at the same time a courtier and ecclesiastical politician; since his youth he had been a friend of the king. It was due to his influence that King Abgar the Great in about A.D. 200 embraced Christianity; for the first time Christianity had become an official State religion. An "original portrait" of Jesus Christ was placed in the palace, and on his coins Abgar wore a tiara with a jewelled cross. Edessa became the first Christian city of the Ancient World, and here originated that Eastern form of Christian culture which was in time to stretch from the Mediterranean to Ceylon and China.

Edessa and Asia Minor co-operated to pass the message on to Armenia. When King Tiridates of Armenia was converted in *c.* 300 (by the agency of St. Gregory the Illuminator) he at once began, with the zeal of a new convert, to destroy idols and convert pagan temples into churches. As in Edessa, the conversion of the King meant to all intents and purposes that the whole country accepted the new religion.

The Eastern Syriac liturgy was further carried into Persia, where the Church grew rapidly, despite official opposition and the persecution of individual Christians. This church was later to be of considerable importance, on account of its missionary activity in Central Asia and China. In 410 the Bishop of Seleucia-Ktesiphon was made *Katholikos* (for national reasons), with a high degree of independence over against the Syriac-Monophysite province of Antioch. The virtual independence of the Persian Church made it easier for them to accept the Nestorian form of Christianity—a step which cut their lines of communication westward, but opened doors eastward, to India and China.

In 190 Pantaenus penetrated to "India" (probably the

Yemen in S. Arabia). Following him the first ships carrying Christian merchants reached South India. By this means the foundations were laid of the Syrian Church in India. A further important result was the "Christian Topography" of Kosmas, which dates from *c.* 540, and which was of fundamental importance for travellers throughout the Middle Ages.

Indian Christians regard the Apostle Thomas as their first missionary, and hold that he was martyred in India. This is a tradition which has often been called in question, but is not one which can be rejected out of hand. There were Jewish *diaspora* groups in Travancore by A.D. 70, and archaeological evidence has shown the Syrian Church in India to have been of extreme antiquity. Recently the remains of an old church have been found at Nilackel in Travancore, 25 metres long and 9 metres wide. The site of the chancel is shown by a raised section of the floor at the east end, 6 metres long. It is interesting to note that the remains of an ancient Hindu temple have been discovered hard by, and it is tempting to assume that the Christian church was built on the approximate site of the abandoned pagan shrine.

The Church of Antioch seems also to have had some contact with Africa. Acts 13: 1 mentions among the "prophets and teachers" of the church there one Lucius of Cyrene. And the Gospel reached Africa at a very early date, perhaps through the witness of Simon of Cyrene, who carried Jesus' cross. Alexandria, with its flourishing catechetical school, we know to have formed the centre of a mission; however, we know nothing of its details. Tradition has it that it was from Alexandria, in the 330's, that Adesius and his brother Frumentius reached Ethiopia by sea. Frumentius was consecrated Bishop of Ethiopia by Athanasius, and became the founder of the Coptic Church in that country.

The Church's language situation in the Orient was complicated. Christianity could be proclaimed in Greek—

and only Greek—in these countries in which Hellenism was the dominant culture. This applied, for instance, in Asia Minor, where the Church encountered languages having little or no cultural background, and hence little future. Such were the Phrygian and Lycaonian languages. In these countries Hellenism and Christianity conquered hand in hand.

But in Egypt and Syria the Church had to face an entirely different situation: ancient cultures and languages over which the veneer of Hellenism was thin. The Church's solution was to make use of the ancient languages. True, they had been neglected and despised since the conquest of Alexander, but the Church took and made of them elaborate, learned, sacred languages. The Bible was read, the liturgy sung and the Gospel preached in Coptic and Syriac.

This bold solution was not without its difficulties in Egypt, and later in the remainder of North Africa. We know from the Egyptian *Acts of the Martyrs* that a large number of Egyptian villages had accepted Christianity by the early fourth century, but Coptic, unlike Syriac, never became the vehicle of original theological thought. It was a translators' language, far removed from the speech of the common people. This is one of the reasons why the first conquest of North Africa by Islam could take place almost without opposition. Ethiopia, on the other hand, was a striking exception.

In North Africa the Church reached just so far as Latin was spoken; so far and no further. Latin was the language of the soldiers, the colonists and the merchants; here too Christianity was the religion of immigrants and foreigners. The Bible was never translated into Punic, and though there were large numbers of Bishops (*c.* 100 in A.D. 250; 165 after A.D. 400), most were totally unable to speak to the people in their own language. Augustine of Hippo was an exception, however. He divided up his diocese in order to ensure that the people would be served by priests conversant with the local language. But the Church's language policy as a whole, from which Carthaginians and Berbers were practically excluded, called forth in time a nationalist reaction; the under-privileged groups abandoned orthodox Christianity for anti-imperialist forms of religion, first Donatism and later Islam.

During the first five generations of its existence, the Church of Rome was not Latin, nor was it even an intrinsic part of the life of the city. The Roman Church was part of a Greek colony, an intermediate station for a host of Oriental, Greek-speaking Christians, who spent varying periods in the metropolis. The Christian congregation was recruited from many groups, one of the most important being the slaves. These came mainly from the East, and spoke Greek. The Church's leaders, too, were for the most part Greek-speaking Orientals. This long Greek tradition in the Roman Church was begun by St. Peter and St. Paul. Of the first thirteen Bishops of Rome, only two had Latin names, and it is probable that most of the others came from the East. The cosmopolitan and bizarre character of the Christian immigrant body, among whom Gnostic tendencies were rife, impressed upon the leaders of the Church the need for a fixed Canon Law. After A.D. 200 there began a period of reaction against foreign influences in the Church of Rome. Bishop Victor, a native of North Africa, was largely responsible, towards the end of the second century, for ensuring the victory of Latin as the language of canon and dogma. The martyrdom of St. Peter and St. Paul also contributed to the establishment of another important tradition in Rome.

The immigrant colony had various ways of reaching the permanent population of the city with their message. They met together with their Christian friends and acquaintances for worship, and above all for the liturgical Eucharist, at which bishop, priests and deacons all served.

Shortly before his martyrdom Justin was asked by his

judge, "Tell me, where do you usually meet? In what place do you assemble your disciples?" Justin answered, "This is my second visit to Rome, and I have a first-floor room in the house of one Martin, near the Timiotinian Bath. During all my stay here I have known no other place. When anyone came to me, asking to be taught the truth, I was in the habit of teaching him." "Are you then a Christian?" "Yes, I am a Christian." This confession was sufficient to sign Justin's death-warrant, but it had a power of attraction, limited to no particular class of society. Celsus looked upon Christian converts as an unattractive group: "We see them in private houses; weavers and tanners, launderers and the most uneducated and rustic persons. They dare not open their mouths in their masters' presence. But they go to women and children, who are as ignorant as they themselves, saying, 'We are the only ones who know how men ought to live.'"

Most Christians belonged to the proletariat. But the house-church in which the bishop met his people might well be the property of a rich Roman *matrona*. She, and others like her, had seen through the cult of the emperor: not even the emperor himself and his court took it seriously any more. No one believed in the old classical pantheons. But this Saviour, in whose name so many had gone singing to their death—He must be the King of Truth. "Christianity bore witness to the truth in a world given over to the lie. That was why it overcame the ancient pagan religions." (Stauffer).

In A.D. 250 the Bishop of Rome was able to report (in Greek) to his colleague in Antioch that in his diocese he had more than 150 priests and other clerics, including acolytes and exorcists. It has been estimated that Christians numbered between 30,000 and 50,000. And while they were still meeting in houses, under the sign of the "fish" ($\iota\chi\theta\upsilon\varsigma$ was the monogram of Christ), a start was being made with the building of basilicas. But by A.D. 300 there were still very few of these; at this time there were

77

only about 20–25 Christian places of worship in the whole of Rome.

It was not only in Rome that foreigners and immigrants set the pattern for the young Christian Church. The Church in Gaul was planted by colonists in the name of the Church of Rome. Irenaeus, who was Bishop of Lyons from 178 to his death in *c*. 220, came from a Greek and Eastern background. He came from Asia Minor; in his youth he had been a pupil of the martyr Polycarp of Smyrna; he spoke Greek. His predecessor in the See of Lyons, Potinus, came from the same part of the world. Irenaeus, though primarily a theologian and church leader, regarded himself as a missionary. He was the first of many missionaries throughout the history of the Church to recognize that a long period spent in work on a mission field has an adverse effect on the missionary's capacity for speaking and writing his mother-tongue. In the foreword to his *Adversus Haereses* he excuses himself for his bad Greek; constantly speaking the "barbaric dialect" of the Celts, he had lost his sense of classical style.

The Church made slow progress through Gaul and beyond, but the Synod of Arles in 314 was attended by no less than sixteen Frankish Bishops, two from Germany (Trier and Cologne) and three from Britain (London, York, and Lincoln). Thus we see that important bridge-heads had been captured in the struggle for the kingdoms of the Germans and Angles. The towns had been partly occupied; but not the country districts. When the Emperor Constantine the Great made his peace with the Church it is hardly possible that more than 10–15 per cent of the population of the Roman Empire were Christians. But the situation changed radically during the later part of the fourth century, particularly as a result of the Edict of Theodosius (380). Now the hitherto despised religion of Christ was the official religion of the Empire, and paganism very soon felt the force of the Emperor's repressive measures. Tradition has it that the Emperor Julian was the one who confirmed the victory of the Church over the Empire with the bitter words, "Thou hast conquered, Galilean."

Why were the men and women of the ancient world attracted to this new faith? For a variety of reasons. The Emperor's claim to be divine had become more and more hollow as the years passed; and viewed against this background the Christian martyrs' confession of Jesus as King came to be regarded as nothing less than an assertion of the truth. The arguments of the apologists and the theologians strengthened this impression among the intelligentsia. Men and women were persuaded, not by organized missionary effort, but by the evidence of the Christian life, the willingness of groups and individuals to help one another, and the exercise of the Christian virtues. But if Christians out-lived their contemporaries, they out-died them too. Many were more impressed by the new death, than by the new life. Where before had men and women met death with a song on their lips? Pascal has gone to the heart of the matter: "I believe only that history whose witnesses are prepared to risk their lives for its truth." Even the way the Christians buried their dead was not without its significance—a circumstance which can be paralleled in Africa and Asia today. In Alexandria, during the great plague of *c*. 200, it was nothing short of a sensation that the Christians, instead of leaving their dead to lie where they had fallen in the street, took and buried them reverently.

The fellowship enjoyed within the congregation and their worship were further important collective factors. Catechumens were only allowed to be present at the first part of the service; not until after their baptism (which often took place on Easter Day) were they permitted to take part in the believers' Mass. Here we may see one of the sources of the numinous attraction to the Altar and its Sacrament which was, and still is, a necessary part of the life of the Church. The church year, which often linked up

79

with the feasts and festivals of the traditional religion, and which may be regarded as in some sense a projection of the Church's collective missionary situation, was another powerful missionary factor. The sacred rhythms of the year, the week and the day consecrated the passage of time; they lent resilience, energy and content to the religious life of the group.

CHAPTER 6

THE CHIEFTAINS AND THE WHITE CHRIST

Europe

The Middle Ages! First of all, a *caveat*: there is a traditional view of the Middle Ages, which looks upon this epoch as "static" or "conservative". From the missionary point of view this is wholly mistaken; the Middle Ages were anything but static. The Church was on the march, westward and northward and eastward. Its leaders and its servants had no permanent resting place, but had to be constantly prepared to travel, far and wide in the service of the Gospel. But we might equally well say that it was the Germanic peoples, in the course of their migration southward, who met the Church and Christianity. K. D. Schmidt has said that "there was a centripetal movement in the Middle Ages": a movement towards the Church's cultural centres in France and Italy. However this is to be interpreted, we cannot help but be impressed by the constant peregrinations of the early Middle Ages: by the sight of men on the march for the sake of Christ. And this movement created civilization. Temporary stave-churches or plain stone basilicas were built to house the worship of the faithful, yet after a few short generations the young Church was ready to build its glorious Romanesque cathedrals over its cloisters and its city walls.

The Middle Ages were one of the Church's great missionary epochs. While the old Church looked after men and women in the classical civilizations, the Medieval Church turned to the barbarians—Germans and Slavs— and fought with heretics (the Arians) and unbelievers

(Islam). Its mission field was Europe—Europe north of the Alps.

A key position in the christianization of the masses was played by the kings and chieftains, and no less by their queens. Seldom was any direct missionary initiative taken centrally by the Pope in Rome; the missionary impulse came rather from local bishops and abbots.

An important era began on Christmas Day, 496, with the baptism of Clovis, King of the Franks. Fifteen years before, when he had become king, Remigius, Bishop of Reims, had sent him a fatherly letter: "Always show respect for the Bishops, and always follow their advice. If you do that, all will be well with your country." In 493 the marriage of Clovis and the Catholic Clotilda of Burgundy had been arranged by Bishop Avitus of Vienne (on the Rhône); the young queen proved to be a purposeful missionary. To win Clovis for the White Christ was no easy matter, however. Difficulties and crises, such as every missionary knows, came and went. When the young couple's first child fell ill and died, the King interpreted the misfortune in the same way as many an African or Indian villager today: "My gods could have saved the child; your god would not." But the faith and prayers of the Queen had made a deep impression, and Clovis was finally baptized by Remigius, who called out during the ceremony, "Bow your head, Sicamber, worship what you have burnt, and burn what you have worshipped." Ten years later, when Clovis conquered the Visigoths, the Church was able to see the beginnings of *Gesta Dei per Francos*, the mighty works of God through the Franks.

In France, England and Germany the conversion of the kings set the seal on the people's christianization. A collective vow of allegiance to the White Christ was often regarded as being the obvious religious consequence of the political and social loyalties of the feudal system. In Denmark and Norway, too, the conversion of Harald Bluetooth and Olav Tryggveson respectively was decisive. In

Iceland, however, a formal decision to embrace Christianity was taken in 1000 by the Althing, after a mere two decades of direct missionary work. In Sweden, the missionary period proper did not start until the eleventh century. There had been earlier missions, of course, but Ansgar and Unne were little more than temporary visitors who only succeeded in scratching the surface of paganism. The highly complex missionary situation in eleventh-century Sweden must be viewed against the background of the struggle for power in the royal house.

The Venerable Bede, in his *History of the English Church and People*, relates how King Peada of the Middle Angles, was baptized by Bishop Finan, "together with his companions, thanes and servants". The reference to the thanes is not without its special significance. The noblemen, standing as they did on the highest level of public life, were important for the process of christianization, which began with the upper classes and worked its way down. Indeed, at that time, and in that type of society, it could not have taken place at all otherwise. When Wilfrid, Archbishop of York, arrived in the province of the South Saxons in *c.* 678, he succeeded in baptizing a large number of thanes and soldiers, leaving to other priests the task of baptizing "the remainder of the people". The work was facilitated by the coming of timely rain; and by a good haul of fish. As Bede says, "the people began to listen more readily to his teaching, hoping to obtain heavenly blessings through the ministry of one to whom they already owed their material benefits". But it must not be supposed that this was an automatic or a sudden process, or that conversion was absolute. Christianity and paganism lived side by side for generations: *vide* the people's burial practices.

Special attention must also be paid to the missionary contribution of the Christian queens. The religious influence of women has always been great, particularly when the religion in question has claimed sole and absolute validity. We recall Clotilda of the Franks, Theodelinda of

83

the Lombards, Ethelberga of Northumbria, Bertha of Kent, Alchfleda of the Middle Angles, and Queens Olga and Anna in tenth-century Russia—all consecrated Christian women prepared to work and sacrifice for their religion. The marriage of a pagan king with a Christian princess is an important fact in the history of missions. For when the princess in question left her home and her church, she was as a rule accompanied by a bishop. Thus the Frankish Bishop Lindhard came with Bertha to Kent, and Paulinus with Ethelberga to Northumbria, where he later became Bishop of York. Many of the Christian queens of the early Middle Ages became famous for their monastic foundations, the mission stations of that period.

While Christian queens often occupied the forefront of the missionary advance, particularly in the capitals, the work of converting the common people was entrusted to the monks. Eremites and anchorites were the first. Wandering monks of the Celtic tradition held fast to their own method: *peregrinari pro Christo*. When Benedict of Nursia established his first monastery and drew up his rule (*c.* 529), he was laying the foundations of many a mission station: centres of light and civilization in a largely barbaric Europe. Benedict's own Monte Cassino was built on the site of the temple of the sun-god. Europe was converted to Christianity by Benedictine monks. On foot or on horseback they penetrated the great forests of Germany and France; in frail boats they navigated Europe's rivers. The wandering monk lived simply, sheltered in some hut or cave. Most are unknown and unhonoured, but the greatest among them may be mentioned: Wynfrith, born in Devonshire, England, and better known as St. Boniface, the apostle of Germany, organizer of the Frankish Church, and later Archbishop of Mainz. He was martyred in Holland in 754.

Of no less importance were the missionary bishops, some of whom had previously been monks. The Papacy at Rome, on the other hand, made little or no contribution to the Church's missionary expansion at this early date, in striking contrast to the Papacy of later periods. The early Middle Ages may perhaps be characterized as a period of dispersion and flexibility in missionary work, rather than as a period of centralization. An important exception to this general rule is however provided by Gregory the Great, who was Pope from 590 to his death in 604, and his initiative towards the christianization of England. Gregory had planned his campaign in detail, even before he sent Augustine, Prior of St. Andrew's Monastery in Rome, to England in 596. He had bought young Anglo-Saxon slaves on the market-place in Rome, and had them brought up and baptized as Christians in order to be able to serve as interpreters for the missionaries. Augustine set out with forty priests, most of whom feared the worst of the unknown heathen country in the north-west. When they came to France they heard rumours that the Angles were in the habit of tearing out and devouring the hearts of their enemies, and that Britain was the very kingdom of the dead. But in the event, they were agreeably surprised. The life and witness of Queen Bertha had done much to pave the way for the missionaries. Whitsun, 597, saw the baptism of the king and his monks. At Christmas of the same year Augustine baptized no less than ten thousand Anglo-Saxons. "Nothing less than a river would suffice" for so many (Daniel-Rops). The Pope sent the *pallium* to Augustine, who thereby became Archbishop of Canterbury—the first in a succession of which the present Archbishop, Dr. A. M. Ramsey, is the hundredth. With the *pallium* Gregory sent instructions as to how the Church in England was to be organized: two Archbishoprics, London (or Canterbury) and York, each with twelve dioceses.

Gregory was a sick man, but his iron will and personal discipline enabled him to keep his affairs in order: from his bed, he wrote many letters to Augustine, directing him how best to carry out his mission. A particularly important

letter is dated July 18, 601; it is addressed to Abbot Mellitus on his departure for Britain and contains instructions
for Augustine and his fellow-workers in England:

To our well loved son Abbot Mellitus: Gregory, servant
of the servants of God.

Since the departure of yourself and your companions, we
have been somewhat anxious, because we have received no
news of the success of your journey. Therefore, when by
God's help you reach our most reverend brother, Bishop
Augustine, we wish you to inform him that we have been
giving lawful thought to the affairs of the English, and have
come to the conclusion that the temples of the idols in that
country should on no account be destroyed. He is to destroy
the idols, but the temples themselves are to be aspersed with
holy water, altars set up, and relics enclosed in them. For if
their temples are well built, they are to be purified from
devil-worship, and dedicated to the service of the true God.
In this way, we hope that the people, seeing that its temples
are not destroyed, may abandon idolatry and resort to these
places as before, and may come to know and adore the true
God. And since they have a custom of sacrificing many oxen
to devils, let some other solemnity be substituted in its place,
such as a day of Dedication or the Festivals of the holy
martyrs whose relics are enshrined there. On such occasions
they might well construct shelters of boughs for themselves
around the churches that were once temples, and celebrate
the solemnity with devout feasting. They are no longer to
sacrifice beasts to the Devil, but they may kill them for food
to the praise of God, and give thanks to the Giver of all gifts
for His bounty. If the people are allowed some worldly
pleasures in this way, they will more readily come to desire
the joys of the spirit. For it is certainly impossible to eradi-
cate all errors from obstinate minds at one stroke. And whoever wishes to climb to a mountain top climbs gradually step
by step, and not in one leap.[1]

These instructions, though fascinating in themselves,
must not be projected on to the historical course of events;

[1] The authenticity of this *libellus responsium* has been called in question, and some scholars are of the opinion that it dates from *c.* 750.

in other words, we must not assume from this letter that the continuity between pagan cult-centre and Christian Church was always observed. The nature of the Germanic and Nordic religion must be kept in mind. It was freely syncretistic, and had no difficulty in assimilating new concepts—even the radical concept of the White Christ— into its world of ideas. But the cult was a different matter. Interference with, or alteration in, the pattern of cult observance brought forth an immediate and violent reaction from the people. Nordic religion was tolerant in its beliefs, but exclusive in its cults; the Medieval Christian mission was exclusive in its beliefs, and tolerant in its cultus. This had a direct effect on the relation between cult-centre and church. In Sweden, for example, although churches were built as near as possible to the old cult-centres (an obvious move in the strategy of missions), the two sites were nevertheless kept slightly apart, with a view to the cultic exclusiveness of the old religion. This applies even in the celebrated case of the temple in what is now Gamla Uppsala. The Christian church there was not built until after the power of heathenism had been finally broken. From the point of view of the history of religions, the building of a church on the exact site of the Uppsala temple was proof of the fall of heathenism.

Who is stronger, Wotan-Odin or the White Christ? That was the decisive question. Which of the rival gods was the mightier warrior, the greater healer, the true conqueror of death? The riddle of death could not be forgotten or ignored. An English warrior in Northumbria may be taken as spokesman of the Germanic peoples in face of the inescapable reality. He said to King Edwin:

"Your majesty, when we compare the present life of man with that time of which we have no knowledge, it seems to me like the swift flight of a lone sparrow through the banqueting-hall where you sit in the winter months to dine with your thanes and counsellors. Inside there is a comforting fire to warm the room, outside the wintry

87

storms of snow and rain are raging. This sparrow flies swiftly in through one door of the hall, and out through another. While he is inside, he is safe from the winter storms; but after a few moments of comfort, he vanishes from sight into the darkness—from which he came. Similarly, man appears on earth for a little while, but we know nothing of what went before this life, and what follows. Therefore if this new teaching can reveal any more certain knowledge, it seems only right that we should follow it."

Formerly, men placed their confidence (*fulltrui*) in Frö or Tor or some other god in the Germanic pantheon. But now they were prepared to repose *fulltrui* in the White Christ. It is characteristic that the Germanic peoples' confidence in power creates a corresponding image of Christ. The image of Christ held by later Antiquity was replaced by the heroic Christ, in triumph while yet on the cross; a crown on His head, His arms outstretched not in torment, but in a gesture of victory. But triumph did not come without bitter conflict, and something of the personal struggle involved is sometimes reflected in the ancient documents. Olav Tryggveson's *skald* Hallfred has embodied his own feelings in these unforgettable lines:

> All men have made songs
> To win the favour of Odin;
> It is hard for me to hate
> The husband of Frigg (Odin)
> Because I am a servant of Christ.

> Frö and Freja may pour their wrath upon me;
> I leave the temple of Njord.
> May the trolls help Odin
> And Tor the strong.

> I will pray to Christ above
> And to God for the love of them all.
> I fear the wrath of the Son,
> Whose Father has given him
> Power over the earth.

88

All men abandon the house of Odin;
I too must leave the friends of Njord
And worship Christ.

But it would be wrong to suppose that all those caught up into the conflict between Odin and Christ underwent a struggle of this kind. Mass conversion was the rule, rather than the exception, among the Germanic peoples. As Wilhelm Grönbech has graphically said, "One-two, one-two: there they go, clans, counties, nations, marching over to Christianity."

The religious conflict in early Medieval Sweden is not without profound significance for corresponding situations in the Cameroons or in New Guinea today. Although the Nordic religion had in principle been conquered, many of its patterns and its ideas lived on under a veneer of Christianity. The conversion was neither sudden nor complete. Only gradually did pagan beliefs, customs and ceremonies fall into abeyance, particularly since the protagonists were an ancient popular religion and a Church prepared to exercise a measure of cultic tolerance. A great deal of popular magic was tolerated, if not accepted; for instance, the signs of the Zodiac were given a Christian terminology. Some have even gone so far as to ask whether the popular religion became christianized, or whether Christianity became paganized in Scandinavia.[1] As late as during the Reformation and Orthodox periods in Swedish church history we find examples of sorcery and magic, and though the Church fulminated against them, they were not at once uprooted. Modern missionaries in Africa and Asia would do well to ponder this development; there is no lack of parallel instances in the young churches.

Beyond Europe

From 500 to 1200, Europe was the Church's principal mission field; but the field was not altogether confined to Europe. In North Africa, the Church was forced to con-

[1] Emil Birkeli, *Fedrekult i Norge* (Oslo, 1938).

cede an overwhelming victory to Islam, which during the seventh century swept away what had once been a relatively flourishing Christian Church. The Christian mission had been successful in Northern Europe, it is true, but that did little to mitigate its decisive defeat in the Mediterranean basin. From that time, the fragments of the Church which managed to keep their separate existence amid the world of Islam did so only with extreme difficulty, particularly since the Muslim majority forbade all forms of missionary work. Eastward the Christian message was carried into South India by Persian Christians and by monks of the Syrian Jacobite tradition, and we have already noted the tradition that the Apostle Thomas himself was India's first missionary. Monks of the Eastern tradition even penetrated as far as China. Nestorians reached China along the ancient silk road through Central Asia. A Bishop was consecrated in 550, and an intermediate station established on the road to the Far East.

The earliest Christian traditions in China date back to about A.D. 635. In 1625 there was discovered the "Hsianfu stone", which tells of the earliest Christian missionary history of China. Hsianfu or Ch'ang-An was the capital of China in the seventh century. The monument. which was erected in 781, and which refers to the events of the 630's, is a ten-foot-high slab of granite, bearing a cross and the inscription: "Table of the spread of the honourable Syrian religion to China." One of the points mentioned is that the Christian missionaries were granted by the Emperor of China the uses of a monastery for more than a score of monks in the capital. The inscription also has something to say about the good influence of Christianity:

> If the Kingdom has peace,
> if men act uprightly,
> if the living can flourish,
> if the dead can rejoice . . .
> this is the mighty task and the power
> of our Honourable Religion.

The country—China: the year—A.D. 635. At that time Roman monks were penetrating the forests of the English Midlands, and building churches in York.

New contacts with the Near East were created by the Crusades. The mendicant orders sensed the missionary opportunity here, an opportunity of which they were not slow to take advantage. The missionary epoch from 1200 to 1400 is dominated by Franciscan and Dominican friars.

St. Francis himself went to Egypt in 1219 and preached to the Sultan; two years later he amended the Rule of his order to allow any brother "inspired by God" to go to "Muslims and others of the unfaithful". Raymond Lull, a Franciscan tertiary from Mallorca, studied Arabic and founded a school for missionaries to Islam. He himself spent three periods in North Africa, where he met with violent opposition; he was imprisoned, but never tired of demonstrating the superiority of the Christian doctrine over Islam. Finally he was stoned to death, in Algiers in 1315.

Dominican preaching brothers also undertook the journey to North Africa and the Near East. At an early stage they became aware of the value of a thorough mastery of Arabic and Hebrew, laying the foundations of a tradition the Dominican order still maintains.

Franciscans and Dominicans even penetrated into East Asia. The legend of Prester John, a mythical Christian King somewhere in Central Asia, was a constant stimulus to the imagination of the faithful at this time; the mendicant friars asked nothing better than to lend their assistance to this King. Their journeys brought them to the boundaries of the Mongol Empire of Genghis Khan. One Franciscan, Vilhelm de Ruysbroeck, reached the Mongol capital, Karakorum (now Edeni Tsu) in about 1250. He found a fair number of "Christian tribes" and individuals scattered over Central Asia.

Another Franciscan, John of Monte Corvino, reached

Cathay (China) by sea in 1289. He later described how he had encountered opposition from the Nestorians, but managed nevertheless to establish himself there. His main work was translation: he translated the New Testament and the Psalter into the Mongolian Wigur dialect, and even celebrated the Mass in that language—a remarkable departure. In 1307 the Pope, encouraged by these reports, sent seven more Franciscans to China, after having first consecrated them bishops. However, only three survived the perils and dangers of the way and arrived in Peking. Their first action was, on behalf of the Pope, to consecrate John Archbishop of Khanbalik (Peking). By the middle of the century there are said to have been 30,000 Christians, mostly Mongols, in China. But hard times were in store. In 1368 the Mongols were dispossessed by the Ming dynasty, and for the Christians there remained only martyrdom.

The missionary cause was dear to the heart of Erasmus of Rotterdam, the most learned man of his time—the threshold of the modern age in the West. He was not satisfied with what he knew of the mission to Islam; it was not to be carried out by force. "Multitudes go every year to view the ruins of Jerusalem," he wrote in his *Homiletics* of 1536, "but is not the task of building a spiritual Jerusalem immeasurably greater? Rise up, then, you courageous and noble leaders of the army of Christ. If you wish to pull down, quench and destroy, turn your attention not towards men, but towards their ignorance, godlessness and other sins. It is a difficult task to which I am calling you, but it is the noblest and highest of all. O that God had accounted me worthy to die in so noble a cause!"

CHAPTER 7

THE EMPIRES AND THE KINGDOM OF GOD
1497–1947

Rome, May 4, 1493

Just over a year had passed since the Coronation of the new Pope, Alexander II. They could say what they liked about his morals, there could be no doubt that Rodrigo Borgia was born to rule. If there had been any doubts on that score, they were dispelled on May 4, 1493, when the Pope imperiously affixed his signature to the *padroado* document, dividing up the entire world outside the boundaries of Europe according to a medieval legal tradition in the Church. The Portuguese had a bridgehead in West Africa, and were preparing to journey far beyond Africa. A Genoese adventurer in the service of Castilia, one Columbus, had just found a New World to the west. Thus by virtue of his Apostolic office the Pope "granted" (for such was the word used) the west to Spain, the east to Portugal. The line of demarcation was carefully laid down in the document; it ran from the North Pole to the South Pole, a hundred leagues west of the westernmost island of the Azores. This generous division of the world was made on one condition: that the Spanish and Portuguese Kings were to be responsible for propagating the Christian faith in the newly-discovered countries.

London, October 17, 1841

The private chapel of Lambeth Palace: thirty-three-year-old George Augustus Selwyn had just been consecrated Bishop of New Zealand. His letter of appointment was signed by the "Defender of the Faith", Queen Victoria. The new Bishop protested against the terms of his appointment, according to which the power to ordain priests was granted by the Queen. His protest went unheard: why then should he draw the authorities' attention to a minor error in the same document? Selwyn had been granted episcopal jurisdiction over an area stretching from 50° S. to 34° N.—not to 34° S., as had been intended. It was a mistake, but a generous mistake, for it gave the new Bishop the greater part of the island world of the Pacific, and enabled him later to found the mission to Melanesia.

Pope Alexander VI and Queen Victoria had one thing in common (and presumably only one!). They shared the same attitude to the coloured population of the world. Western Europe looked upon itself as the Metropolis of the world, with an incontestable right to control the destiny of the countries on the coloured periphery of the map of the world.

Bombay, August 15, 1947

An Indian—evidently with a sense of history—was standing on the quay at Bombay on August 15, 1947. It was the greatest day in the modern history of India: India's independence day. He saw a British ship leaving harbour, on her way to the West. Thoughtfully he said, "Well, Vasco da Gama has gone home now." In those few words he summed up the feelings of Asia about modern history; and at the same time revealed something of the new era in East-West relations. In 1497 Vasco da Gama of Portugal had been the first to find his way round Africa and cross the Indian Ocean to India. In so doing he had ushered in the period of Western dominion in Asia, the colonial epoch—the "da Gama epoch".

The discovery of new continents, new peoples and new treasures in the East—and at the same time, through Christopher Columbus, in the West—widened Europe's horizons, opened new economic perspectives and soon led to new world-wide power-political constellations. But the discovery of the new continents did more: not only did it affect politics and economics; it had a profound effect on theology, too. For the very first time Europeans became aware of mankind as a whole—or at any rate, it now became possible for them to recognize this fundamental fact, not merely in theory, but as a practical and demanding reality.

The essence of the developments of the New Age, seen as a whole, is to be found in the fact that during this period West Europe, little as it was, colonized, governed and evangelized the greater part of the coloured world. First it was the turn of Portugal and Spain; then of Holland, Great Britain and France; and finally, for a brief and hectic generation, Germany. And on the same overall view it is true to say that the New Age, which began in 1497, and which culminated in the developed colonization of the nineteenth and early twentieth centuries, came to an end in 1947. This also means that the geo-political changes which have come about in our own day in the matter of East-West relations have helped to create another new epoch, newer even than the New Age, in which many things—missions included—are faced with entirely new situations and conditions.

Here we shall concentrate on one single aspect of the missionary history of the New Age: the relation between mission and colonial politics. This is a distinct limitation; it is, however, consciously so. The changes and chances of colonial power-politics, and the positive or negative attitude taken by the mission towards these, provide the necessary background against which to view the history of missions in this period. But it is not merely an outer framework, an incidental background to the various missionary contributions. The Church, which is not "of this world", is called to labour and to bear witness "in the world". She is sent to the world, but she cannot avoid being in some way influenced by "the world". Political events have influenced missions decisively: conditioning, facilitating or limiting what has had to be done. This applies equally to Catholic and Evangelical missions. What we shall try to do in this chapter is to follow some of the most important lines along which the development has taken place.

First, a few words about the conditions obtaining at the start of the New Age. Portuguese and Spanish galleons ruled the seven seas. These two Catholic states had control over strategic points—harbours and islands—in the East and South and Central America. And their strategy was rendered all the more confident by the knowledge that they were acting in accordance with the Papal *padroado* decree concerning the division of the coloured world.

This places the problem of "reformation and mission" in its proper perspective. It is true that the reformers were not unaware of the missionary obligation as such. Luther's rediscovery of the dynamic character of the Gospel led in principle to the new understanding of the expansive power of the preached word. "Preachers shall fly round the globe, and find those who are awaiting them and also receive them joyfully," he wrote: the challenge was provided by the Turk and by Islam. But this insight failed to lead to any practical missionary contribution, for two reasons. First, because Luther and to an even greater extent Calvin, and later the whole of Lutheran Orthodoxy, believed in the mediaeval idea that missionary preaching as such was the especial privilege of the Apostles. It was, of course, through the Apostles that the Gospel had been preached to all peoples in the early days of the Church, but geographical discoveries had opened new horizons, as a result of which the traditional view came to be called in question. However, Calvin was still able to refer to missionary preaching as the extraordinary privilege of the Apostles. But secondly, we must bear in mind, alongside this theological argument, the constitutional and geopolitical aspect. The Reformation led to the formation of local national churches and semi-theocratic ecclesiastical states, the German *Landes-kirchen* and the English Established Church. These national churches controlled the office of preaching; but in point of fact the states in question were not at that time colonial powers. During the first century of the New Age mission could be carried on only under the auspices of one or other of the colonial powers; these, however, were all Catholic. The defeat of the "invincible" Spanish Armada by England in 1588 was of immeasurable significance, for missions as well as for secular history. The control previously exercised by Catholic South Europe over the overseas colonies was broken, and Protestant West Europe, led by England and Holland, took over. With the dawn of the seventeenth century the Protestant powers were able to enter the colonial picture— and the question of missionary responsibility arose simultaneously.

Catholic South Europe

In the Roman Catholic countries the relations between the State and the missionary church were intimate. In Spanish South America rapid colonial expansion and mission went hand in hand. In the space of a few short decades the *conquistadores* brought South and Central America and Mexico into subjection to the Spanish crown. The King of Spain appointed bishops, created new dioceses and determined their boundaries. Even the simplest and most elementary of appointments and dismissals (sacristans, for example) was a matter for the Crown to decide. The Papacy was virtually powerless in face of the influence of the Spanish throne over the Church in Latin America.

But it would be wrong to assume that mission and colonial politics coincided on all things. Divergent intentions came to light rather often, and the apostolic fervour of the missionaries, "the conquerors of the faith", may be illustrated by the case of the Dominican monk, Bartolomeus de Las Casas (d. 1566), who was of Spanish aristocratic blood, and who tried to protect the Indians from the rapacity of their white overlords. Incidentally, the two mendicant orders, together with a number of new orders founded in the sixteenth century, played a prominent part in the missionary expansion of the sixteenth and seventeenth centuries. A common goal was work in "the two Indies" (the West Indies, i.e. America, and the East Indies). But by far the most important missionary instrument at the disposal of the Roman Catholic Church at that time, in Latin America and elsewhere, was Loyola's Society of Jesus, the Jesuits. In Paraguay the Jesuits created "reductions" for the Indian population. Here, in the early seventeenth century, they assembled some 150,000 Christians from 40 villages, thus forming a Jesuit state. But the expulsion of the Society of Jesus towards the end of the eighteenth century was fatal to this organization, which had been one of the most remarkable social manifestations in the missionary history of this or any period.

Africa and Asia fell to the lot of Portugal. The River Congo was discovered by the Portuguese in 1482. Ten years later they began missionary work among the Congo tribe, and baptized their king. In 1521 his grandson, Henry, was consecrated as bishop, with his cathedral in San Salvador (situated on the extreme north of what is now Angola). Here, too, the main burden was borne by Jesuits. Others beside the Portuguese were active in this area, but the decisive influence was that of the Portuguese royal house. It seems that by the seventeenth century the Congo church had about 20,000 members, but a decline set in in the following century. When Livingstone came to San Salvador in 1856 he found the ruins of the cathedral (which can still be seen), and crucifixes and images of the saints being used as fetishes. They were held to be particularly effective as a charm against drought.

We have said that the period of Western influence in

Asia began with Vasco da Gama. A Portuguese colony was founded in Goa, south of Bombay, to which there came, in 1540, Francis Xavier, the greatest Roman Catholic missionary of the New Age. Xavier based his strategy on Portuguese trading stations in Malacca, the Moluccas and Macao, and on the Japanese port of Nagasaki, at which Portuguese traders often called.

Xavier was of noble Basque stock, and studied at the University of Paris from 1525 to 1536, where he came into contact with Ignatius Loyola, whose influence turned him from incipient Protestantism to the wholehearted service of the Roman Catholic Church. The young Xavier's decision he afterwards formulated in a prayer, the missionary implications of which are little short of breathtaking. "Lord, here am I. What wouldst Thou have me to do? Send me where Thou wilt, even, should it be Thy will, to India."

"India"—still the symbol of the supreme sacrifice. In 1540 Loyola determined to send his colleague Bobavilla to India as a missionary, but at the last minute, just before his ship was due to set sail, Bobavilla was taken ill, and Xavier was given twenty-four hours to prepare himself for the long voyage—a striking example of the mobility which has always been one of the strong points of the Jesuit order.

His twelve years as a missionary may be divided into three periods: from 1540 to 1544 in South India; 1544–1548 in the Moluccas and in Malacca, and 1549–1551 in Japan. After a further short visit to India he died in the island of San Chao off Canton. He was never able to fulfil his dearest wish by working in China. He regarded himself as a missionary to the whole of Asia, and as a *conquistador* of souls he was responsible for missionary work from the Cape of Good Hope to Japan—no insignificant parish.

Xavier's missionary methods may now appear superficial. In point of fact, however, his intensive, practical missionary work was precisely designed to combat the shallow Portuguese missionary methods, as applied in the 1530's. This was particularly noticeable in the case of the Paravas of Travancore, 20,000 of whom had been baptized without any real preparation. Xavier went to these. Although he does not appear to have had any great gifts as a linguist, he had soon translated the "prayers" into the Malabarian language. "I learned the text by heart, and ran with a bell in my hand through the whole of the village, and collected as many boys and girls as I could." He hoped by first reaching the young people to reach their elders through them. On the Moluccas he wrote a rhymed catechism, containing the basic truths of Christianity and the most important elements in the Biblical history, from the Creation to the Last Judgment. This catechism was arranged in such a way that by learning twenty words a day, the whole could be mastered in a year.

In Asia, too, the Society of Jesus was a flexible instrument in the expansion of the Roman Catholic Church. "Flexible" is indeed the word, as may be seen from the controversy attending the question of "rites"—the century-long discussion on the subject of missionary accommodation in the Asian cultural milieu. Two names must be mentioned: those of the Roman nobleman Roberto di Nobili, who worked in South India between 1606 and 1646 and Matteo Ricci, who was in China from 1583 to 1610. Both were concerned to try and reach the highest levels of Asian society, the Brahmins and the Mandarins respectively. And in Japan the Jesuits, following Xavier, made a notable contribution; towards the end of the sixteenth century large numbers of converts were gathered in, and it is estimated that there were between half a million and three quarters of a million Christians in Japan. But despite the Jesuits' extensive attempts to "accommodate" their message to Eastern conditions, the Christian groups in both China and Japan were regarded as foreigners, representatives of Western imperialism. Persecution began in Japan in 1612: Christianity was proscribed—a situation which lasted for 250 years. And the Chinese had a Portuguese name by which they called those of their own numbers who had gone over to the "foreign devils" and their religion: *compradore*. The word was originally used for the Chinese crews of Western merchant vessels but came in time to be applied to all Chinese having direct contact with the West, missions included. In recent years the term has taken on a new currency. Communist China is now condemning contact with the West—for example, via Western missionaries and churches—as attempts of *compradore* to bring China once more under imperialist slavery.

Protestant Western Europe

We have already mentioned the defeat of the "invincible" Spanish Armada in 1588 as an event of primary importance. Queen Elizabeth I of England had permitted English venturers to encroach upon Spanish territory in the West Indies. Philip II of Spain sent his "invincible" Armada of 130 warships to England, partly by way of reprisal, and in an attempt to crush English sea-power once and for all. The Armada was defeated, however; the consequence being that England—and Protestant Europe generally—came for centuries to control the seven seas, world trade and—world mission.

The Puritan spirit was a spirit of commerce, among other things, and Puritans were responsible for extensive overseas trade. Amsterdam and London were bases of trading companies, having connexions in the East Indies, the West Indies and North America. East India Companies were formed: in England, 1600; Holland, 1602; Denmark, 1612. These were semi-official enterprises which enjoyed considerable privileges, principally an absolute monopoly of trade, in return for which they had to pay a certain sum of money to the State. Sweden later came into the picture—the Swedish East India Company was founded in 1731 and dissolved in 1813.

The earliest chapters in the missionary history of the Dutch East India Company in Indonesia are not altogether edifying. The Company was more interested in commerce than in Christianity; nevertheless they expelled the Portuguese from the colony to the greater glory of God, and made Protestants of the Catholics among the native Indonesian population. Western Europe was of course governed on the basis of *cuius regio, eius religio,* and this same principle was extended to the non-Christian world. Christianization of the island population of the East Indies proceeded apace. At about the same time, in 1652, a group of Dutchmen settled in South Africa on the Cape, thereby inaugurating a further chapter in the dramatic relationship between mission and politics—a chapter to which we shall soon have occasion to return.

Holland also possessed a number of gifted theologians who were interested in the question of missionary training. In 1622, the year in which *Propaganda Fidei* was founded in Rome, there was opened a *Seminarum Indicum* in Leiden, under the direction of Professor Waleus. This was however no more than a brief episode; the seminary closed a mere ten years later. But the seventeenth and eighteenth centuries saw the sending out of no less than 250 "preachers" from Holland to the East—to Indonesia, Ceylon and Formosa.

Protestant missionary activity in North America was not faced with the same difficulties as in the East Indies, controlled as they were by thrifty Dutch businessmen. To be sure, things looked somewhat unpromising in 1637, when the fanaticism of a body of English Puritans resulted in the extinction of a whole tribe of Indians. The Indians in Delaware fared better; there in 1638 a group of Swedes, influenced by the Dutchman, Willem Usselinx, founded New Sweden. This was in the period of Lutheran Orthodoxy, though Orthodoxy was for the most part little concerned with missions. But the National Church of Sweden followed hard on the heels of Swedish colonialism—just as the Lapps had been incorporated into the fellowship of the Church of Sweden. A Swedish priest, Johan Campanius, was the first Lutheran to start a mission outside Europe; he worked in America for five years. This mission later aroused episcopal interest. Jesper Svedberg (d. 1735) Bishop of Skara and hymn-writer, had pastoral oversight over the Swedish immigrants, and called himself "Bishop of America". However, the Swedish colony was soon occupied by the Dutch.

The noblest figure among British missionaries to the American Indians was the Presbyterian, John Eliot (d. 1690), whose labours stretched over a period of practically sixty years. Cromwell was Eliot's ideal, and the Long Parliament agreed, on Cromwell's suggestion, to support Eliot's mission. The question of the relationship between worldly rule and the Kingdom of God he solved along theocratic lines. His "fourteen praying Indian villages" in Massachusetts became a New Jerusalem, a Protestant theocracy in miniature; from their 1,100 Indians there spread a living Christian influence to some 70,000 of their fellow-tribesmen. The law of the State was simply the five books of Moses, and the villages were organized, following Exodus 18, into groups of ten, fifty and a hundred. The Indians were to be ruled by Holy Writ, and by no other law; the Lord Himself was to be their lawgiver, their judge and their King. But this Old Testament order was destroyed by the Indian wars of the years around 1675. Eliot's New Jerusalem was in New England. His Indian converts were suspected, both by their unconverted fellow-tribesmen and by White Christians; by the first, because they had embraced the faith of the "palefaces' " White Christ; by the latter, simply because they were Indians. Seven of the fourteen Christian villages joined the rebels, and together with the rebels were exterminated by the colonial government troops. For Eliot, this was practically a death-blow to the mission he had attempted, at such great cost, to build up.

An interesting anticipation of the type of mission later carried on by the Pietists is seen in the work of Justinianus von Welz, an Austrian nobleman who laboured in Germany and Holland (1621–1668). His proposal was for the formation of a "Society of the Lovers of Jesus", the object of which would be the carrying out of mission at home and abroad. His bold strategy presupposed some form of link with the government authorities. He proposed the appointment of missionary attachés to the embassies of London, Amsterdam and Paris, and also in Constantinople, the East Indies and the West Indies. Many years later, in the early twentieth century, this idea was partially realized when "missionary consuls" were appointed in the Dutch Indies, their task being the maintenance of contacts between the colonial government and the missionary bodies.

Another pioneer was the philosopher G. W. von Leibniz (d. 1716), who succeeded more than most of his contemporaries in interesting the European intelligentsia in the problems of missions. In Rome Leibniz had met the Jesuit missionary, Claudius Grimaldi, newly returned from China, and in his book *Novissima Sinica* gave an account of the scientific and missionary information gathered by Father Grimaldi. But he was not satisfied with second-hand accounts. The experiences of the Jesuits inspired him to formulate an ambitious programme for Protestant missions to be carried out in conjunction with the State and the universities. The King of Prussia, he suggested, ought to send out a missionary caravan to China, via Russia. And on the draft constitution he prepared for the Prussian Academy of Sciences he laid down as one of its objectives the task of *propagatio fidei per scientias*, the propagation of the faith by means of the sciences—a clear expression of his view of the relationship between mission and science.

Pietism

Both Roman Catholic and Evangelical missions during the sixteenth and seventeenth centuries were closely connected with national and colonial interests. This connexion was broken in the eighteenth century by Pietism and by the movements which descended from Pietism, and shared its ideals. These ideals were twofold: the salvation of the individual and the setting up of the *ecclesiola in ecclesia*. Pietist missions were concerned not at all with the kingdoms of this world; but certainly with the Kingdom of God, envisaged as the sum total of the converted, as those saved from the world, or, in the case of Württemberg Pietism, as a purely futural, eschatological entity. The conversion of the individual "heathen" was seen in this vast perspective.

The Pietists saw far beyond the parish boundaries of the Orthodox, or the State boundaries of the petty princes. For a Zinzendorf or a John Wesley, the world was his parish. That was all; but it was enough. They needed no further credentials. Contact with the State was a hindrance rather than a help, since as Zinzendorf put it, the missionary was "the Holy Spirit's bag-man". Further, they had to avoid all contact with worldly authorities: "Under no circumstances must you become involved with the outward or the worldly." But most important of all, Zinzendorf stressed that they must not endeavour to exercise any influence on "*Politicum* or *Commercia*"—a conscious polemic against earlier missionary practice. This theme was worked out in apocalyptic terms by J. A. Bengel and the Württemberg Pietists. The Kingdom of God stood in the forefront of this theology, and it was considered that the conversion of the heathen belonged to the eschatological last days. "The time is not yet ripe for missions among the heathen and the Jews." And yet, despite this attitude, Bengel was deeply interested in Pietist missions, such as that in Tranquebar.

An *ecclesiola*, or society of the redeemed, instead of State-directed missions; and a Kingdom of God sharply distinguished from political and financial interests—such was their view. But even the Pietists had to realize in time that politics and commerce, too, are the stuff of which missionary history is woven. They founded churches—unwillingly—in Africa and Asia; and the missionaries followed reluctantly in the footsteps of the soldiery and the importers of spices.

The relations, positive as well as negative, of the missions to Palace and Parliament (we may compare the Middle Ages, in sixteenth-century Spain), came into prominence at the time of the Danish-Halle mission, the most important of the eighteenth-century Pietist missionary enterprises. We have seen that Pietism was opposed in principle to missions run by national churches, or by governments; it was nevertheless characteristic of the royalism and aristocratic connexions of Halle that this mission operated officially "at the most gracious command of His Majesty King Frederick IV of Denmark and Norway", and that its missionaries were sent to the Royal Danish colony of Tranquebar, in South India. King Frederick, had, when Crown Prince, been sufficiently influenced by Pietism to think of sending missionaries to the little Danish possessions in the West Indies, Africa and India. The King's German chaplain, Lütgens, made contact with August Hermann Francke, at that time the leader of the Pietists in Halle, and with the first German missionary candidates. The mission was also granted some slight financial support from public funds.

In 1707, the Danish court sent 2,000 *riksdaler* to the mission-field. However, the money never reached India, the ship sinking *en route*. Three years later, the court sent a further 1,200 *riksdaler*. King George I of England was also interested in Francke's mission: he wrote letters to the missionaries, and provided sums of money to help with their expenses. But they found a more reliable source of income after 1711, when they were granted 2,000 *riksdaler* a year from the profits of the Danish postal department. A similar contribution, though of only 1,000 *riksdaler* a year, came after 1736 from the Norwegian postal department. This is enough to demonstrate the official character of the mission; but in the long run these sums were insufficient to guarantee the continued existence of the mission.

The official headquarters of the mission was in Copenhagen. But the "Danish-Halle" mission was in fact far from being Danish. Practically all its missionaries were Germans; and most of its money came from the Society for Promoting Christian Knowledge in London—an interesting anticipation of later "joint actions for mission".

The mission's contacts with the pious Danish royal family did not succeed in winning the favour of the local Danish authorities in India. These were in fact particularly ill-disposed towards the missionaries. In 1621 the Danes had bought from the Rajahs of Tanjore a little strip of coast called Tranquebar ("the town of the waves"), south of Madras. Here they built a fort called Daneborg. Here, too, there was a small harbour, and in 15–20 nearby villages lived some 20–30,000 Tamils. The whole amounted to a diminutive Danish trading colony, and its commander, Hassius, was concerned to see that nothing stood in the way of trade. The Christian mission he regarded as a potential danger to commerce; he threw the missionaries into prison on a number of occasions, and otherwise did all he could to discredit their work.

One of the first two Tranquebar missionaries was Bartholomaus Ziegenbalg, who was only just 23 when he came to India in 1706. He died thirteen years later, in 1719, at the age of 35, by which time he had succeeded, despite all opposition, in making a contribution of very great importance indeed. He was a gifted linguist, and translated the whole of the New Testament and large parts of the Old Testament into Tamil. He also published catechisms, tracts and textbooks in Tamil for use in his school. At the same time he was deeply interested in the study of Hinduism, and wrote a number of large-scale works on its history and practices. When the manuscripts reached A. H. Francke in Halle, the Pietist missionary leader was shocked, and wrote chiding the young missionary: "You were sent out to destroy heathenism in India, not to spread heathen superstition in Europe." The manuscripts were put away, and remained hidden for more than 150 years, until they were finally published. The year before he died, Ziegenbalg was able to consecrate Jerusalem Church in Tranquebar, which is still, 250 years later, used as a place of worship. But while all these schemes were in progress, he had to be constantly on the watch against the intrigues of the colonial officials.

The Halle Mission sent out 57 missionaries in a period of 140 years; as a result of which some 35,000 persons were baptized, 23,000 of them in the vicinity of Tranquebar and Tanjore. The first Tamil minister, Aron, was ordained in 1733, and thirteen more were ordained in the period up to 1813.

Two other missionaries deserve special mention: Philip Fabricius and Christian Friedrich Schwartz. The former, who served in Madras for almost half a century (from 1742 to his death in 1791), made a masterly translation of the Bible into Tamil—an interpretation which, in the intensity and clarity of its language, achieved a position of authority among the Tamils which it still holds. Schwartz, the greatest name in the history of the Halle Mission, arrived in India in 1750 and died there in 1798. His work was mainly in Tanjore, though he spent some time in Tranquebar itself. At this time the political situation in South India was extremely precarious and tense. The Muslim Nawab of Tanjore and the commander-in-chief of the British forces in Tiruchirapalli were contending for power; the situation at that time was one of uneasy compromise. Schwartz succeeded in winning both. Apart from Tamil, English and Portuguese, he learned Hindustani and Persian in order to be able to converse with the Nawab. He was appointed British garrison chaplain, and accompanied the British troops as chaplain and medical assistant to Madura. He agreed to be sent by the British as political agent to a rebel leader in Mysore, and used this expedition as an opportunity to preach the Gospel. He lived a life of apostolic simplicity and poverty, wholly taken up with the problems of evangelization and popular education. Schwartz was one of a group of Halle missionaries who founded "English stations" under the SPCK within the German area, thus laying the foundations of later powerful Anglican influence in South India. Schwartz (who soon altered the spelling of his name to Swartz) might perhaps be described as an early ecumenical Lutheran—a type of missionary which was common in the Halle mission. Another missionary of the same type—a Continental Lutheran in the service of a British missionary society—was the Swede Zacharias Kiernander, who came to South India in 1740 and died in Calcutta in 1799.

The Halle Mission concentrated on *one* field. The opposite tendency—febrile activity on a large number of fronts —is to be seen in the case of Herrnhut. Twenty-eight mission-fields were occupied in the space of the same number of years, from 1732 to 1760. It is characteristic that here, too, a start was made in Danish colonies, St. Thomas in the West Indies (1732) and Greenland (1733), but they also reached South Africa (1736) and Asia. Herrnhut, who called and sent all these missionaries, was in 1732 no more than a little village with 500 inhabitants and 50 houses; but by 1760 its population had reached 1,200. The actual missionary contribution made by the Moravian missionaries in a number of fields became a factor of great importance, while the role of the Herrnhut community in arousing missionary interest in Europe during the eighteenth and early nineteenth centuries was at least as important. In their practical work, the Moravian missionaries did their best to follow the advice of Zinzendorf, and avoided politics.

The modern period in Protestant missions dated from 1793 and the coming of William Carey to India. William

Carey (1761–1834), a Leicester cobbler, was born into an Anglican family, but on his conversion at the age of 15 joined the Baptists. He was self-taught, but succeeded in acquiring a high level of proficiency in geography and languages. He was a constant and careful reader of the Holy Scriptures. His missionary manifesto, *An Enquiry into the Obligation of Christians to use Means for the Conversion of the Heathen* (1792), is in every way an impressive feat. His interest in missions had been stimulated by a number of factors: by Captain Cook's voyages in Oceania; by the new spiritual climate called forth by the Wesleys; and by the evangelical awakening generally, which created a concern in social matters reaching far beyond the British Isles. But above all he had been inspired by the record of the Moravian missionaries. Carey was no superficial "enthusiast": it was a solid and far-sighted Christian with great intellectual and spiritual gifts who in 1792 formulated the great motto of Evangelical missions: "Expect great things of God. Attempt great things for God."

Carey, like the Herrnhut missionaries he admired so much, was unwilling in principle to become involved in politics. But he was destined to make the acquaintance of its harsh realities. Bengal had been under British rule ever since the victory of Robert Clive in the battle of Plassey in 1757. The East India Company had long had its own chaplains in Calcutta, and some of them had been effective missionaries, but the general attitude of the Company towards Christian missions was negative. In the year of Carey's arrival in India the Company stated that although they were "very far from being averse to the introduction of Christianity into India or indifferent to the benefits which would result from the general diffusion of its doctrines", they were convinced "that nothing could be more unwise or impolitic, nothing more likely to frustrate the hopes and endeavours of those who aim at the very object —the introduction of Christianity among the native inhabitants—than any imprudent or injudicious attempt to introduce it by means which should irritate and alarm their religious prejudices."

Thus the arrival of the English Baptist preacher in Calcutta was not received with any great measure of enthusiasm by the authorities. Missionaries were dangerous; they might put revolutionary ideas into the heads of the Indians; and that would be bad for law and order—and for trade. Indeed, the Company was so anxious to preserve the contentment of its "subjects" that it gave considerable sums of money to the upkeep of Hindu temples and practices—a remarkable situation which persisted well on into the nineteenth century. Peace at all costs: such was "John Company's" policy. Most shared the opinion of Warren Hastings, that it was possible to fire a pistol into a barrel of gunpowder without it exploding, but that no man in his right mind would try it. India was the powder-barrel; the missionary message the pistol. A Brahmin non-commissioned officer who submitted to baptism was in 1819 dismissed the service, as a warning to others. In face of such prejudice it is not surprising that Carey tried for seven years to gain a foothold in Calcutta, without success. In fact a practical missionary effort was only possible thanks to another little Danish trading station, Serampore, to which Carey and his fellow-workers Marshman and Ward moved in 1800.

The achievements of the Serampore Trio—Carey, Marshman and Ward: the cobbler, the board-school teacher and the typographer—were considerable. Carey soon became one of his day's foremost authorities on Indian languages, particularly Sanskrit and Bengali; he had some knowledge of thirty Asian languages, including Chinese. By 1832 various parts of the Bible had been translated into forty languages and dialects, and printed on Ward's press in Serampore; a number of grammars and dictionaries had also been published. As professor in Calcutta Carey was able to exercise considerable cultural influence. The prohibition by the British authorities of the burning of widows (*sati*) was very largely a result of Carey's influence. He laid the foundations of theological education in India. Serampore College was given its first charter by the King of Denmark in 1827, and theological degrees, including doctorates, awarded by India's Christian college still bear Serampore's royal Danish seal. Carey's hobby was botany, and the Calcutta Botanical Gardens owe their existence to his love of flowers. And finally, it was very largely thanks to Carey that the monopoly of the East India Company was broken in the matter of missionary access to India, so that missionaries of all nationalities were admitted to India. The Act authorizing this measure was passed in 1833, a year before Carey's death. Carey had made his point.

The Nineteenth-Century Missionary Societies

The missionary enterprise of the Pietist and Evangelical periods is characterized, apart from its negative attitude to the political and economic responsibility of mission and the missionary, by its structure, in voluntary societies. There were of course Protestant missionary societies before Carey. The Halle mission was one of them; another we have already mentioned, the Anglican tract society, the Society for Promoting Christian Knowledge (SPCK). This had been founded in 1698 for the purpose of providing New England (i.e. America) with Christian literature, but later extended its sphere of activity to include India. Another Anglican society, the Society for the Propagation of the Gospel (SPG), of which the Archbishop of Canterbury was Chairman, had as its original object (it was founded in 1701) what we might call the spiritual aspect of colonialism: pastoral care for British subjects abroad, and the winning of "Indians and negro slaves" for the Christian faith. During the eighteenth century the SPG was most concerned with the spiritual welfare of British colonists, particularly in America. These were however soon in a position to be able to found their own missionary societies. America can in fact claim the honour of founding the world's first missionary society, the Society for the Propagation of the Gospel in New England, which dated from 1649. The coming of American independence led to fresh activity in this field, and two new societies for missions to the Red Indians were founded in 1787.

Both the SPCK and the SPG were in a sense reminiscent of another contemporary colonial phenomenon, viz. the trading companies. The analogy must not be pressed too far; nevertheless, the missionary societies and the trading companies had this much in common, that both were characterized by individual enterprise and private initiative. They were no longer prepared to rely on the favour of princes or the authority of the state. The modern missionary societies, which began to emerge in the last decade of the eighteenth century, were the fruits of the Pietist and evangelical awakenings on the Continent and in Britain respectively. Pietism had created the conventicle, the society of the saved, and it was out of this form that the missionary societies grew. The missionary society is in essence the conventicle enlarged.

Two kinds of missionary society may be distinguished: interdenominational societies, based on the principle of "alliance"; and denominational or confessional societies. The London Missionary Society, founded in 1795, stated in its "fundamental principle", adopted the following year, the grounds on which an interdenominational society was based:

As the union of God's People of various Denominations, in carrying on this great Work, is a most desirable Object, so, to prevent, if possible, any cause of future dissension, it is declared to be a fundamental principle of the Missionary Society, that our design is not to send Presbyterianism, Independency, Episcopacy, or any other form of Church Order and Government (about which there may be differences of opinion among serious Persons), but the Glorious Gospel of the blessed God to the Heathen.

H 113

The Society was staffed by Anglicans and Free Church-men jointly, and its interdenominational principles were to have a considerable effect on missionary organizations in other countries.

But William Carey, in his *Enquiry* of 1792, had claimed that the most practical and effective method of missionary work would be the foundation of denominational societies. Thus it was that he advocated the foundation of a speci-fically Baptist Missionary Society. The London Missionary Society was soon faced with the fact of its Anglicans founding their own society, the Church Missionary Society (1799), whose first field was the territory given to the freed African slaves, Sierra Leone. However, the steady growth of the Tractarian movement after the 1830's resulted in the CMS being regarded as too low-church by influential and growing groups in the Church of England. The high-church party—and later Anglo-Catholicism—infused new life into the old SPG, which became a lively and effective organization. Other Anglo-Catholic missions included the Universities Mission to Central Africa (UMCA), founded in 1859. The two merged as the United Society for the Propagation of the Gospel in 1965.

The most notable feature of the corresponding develop-ment in Lutheran Europe was the tension between inter-denominational and confessional societies. Among the organizations following the LMS principle may be men-tioned the Basel Society (founded in 1815) and the Swedish Missionary Society (1835), on whose first board Swedish bishops, a member of the Herrnhut Brethren and a Metho-dist minister worked together amicably. But Lutheran confessionalism was on the increase, and new organiza-tions came into being about the middle of the nineteenth century. Karl Graul was the first great leader of the Leipzig Missionary Society. Four years in South India had given him an excellent insight into the practical problems facing the work of missions. The Leipzig Mission wanted their missionaries to have academic training. Ludwig Harms'

Lutheran Herrmannsburg Mission, on the other hand, which was supported mainly by the peasants of the Lüneburg Heath, aimed at sending out faithful and reliable peasants to build churches in Zululand. Another prominent Lutheran missionary leader was Wilhelm Löhe, who was strongly opposed to interdenominational missions in general, and the Basel Mission in particular; Löhe's wish was to bring about an integration between German Lutheran emigrant churches and mission. In 1841 he founded the Neuendettelsau Mission, which enjoyed success in a number of fields, particularly New Guinea. The formation in 1874 of the Church of Sweden Mission Board was a new departure, taken on the initiative of South and West Swedish confessionalism; its main object was to overcome the "conventicle" character of the missionary societies, and at the same time to integrate mission into the work of the Church as a whole. Ideally, every Swedish clergyman was to be a mission worker by virtue of his office. The Archbishop of Sweden is *ex officio* Chairman of the Church of Sweden Mission Board.

The most important of the European missionary societies formed during the nineteenth century are as follows:

TABLE OF MISSIONS

BODY	FOUNDED	MAIN WORKING AREA(S)
1. *England*		
Interdenominational		
London Missionary Society (LMS)	1795	South Africa 1799, Madagascar, Oceania, South India (→CSI), China
China Inland Mission (CIM)	1865	China. After 1950: Japan and South-East Asia
Church of England		
Church Missionary Society (CMS) [Evangelical]	1799	Uganda, East Africa, Sierra Leone and Nigeria, Egypt-Sudan, South India (→CSI), China

Society for the Propagation of the Gospel (SPG) [Anglo-Catholic] (1840)	1701	Southern Africa, West Indies, India, Malacca, Borneo, New Guinea, Japan
Universities' Mission to Central Africa (UMCA) [Anglo-Catholic] SPG + UMCA = USPG	1859	Tanzania, Nyasaland, Northern Rhodesia

Nonconformist

Baptist Missionary Society (BMS)	1792	Bengal, Ceylon, China, Congo
Methodist Missionary Society (MMS)	1818	West Africa, West Indies, South India (→CSI), Ceylon, China

2. *Scotland*

The Church of Scotland Mission	1824	South Africa, Nyasaland, Arabia, North India, South India (→CSI), China

3. *The United States of America*

American Board [Congregational]	1810	Oceania, South India (→CSI), Southern Africa

Each church now has its mission board integrated into the overall activity of the church. Some examples:

Methodist Episcopal Church	South and Central Africa, West coast of India, Latin America, Japan
Presbyterian Church in the U.S.A. Board of Foreign Missions	Cameroons, Congo, Japan, Latin America
Baptist General Conference Board of Foreign Missions	Congo, South India, China, Burma
Southern Baptist Church	World wide
The Episcopal Church	Liberia, Japan

4. *The Continent of Europe*

Interdenominational

BODY	FOUNDED	MAIN WORKING AREA(S)
Basel	1815	China (Shantung), Ghana, Cameroons, South India (→CSI), Borneo
Berlin	1824	South Africa, Tanganyika, China
Barmen	1828	South West Africa, Indonesia (the Batak Church)
Bethel	1886	Tanganyika (with Swedish and Danish missions)
Gossner (Berlin)	1836	Chhota Nagpur (Central India)
Paris	1824	French empire, now Communauté Française: particularly Madagascar, but also Basutoland and Northern Rhodesia; Oceania

Lutheran

Leipzig	1836	South India, Tanganyika, New Guinea
Hermannsburg	1849	South Africa, Ethiopia
Neuendettelsau	1841	New Guinea

Reformed

Netherlands Missionary Society	1797	Indonesia

5. *Northern Europe*

Danish Missionary Society	1821	South India, Manchuria, Arabia, Tanganyika
Norwegian Missionary Society	1842	South Africa, Madagascar, Cameroons, China (Hunan)→Japan
Finnish Missionary Society	1859	South West Africa, Tanganyika, China (Hunan) →Japan

BODY	FOUNDED	MAIN WORKING AREA(S)
Swedish Missionary Society	1835	Its foreign missions were transferred to the Church of Sweden Mission in 1875 thereafter work among Lapps
Evangelical National Missionary Society	1861	Ethiopia, Tanganyika, Central India
Church of Sweden Mission Board	1874	South India, Malaya, South Africa, Southern Rhodesia, Tanganyika, China (Hunan)→Hong Kong
Mission Covenant Church of Sweden	1881	Congo, China (Hunan)→ Japan, East Turkestan→ India

Before going on to discuss the problem of mission and politics between 1850 and 1960, we shall make one general observation with regard to the geographical situation of nineteenth-century missions. As late as the 1870's Christianity in Africa and Asia was still largely a *coastal religion*. The missionaries came by boat in "the ship of the Church". It went without saying that the first mission stations were founded in or near ports—in East Asia, West, East and South Africa. In Africa, it was the journeys of David Livingstone which opened the way for missions to the interior. It is characteristic that missionary societies after Livingstone tended to call themselves by names such as "Africa Inland Mission" or "The Heart of Africa Mission". A plan—or perhaps it would be better to call it a dream— which occupied the attention of certain missionary societies in those years was the "trans-African apostolic road", a chain of light, formed by a thousand mission stations, from the East to the West of the African continent. Henceforth, missions attempted to establish themselves along the inland waterways, particularly the River Congo and the Central African lakes.

These mighty lakes were discovered by R. F. Burton

and J. H. Speke in 1858—a further example of the explorers' role in widening the horizons of the missionary world. Africa's lakes—in an Africa which, it must be remembered, was still largely unknown—exerted a powerful attraction over a generation which had just learned to appreciate the value of the steamship on the Thames, the Rhine and the Göta Canal.

The voyages of Captain James Cook in the Pacific led to the LMS and other societies equipping sailing-ships for use in the Polynesian archipelago. One such was the *Messenger of Peace*, the ship which John Williams built, and in which he sailed tirelessly from island to island, founding fast-growing churches. But now the missions changed from sail to steam. The LMS launched a steam-packet on Lake Tanganyika, and many of the missions preparing to work in Central Africa and the Congo equipped their own steamships. The UMCA even went so far as to place their theological college on the SS *Chauncy Maples* on Lake Nyasa. Unfortunately for this enterprising idea, the floating college was lacking in stability; seasickness was rife among the African students, and there was great rejoicing when theology was once more restored to dry land.

CHAPTER 8

MISSIONS AND COLONIAL POLITICS

1850–1950

WE HAVE NOW SEEN THE MOST IMPORTANT WAYS in which the missionary enterprise was conducted during the eighteenth and nineteenth centuries—by missionary societies, as distinct from the national missions of the sixteenth and seventeenth centuries—and can return to the main line of our discussion: the relation of missions to Western imperialism in Asia and Africa.

On the subject of colonial politics proper (1850–1950) we must begin by drawing an important distinction. We shall be concerned with missions and politics in two separate and distinct situations: on the one hand, in those territories which were under direct Western colonial rule: India, South East Asia, Indonesia, Africa; and on the other, in countries such as China and Japan, which although they were subject to powerful and irritating political and economic pressures from the side of the Western powers, never became colonial powers in the accepted sense. But at the same time it is noteworthy when comparing India and China that India was never subjected to the same degree of violence as was China. And China's reaction, in its turn, was equally violent—the violence of long-pent-up bitterness.

To Africa and Asia, Christian missions in the colonial epoch appeared to be largely a religious accompaniment of the political, economic and cultural expansion of the West. The clearly national limitations, though frequently unconscious, of the individual missionary and the missionary organizations, stand out sharply in the light of history. The missionary knew of course that he had been sent to serve the Kingdom which is not of this world. But the land of his birth—England, Scotland, Holland, Germany, France, America, Scandinavia—had inevitably left its traces upon him; and he took with him to his mission-field many of its ideals and prejudices. And he was frequently careful to further the interests of "the Christian West" *vis-à-vis* the ancient régimes of the East.

We have said that the colonial period proper extended over approximately a century, from 1840–50 to 1950. It was during the 1850's that David Livingstone, perhaps the most important figure of the nineteenth century, began his journeys in the interior of Africa, thus opening the previously unknown continent to Western politics, trade— and mission.

Three dates—1833, 1842 and 1853—mark the stages by which Western missions entered Asia: India 1833, China 1842, Japan 1853. In India, the East India Company was long able to bar Christian missions from most of the sub-continent, but was finally compelled to accept the Act of 1813, granting British missions the right of access to India. In 1833 this access was extended in principle to all Christian missions.

The China of the Manchu dynasty was bitterly opposed to British trade, particularly in view of the British determination to import opium from India into China. But the Opium War of 1840–42 ended with the defeat of China, and by the Treaty of Nanking (1842) China undertook to open five harbours, among them Canton and Shanghai, to Western trade, and mission. In Sweden, a Swedish vicar, Peter Wieselgren in Västerstad, meditated over the news from the East, and wrote, "Trade shall be a vehicle for mission"—an interesting anticipation of a later terminology. In Japan, too, the way was opened with the assistance of military power. The American Commander Perry took a squadron into the harbour of Nagasaki in 1853, where-upon the Emperor decided to open these harbours for Western trade. The first missionaries arrived in 1859, and found what they called "an open door for the Gospel".

We cannot in this context hope to describe in detail the rise and decline of modern colonial politics. Instead we shall point out what were the most important features of the period, from the point of view of the history of mission. We must constantly bear in mind that this period, which was so profoundly affected by the link between colonial expansion and Western mission, was also a time of national renaissance and increasing political consciousness in those areas of Asia and Africa which were controlled by and from the West. India was subject to the British Crown from 1858 to 1947; for the latter half of that period Indian nationalism was an active, and growing, force. The desire for political independence received its official organ, the Indian National Congress, in 1885, though its constitutional methods were too mild for some nationalists, particularly after Japan's victory over Russia in 1905 had given nationalism a new impetus. The greatest of its leaders was Mohandas Karamchand Gandhi (d. 1948), its weapon civil disobedience and *ahimsa*, non-violence. In 1947 Gandhi won his victory; but it had to be paid for. The country was divided along a religious boundary, into the Hindu Bharat (India), and the Muslim Pakistan. The tensions between the two are as yet unresolved in a great many cases.

The early years of the century saw political revivals all over the East. The British and Dutch colonies of South East Asia were granted political independence soon after India, and in five years half the population of the thickly-populated area attained a new political status.

The process of granting political autonomy, thus begun in Asia, was completed a decade later in Africa. The political division of Africa had been decided at the Congress of Berlin in 1885. However, the Peace of Versailles in 1919 led to sweeping changes in the political map of Africa, since the forfeited German colonies became mandates under the hegemony of Great Britain, France, Belgium and South Africa. Not until after the Second World War did the Africans' striving after political autonomy become a factor to be reckoned with. Ten years after India's independence the colony of Gold Coast became the State of Ghana, under the leadership of Kwame Nkrumah; the stage was set for political revolution throughout the whole of Africa north of the Zambezi.

In 1955, some thirty Asian and African countries met together in Bandung, Java, for the first great political conference of the coloured world: representatives of "the countries which will never again be called colonies" (R. de Montvallon). Prime Minister Sukarno of Indonesia welcomed his guests, from China to West Africa, with the words, "We are united by race and religion." This was a modified truth, coming as it did at a time when the subject of race was taboo, at least in the West (a reaction, led by UNESCO, against the racial ideologies of the 1930's); while the religious affiliations of the Afro-Asian group were far from homogeneous. But Sukarno's formula had symbolic importance: competing interests were united by their anti-colonial sentiments, and a vast diversity of countries and cultures took on at least the trappings of apparent unity.

To start with, it was only natural for missionaries belonging to the colonial powers to support their own respective political régimes, convinced that the combination of religion and Western civilization was the greatest blessing which could be afforded to the coloured world. We may illustrate this situation by a number of examples.

In British India, British missionaries were in the majority. Their main areas were in South India (Tirunelveli, Travancore, Madras and Mysore) and to a lesser extent, in Bengal and the Bombay area. In the mid-nine-teenth century, of 91,000 Protestant Christians in India, 50,000 were attached to the Anglican mission in South India. The importance of South India for missions is most clearly seen in the fact that at this time only one-fifth of the Protestant Christian population of India was found north of the Province of Madras. American missions—Lutherans, Baptists, Congregationalists—came to South India in these years, as did the important Basel Mission. The numbers of missionaries, and of Christians, grew rapidly towards the close of the century, and by 1914 the Christian community numbered a million. Missionary education was of vast importance in this growth. The Scotsman, Alexander Duff (in India 1829–63, d. 1878) one of the greatest names of the "Great Century" saw in the combination of Christian mission and higher education on the college and university levels the answer to the social and cultural problems of India. Hinduism, he believed, would be unable to withstand this joint impact. The educational pattern laid down by Duff was to have untold consequences—positive and negative—for the future of especially British and American missions in India.

The history of Africa, including its missionary history, is dominated by one great name, that of David Livingstone. The modern missionary history of Africa virtually began with the explorations of Livingstone, and later those of H. M. Stanley, and is thus of quite recent date. Livingstone's three journeys through the interior of Africa were in 1853–56, 1858–64, and 1866–73; Stanley's journeys across the continent and along the River Congo were between 1874 and 1877. One of the most important results of these journeys was the missionary interest they aroused among Protestants and Roman Catholics alike. Livingstone's missionary ideal was characteristically British in that it provided for practical economic aid as well as the preaching of the Gospel. In 1857 he said in Cambridge, "I go back to Africa to try to make an open path for commerce and Christianity." At that time the "path" he proposed seemed to be for the healing of "the open sore of the world"—the Arabs' slave-trade. The Anglo-Catholic Universities' Mission in Tanganyika, Nyasaland and Northern Rhodesia was founded in 1859 in answer to Livingstone's appeal, an appeal which also influenced his Scottish countrymen to found a mission to Nyasaland, in 1875. Among Roman Catholics, Father (later Cardinal) Charles Lavigerie (d. 1892) was responsible for an important missionary initiative in Central Africa, through the founding, in 1868, of the order of the White Fathers, whose main fields were Uganda, Tanganyika and Ruanda-Urundi.

The political problems attending the practice of missions were brought into sharp relief in these and similar cases. In Uganda Christianity and British rule were identified to an extent which was largely hidden from those involved. In 1894 the CMS undertook to start a national fund to keep Uganda in the British Empire, and at the same time to weaken the position of the Arabs, Islam and the slave-trade; £16,000 were collected in ten days. An unconscious characterization of an important aspect of nineteenth-century missions was provided by the author who called the SPG's jubilee volume, issued in 1901 in commemoration of the Society's 200th anniversary, "The Spiritual Expansion of the Empire".

The history of Madagascar in the 1850's was noteworthy for a dramatic struggle for power between British and French colonial interests, who were played off against each other by the Hova kings and queens, holders of the traditional power. An interesting role in this conflict was played by a Congregationalist, William Ellis of the LMS. He was a good Victorian imperialist: that is, he was perfectly sure that by furthering British colonial interests he was acting in the best interests of his Society. In fact he became the friend and personal adviser of the Hova king, and his counsels were given precedence over those of the British ambassador, Pakenham, an Irish Protestant. Pakenham's irritation expressed itself in a conspiracy with the French Catholics against the successful British Congregationalist! When Madagascar became a French colony in 1895, the Catholics maintained that allegiance to the Pope should be an essential ingredient in loyalty to the colonial authorities.

The short but hectic period of German colonialism saw a great influx of German missionaries to their own colonies, Tanganyika, the Cameroons, Togo and South West Africa.

The work of missions, and particularly of educational missions was greatly facilitated by the co-operation of missionaries and administrators, who usually came from the same country, and not infrequently from the same University and even the same College. A British missionary in Malacca or Nigeria, a Belgian missionary in the Belgian Congo, a Dutch missionary in the Dutch East Indies— these were not strangers, in the way in which missionaries from other countries were strangers. He could obtain concessions for his mission: grants, or sites for church, school and hospital. He was at home in his own colony.

Since he held a privileged position, his responsibilities towards Afro-Asian independence movements were all the greater. At this point mission and colonialism often parted company. We may mention the names of some missionaries who, at an early stage, identified themselves with the political aspirations of the colonial peoples, at the risk of being held traitors by their own countrymen.

Perhaps the greatest of these was the Englishman, C. F. Andrews (d. 1940), who in 1914 relinquished his Anglican orders and joined Rabindranath Tagore's *ashram* and school at Santiniketan, thereby identifying himself with one of the greatest spiritual centres of Indian nationalism. Of Catholic Apostolic family, he was a staunch Anglo-Catholic on his arrival in India, but later adopted a theological position which made generous recognition of both Indian and Christian heritages. India interpreted his initials, C.F.A., as meaning "Christ's Faithful Apostle". In East Africa, the name of Archdeacon Owen is worthy of especial mention; Owen was a consistent critic of the British Government's misdemeanours in the matter of social legislation. Also in East Africa we have Frank Weston, Anglican Bishop of Zanzibar, whose book *England's Black Slaves* was a clear challenge to British colonial policy in Africa. The Dutchman, Hendrik Kraemer, gave proof of his personal courage in the 1920's, when he urged his country to bring to an end its 300-year-old history of colonialism in the Dutch East Indies. A Roman Catholic parallel is to be seen in the bishops' pastoral letter in 1954 to the people of Madagascar, in which the bishops looked forward to a national revolution on the island, and declared themselves to be in full sympathy with the aims of the nationalists.

It is thus entirely wrong to assume that the missionary contribution of the nineteenth and twentieth centuries was nothing more than a religious *obbligato* to the theme of colonial expansion. Nor were the missions organized by particular countries limited to those parts of the world in which they had their colonies. Protestant and Catholic missionaries alike found their way to the colonies of foreign powers—and that in itself may serve as a warning against exaggerating the connexion between mission and colonial politics. British and American missionaries came to work in the Belgian and French Congo, where the official language was French (never easy to the English-speaking world), and where legal practice, the educational system, and much else, differed profoundly from what they had been used to. Other examples are the work of the LMS on the French island of Madagascar; the French Protestant mission to British Basutoland and Northern Rhodesia; and the German mission in the Dutch East Indies.

We may also recall that a Swedish Baptist, E. V. Sjöblom (d. 1904) made a courageous appeal to world opinion in connexion with the treatment of Africans in King Leopold's Belgian Congo.

Protestant missionaries at work in areas dominated by Latin colonial governments and the Church of Rome met with special difficulties as for example in the Belgian Congo, in Portuguese Angola and Mozambique, and in what was in the 1930's the Italian colony of Eritrea (from which Swedish missionaries of the Evangelical National Missionary Society were expelled in 1936). Catholic missions enjoyed a privileged position in the Belgian Congo. Up to the Second World War fifty Catholic missions had received territorial concessions amounting to 120,000 *hectares*; while thirty-one Protestant missions had had to be content with 5,000 h. During the same period Catholic missions received State subsidies to the tune of more than 30 million francs annually; the highest annual subsidy granted to Evangelical missions was 77,500 francs. Up to 1948 Protestant missionary schools received no official financial support, while Catholic schools received 16 million francs annually. All Catholic missions, whether run by Belgians or not, were classified as "national missions"; Protestant missions were "foreign missions", and as such agents of a dangerous "denationalization". Hence the two standards of treatment. In 1948, however, there was a marked change of front. Protestant missionary schools began to receive State subsidies. The situation improved steadily during the 1950's. Official contact between the Protestant Churches and the Belgian authorities in the Congo was brought about through the General Secretary of the Congo Protestant Council (a post held during the 1950's by a Swede, Josef Ohrneman). Further, since 1920 the Protestant Churches have had a representative in Brussels; his position was made official in 1948.

Improvements of this kind were scarcely to be expected in the Portuguese possessions in Africa—which incidentally since 1951 have not been called colonies, but Portugal's fifth and sixth "provinces": too great store must not however be set by this semantic modernization. For decades Protestant missions have been regarded in these territories as opponents, endangering the religious homogeneity of the nation. The Protestants' attempts to teach the Bible in the vernaculars were regarded as threatening the spread of the Portuguese language. Protestant teachers and evangelists have been given severe punishments if they have been caught in possession of a Christian book in any of the tribal languages. The Bible is now always printed "bilingually", for example with Chitonga or Chirwa on the left and Portuguese on the right. The freedom movement in Angola in 1961, which was inspired from the Congo, was claimed to be inspired by Protestant elements (which was tantamount to saying that it was communist-inspired), and the Portuguese authorities made examples of a number of Protestant ministers, teachers and other Christians.

We have seen how the Congregationalist London Missionary Society was able to exercise considerable influence on the court at Tananarive, particularly through its arch-diplomat, the missionary William Ellis. It was common knowledge that the London Mission had done all in its power to hinder Madagascar from becoming French, and when the island finally fell into French hands the LMS missionaries were faced with the combined opposition of the secular French State and the Jesuit mission. Their motto was, "Catholic is French", and the British Congregationalists were far from fulfilling either condition. Loyalty toward the new French régime meant breaking with the British missionaries, foreign and Protestant as they were. In this critical situation an arrangement was arrived at which was of great importance as a mark of missionary strategy. In 1896 the French Protestant Paris Mission came to Madagascar, and took over the whole Reformed mission's school system and half of the LMS mission-field. Here was a mission which, though French and utterly loyal, was willing to co-operate with the Protestant foreigners. In fact the Paris Mission has gone down to history as the defender of non-French Protestant missionary interests all over the French colonial empire; similar situations could be described on Tahiti, in the French Congo, the Cameroons and Togo.

But the problems were not all on the side of Protestantism in Catholic territories. We have at least one good example of the difficulties encountered by a Catholic mission on Protestant ground. It is true that the nationalist régime in South Africa practises a policy of religious neutrality and *laisser faire* toward the missions. But its racial and educational policies have been bitterly opposed, particularly by the Catholic missions (Roman and Anglican alike), and its religious policy, inspired as it is by the Dutch Reformed Church, can hardly be called favourable to Catholic activity. These missions are in fact barely tolerated by the Government.

From this analysis of some of the problems of the former colonial territories we pass on to the development in China and Japan, which differs from that of the colonies in many respects. The relation between missions and politics in China is deserving of our attention for other reasons, too. One of the main points of the anti-imperialist catechism issued by the Chinese Communists is that the Christian missions have been the lackeys of Western capitalist imperialism in China. What are we to say about Mao Tse-tung's interpretation of the history of mission?

China and Japan, 1850–1960

Although China and Japan were subjected to considerable political and economic pressure from the Western empires during the nineteenth century, they never became colonies in the sense that Madagascar, Indonesia or Nigeria were colonies. And the pattern of Western missions in these countries differed to some extent from that we have seen to have been operative in "the colonial situation". We shall first of all give a rapid sketch comparing the missionary situation in China and Japan during the past century; then we pass on to a somewhat more detailed picture of the development of missions in the two countries.

The two countries became open to Western influence at about the same time: China in 1842, Japan in 1853. In each case the doors were opened most reluctantly, in the face of superior military strength.

Not until the 1860's was it found possible to begin missionary work in the inland of China. Somewhat later, in 1873, Japan repealed the 250-year-old edict forbidding Christianity in the country. As in China, so in Japan: the 1870's and 1880's were a time of progress for missions. Indeed, a wave of enthusiasm for Christianity swept Japan in the 1880's. In China, at this time, the Christian movement was limited to the country districts, led by fundamentalist missionaries whose interest in questions of culture was slight. However, there were British and American missionaries who, following the example of Timothy Richard (d. 1919), were beginning to devote time and energy to literature, to schools and universities. In Japan, on the other hand, the cause of Christianity was furthered mainly by an intellectual *élite* from poor *samurai* families, and it won most ground in the cities. Leading Japanese Christians had been deeply affected by Christianity in America, with its greater openness to culture, and wished to influence Japanese opinion by means of Christian colleges and Christian literature.

In the 1890's there followed a period of reaction against all the West stood for: in Japan open and categorical; in China hidden and threatening.

The victory of Japan over Russia in 1905 exercised untold influence over the whole of the East, bringing new hope and a new confidence in its train. Japan became more than ever open to Western influence, particularly in the realms of technology and culture; that influence came largely from America. The same was true of missions, in which American influence was outstanding. In 1925, five-sixths of all Evangelical missionaries in Japan were Americans. The pressure of a rapidly expanding population, together with the confidence of Western-inspired technology, led to an unfortunate attempt to realize Japan's dream of a pan-Asian empire, a dream from which she emerged in 1945, on the destruction of Hiroshima and Nagasaki. The atomic bomb, too, was American. The "openness to the Gospel" after 1945 was in no small measure an alternative expression for Japan's hunger for American language and industry.

While Japan was developing, China was almost continually in the throes of revolution; in 1912 the Emperor was deposed, and in 1949 Generalissimo Chiang Kai-shek. Western influence was not able to penetrate the vast country to the same extent as in Japan, but reached the population of the towns to some extent. The Christian Church, on the other hand, was largely confined to the people of the villages than the towns' more sophisticated population. At the end of the 1940's the two countries' ways parted: Mao's China turned to Moscow—a catastrophe for Western Christian mission; Japan became more and more Westernized, in missions as in all else, though at the same time this influence led to dramatic reaction on a number of occasions.

We have said that China became opened to Western missions in 1842. This is an important date in the history of missions, but its importance must not obscure the fact that modern missions to China began much earlier, and that their beginning was both adventurous and heroic. Among the great pioneers must be mentioned the brilliant Scottish LMS missionary, Robert Morrison (1782–1834), whose contribution had been made long before the Treaty of Nanking in 1842. The sole point of contact between the West and China was trade in the port of Canton, and Morrison, who arrived in Canton in 1808, worked as an interpreter for the East India Company there. He learned Chinese, and by 1819 had translated the whole of the Bible into Chinese. The German, Karl Gützlaff (1803–51), an erratic but nonetheless fascinating figure in the history of modern missions, served in the 1830's as an interpreter on board a ship belonging to opium smugglers, and later as an interpreter in the British consular service. By this means he hoped to send evangelists and Christian literature into the hitherto inaccessible China. The American missionary doctor, Peter Parker, who was the great pioneer of medical missions in China, persuaded the American authorities to sign a treaty with China. This was so successful that the American Government appointed the young missionary as their official commissioner. In this office he spoke authoritative words to his American countrymen in Canton: "My method with the Manchu Government is to be friendly, but firm. We have no more time now for nonsense, and empty talk will no longer be tolerated." In concrete terms this meant that more American ships were to be stationed in Chinese waters.

A number of bilateral treaties in the mid-nineteenth century favoured the Westerners, including the missionaries. Among these was the so-called "extra-territorial law", which incidentally also applied to Japan, according to which Westerners were not to be judged on a basis of Chinese law, but by the laws of their own respective countries. The irregularities brought about by these "unequal treaties" were the cause of much bitterness in China, and their consequences were felt in every twentieth-century crisis.

In 1842 China had granted the West access to the harbours of Canton, Amoy, Fuchow, Ningpo and Shanghai. As far as the missions were concerned, this meant that Christianity remained a coastal religion in China during the rest of the nineteenth century, and that its centres of expansion were ports, with their lines of communication westward. But the five ports became more important even than that. For a variety of missions took up work in China in the 1840's and 1850's, and at the close of this period it is already possible to discern the contours of the Protestant geography of that part of the country south of Shanghai. Now the strategic centres of the missions were precisely these five ports, together with Hong Kong, and as soon as circumstances allowed—in this case after 1860—they began to move inland. This general rule was of course subject to variation, but it fits the overall situation at this time.

The plurality of missions compelled co-operation and joint strategy from the very first. For instance, it was held desirable to come to some agreement regarding the Chinese translations of basic Christian terminology. But the solution was not immediately forthcoming. Perhaps the greatest problem concerned the Chinese name for God. Catholics said *T'ien chu*; British Protestants used the name *Shang ti*; Continental Protestants preferred the name *Shen*. Another controversy—this time between Baptists and others—was over the Chinese translation of the word "baptism". But language and literature were the most important problems that the missionaries could tackle in this first period, while they were awaiting the opportunity to move inland. The Scottish LMS missionary, James Legge (d. 1897), who came to China in 1839, proved himself a brilliant linguist, and became an outstanding authority on the Chinese classics. The Germans, F. G. Genähr and E. Faber, were also gifted Sinologists, and did much to help introduce Western culture to China.

A revolutionary folk movement which swept across the Middle Kingdom at this time was scarcely noticed by the few missionaries, absorbed as they were in their language studies. But it has been said that, had the missionaries joined in the Taiping movement in time, the history, and

134

of Church history, of China might have been profoundly affected.

But as it was, they preferred to ignore it. A Swede, Theodor Hamberg, was one of the few who knew the leaders of the movement personally, and even wrote a valuable little book about it, in English.[1] But it was soon evident in China that even those who tried to shut their eyes to political reality were thereby taking up a political attitude. The Taiping Movement was basically the revolt of the peasant population of China against the intolerable economic and political conditions imposed upon them by the Manchu dynasty. Its leader, Hung Siu ch'üan, a peasant youth from South China, was something of a visionary, believing himself to be Taiping-wan, King of the Great Peace. He had received Christian teaching for a couple of months from an American Baptist missionary from the Southern States, but the missionary failed to maintain contact with his young pupil. Hung tried to create a synthesis of Christian and traditional Chinese ideas. He believed that he received revelations from God (*Shang Ti*) direct, regarded himself as the younger brother of Jesus, and declared that Jesus and he were both born of the same mother. The growing army of rebels which joined Hung came through him into contact with a syncretism which went by the name of Christianity. Sacrifices to the ancestral spirits were abolished, as were popular burial rites. The Bible was read and honoured. The ten commandments and a modified form of the Lord's Prayer were taught. Large numbers of soldiers were baptized.

Supported by this ideology, Hung turned on the hated Manchu dynasty. There were times at which it seemed as though he might win. But Western troops, and the missionaries, supported the imperial power, and the Taiping Revolt was crushed. It has been estimated that 20 million people lost their lives in the course of this revolution. The

[1] *The Chinese Rebel Chief Hung Siu-Tsien and the Origin of the Insurrection in China*, (London 1854).

Western missionaries looked upon the beliefs of the peasant army as strange and unchristian, and they were unwilling to maintain the contacts which Hung wanted. His fantastic claims were of course heresy; but they were not merely heresy. They gave evidence of the spiritual hunger of the Chinese peasant—a hunger which expressed itself in an open appeal to the missionaries, the like of which has never been heard since. Perhaps the mission was too Western, too respectable to be able to understand and take part in an Asian popular movement of this kind. But the opportunity came and went, and the end of the Taiping Revolt meant the peace treaties of 1858–60, giving Hudson Taylor and the Western missions exactly what they wanted —the right to penetrate inland. The Yangtse was opened to foreign vessels, and mission stations began to be built in the interior provinces.

The period from 1860 to 1900 in the Protestant history of China was dominated by the name of Hudson Taylor. In 1865 Taylor founded what was to become the most extensive of all Protestant missions to China, with a name which was both a claim and a challenge: The China Inland Mission. Not even Hudson Taylor was immune from the changes and chances of power-politics in his endeavours for the Kingdom. But his Christianity, like that of the majority of Protestant missionaries to China between 1860 and 1920, was of a type which refused in principle to become mixed up in politics—though this was itself a political attitude, as we have seen. When in 1894 he made his famous appeal to the members of the Student Volunteer Movement in Detroit to come and work in China he said:

"It will be the work of Jesus, Jesus in you, if it is ever done. And the Gospel must be preached to these people in a very short time, for they are passing away. Every day, every day; oh how they sweep over! Your great cataract Niagara seems to me to teach us a lesson and to afford us an example. How the water pours over and over ceaselessly by day and by night, over that great cataract! There is a great Niagara of souls passing into the dark in China. Every day, every week, every month they are passing away—a million a month in China are dying without God. And what a wonderful difference there is in dying with God, dying with God as a Saviour, and dying without God."[1]

Hudson Taylor's plan was to bring the Christian message to the Chinese provinces in the shortest possible time. His motto was rapid evangelization—we might almost call it frantic evangelization. He was less concerned with the building of the Church in China, with all that that implies in terms of the training of a Chinese ministry and the like. There was no time for such details. The important thing was to reach out to all the provinces and to all the Chinese people. The task of training and educating those who had been won could be taken over by other missionaries afterwards—though the China Inland Mission was later to modify this ideal somewhat in face of practical necessity. Hudson Taylor, with apostolic enthusiasm, threw himself heart and soul into his work, and his ideal. His mission might not appeal for funds; it was a "faith mission", which lived in prayer and faith: the Lord will provide.

The China Inland Mission was interdenominational, and its staff was made up of representatives of a large number of churches and societies in the West. For instance, the Church of England had its own diocese in the Province of Szechwan, with an Anglican bishop, but incorporated into Hudson Taylor's enterprise. The work grew apace, and by 1895, after thirty years, there were 640 missionaries serving in 260 stations and outposts. There were other European missions co-operating with the CIM.

The expansion of this mission did not of course take

[1] *The Student Missionary Enterprise* (ed. M. W. Moorhead), Boston 1894, p. 48.

place in a politically neutral China. At the same time as the nationalist movements were gathering momentum in India, the hate of the Chinese for the foreigners and their privileges was growing. This culminated in the Boxer Rebellion which ushered in the twentieth century: a bloody episode in China's history.

One of the main causes of the trouble in China, as in Japan, was the "extra-territorial law"; in 1900 there began in three of the provinces of North China a campaign of violence against the "foreign devils". In the course of the Boxer Rebellion about 50 Catholic and 135 Protestant missionaries were killed, together with more than 30,000 Catholic and 2,000 Protestant Chinese. The trading agreements which were signed after the Boxer Rebellion —e.g. those with the United States in 1903 and with Sweden in 1908—included clauses guaranteeing protection of Western missionaries and their Chinese co-religionists.

In 1912 the Manchu dynasty was overthrown, after having ruled in China for two and a half centuries. The leader of the new China was Sun Yat-sen, a doctor who had become a Christian. He was responsible for introducing democratic ideas into China on a scale never seen before or since. His Kuomintang party was based on the three "popular principles": nationalism, democracy and social reforms. His interest in social reforms made him receptive to the teachings of the Russian Communists. Sun Yat-sen died in 1925; he was succeeded by Chiang Kai-shek, who in 1927 broke with Communism and three years later became a Christian. The missionaries and the Western missionary societies were naturally very much in favour of the nationalist régime, particularly since the authorities had treated the missionaries' work with great generosity.

Chinese Christendom was split into some hundred different organizations. It is true that there had been an organ of co-ordination since 1922 in the National Christian Council, but it never succeeded in gathering more than 60 per cent of the Protestants. And in 1926 the China Inland Mission left the Council on account of its supposedly liberal tendencies. In 1927 was formed the Church of Christ in China, in which Congregationalists, Reformed and Baptists united; in 1920 the Lutherans of Central China (comprising Americans, Danes, Swedes, Norwegians and Finns) united to form the Justification by Faith Church. The Protestant missionary body was largest in the 1920's, when it had almost 7,700 members. But this figure later declined considerably, partly on account of the war. In 1948 there were 1,300 British Evangelical missionaries in China; America had 2,100, and the Continent of Europe, including Scandinavia, about 1,000. At that time the representatives of the Chinese Church appealed to the West for reinforcements. At the Whitby Conference of the International Missionary Council in 1947 the Chinese asked for 20,000 more Western missionaries in China. But these speculations came to nothing, thanks to Mao Tse-tung and the people's revolution.

The most striking weakness in the Chinese Church before 1949 was the lack of a sufficiently large number of qualified leaders. In 1938 there were only 2,135 ordained Chinese ministers, and this in a Church of more than 600,000 members. Consequently the Church, as an organization, was weak. The missionaries had long striven after "devolution"—i.e. transfer of responsibility to Chinese leaders—but this was conditioned by outward factors, of which two must be mentioned. First, the political revolution of 1927 made it imperative for the missions to create self-governing churches in China, with responsibility in Chinese hands; and secondly, the economic depression of 1929–33 was felt very keenly, particularly by the numerous American missionaries: grants were reduced and the Chinese churches were compelled to become more and more self-supporting.

The coming to power of the Communists in 1949 was

the start of a new epoch in the history of China. For Western missions—Catholic and Protestant alike—this was a catastrophe comparable in its dimensions only with the destruction of the churches of North Africa by the Muslim hordes in the seventh century. But we must be careful. As a Swedish observer, Bengt Hoffman, has said, "To regard our [i.e. Western mission] absence as a failure would surely be to tempt God."

Since the taking over of power in 1949 by the Communists under Mao Tse-tung the situation of the churches in China has altered drastically, and their opportunities of service have been severely curtailed. Persecution of Catholics and Protestants as "the lackeys of American imperialism" set in. In the cities, churches were compelled to unite without regard to earlier denominational traditions. It seemed for a time as though apocalyptic groups, such as the "Family of Jesus", which worked along Christian communist lines, would have the best chance of survival; however, even this would seem to be doubtful in the long run. Those who accept Communism supported the "Three Self" movement, which was organized in 1950. The classical pattern of Evangelical mission (a self-governing, self-supporting, self-propagating Church) has been reshaped into an ideological instrument for the spread of anti-Western propaganda. The totalitarian control exercised by the Communist authorities over what remains of the churches has been in the hands of a special department of religion since 1960.

In 1948 the Roman Catholic Church had 3¼ million members. There were more than 3,000 ordained missionaries, and almost 2,700 Chinese priests. The Communists' attack on Christianity was aimed especially at the Roman Catholics. According to the official propaganda they were "the tools of an imperialistic Pope". The Papal Internuncio, Archbishop Riberi, was expelled from China in 1952. The Chinese Cardinal Tien, who had been appointed in 1946, left China, but continued to work on the nationalist island of Taiwan (Formosa). The Three Self movement led to the formation of a group of pro-Communist "progressive Catholics". This was condemned by Pope Pius XII in the encyclical *Ad Sinarum Gentes* of 1954, and when in 1958–59 the movement compelled the consecration of schismatic bishops, and revealed the existence of plans to appoint a pro-Communist Chinese Pope, the break became even more marked, as may be seen in Pius XII's last encyclical *Ad Apostolorum Principis* (1958).

The Chinese catastrophe of 1949–50 led to a complete reorientation of the whole of the Church's missionary strategy in East Asia. The Communists deported all Christian missionaries, both Catholic and Protestant. These were for the most part redirected to other countries. The rapid increase in the missionary force at work in Japan during the 1950's was largely due to the arrival of former Chinese missionaries. Many others found their way to Hong Kong and Taiwan, as well as to the great Chinese refugee *diaspora* (more than 12 millions) in South-East Asia. It may be that this *diaspora* is challenging the Christian mission to new efforts, and offering new possibilities.

Now, having dealt with the Chinese situation in some detail, we must give a brief account of developments in Japan during the same period. The Japanese situation is characterized by oscillation between aversion and acceptance in the matter of Western culture and religion. And the missions were faced with perplexing changes, from success to opposition and back. Christianity was not officially recognized as a religion in Japan until 1921, though the 1907 Tokyo Conference of the World's Student Christian Federation had revealed the existence of a certain amount of goodwill. Japanese nationalism, which led to the war with China in 1937, forced the missionaries in Japan into a critical situation. After indirect, but effective, political pressure, most of the non-Roman churches in

Japan joined together in 1941 to form a united Japanese Church, the *Kyodan*. After the war the Lutherans, Anglicans and Baptists left this organization, but it still remains the largest of Japan's non-Roman churches. In 1945 the Emperor of Japan relinquished all claim to be regarded as divine, an event the significance of which can be understood only against the background of the fundamentally sacred role of the Emperor in Japanese religion.

Although the Christian groups were a very small minority, never having amounted to as much as 1 per cent of the population, Christian individuals have nevertheless been able to make a positive contribution to the public life of Japan. Western missionaries played a much more prominent part in Chinese affairs than was ever the case in Japan. In Japan, however, the country's own sons have been able to make striking Christian contributions, leading to social and political consequences. We may mention three names.

Joseph Nisima (d. 1890) was the founder of the Christian college in Doshisha at which many of the leaders of modern Japan were educated. His aim was to combine Japanese patriotism with a modern Western and Christian attitude to life. The importance of Doshisha, as in the case of Duff's Institution in India, was that it set a pattern for other Christian colleges. The most important of these was the Christian University in Tokyo, organized by the Americans after the war. Nisima represented the important link between Western and Japanese culture. *Kanzo Utshimura* (d. 1930), on the other hand, was more concerned with the Japanese interpretation of the Gospel. He had studied in America, and founded the *Mukyokai*, the Non-church movement, in Japan (see p. 290). There are now about 50,000 adherents of this movement—a fairly high number for Japan.

Toyohiko Kagawa (d. 1960), who was brought up in the slums, became one of the greatest prophetic figures of the twentieth century, known the world over for his books and poems. He was inspired by the example of Scandinavian folk high schools and the co-operative movement to work not only for the betterment of the population of the city slums, but also—and primarily—for the country population. The international missionary conference in Jerusalem in 1928 inspired him to start a country-wide "Kingdom of God Movement": an evangelistic campaign of colossal dimensions. His goal was the building up of the Kingdom of mercy and goodness at the heart of the Japanese Empire.

The Roman Catholic Church has grown rapidly since the Second World War. Large numbers of new missionaries have been recruited, as well as those who were redirected from China to Japan. In 1939 there were 325 missionary priests; by the end of the 1950's there were 1,200, drawn from a hundred orders and congregations representative of 25 different nations. For the sake of perspective it would be well to stress that the Roman Catholic Church in Japan is concentrated on the southern island of Kyushu, particularly in and around Nagasaki, and to some extent in Tokyo. It was on Kyushu that the *Kirishitan*, a group of "Old Catholics", were discovered in 1865. Despite 250 years of intensive persecution, small pockets of Catholics had succeeded in preserving their faith and their religion. Not until a number of years after Japan was opened to Westerners did they make a tentative attempt to come in contact with the Church, through the French missionary, Père Petitjean; at that time their number was some 25,000. In 1954 another group of surviving "Old Catholics" was discovered, again on the South Island

The New States and the Universality of the Church

In our day there has taken place a "Copernican revolution" in relations between the West and the East and Africa. The traditional hegemony of the West has been broken. New independent Asian and African states have emerged. It is important to stress, from the missionary point of view, that the problem of missions and politics is very far indeed from having been finally solved by the decline of Western imperialism. The Christian mission and the Church are faced with new and difficult problems in respect of their relations to the new autonomous Asian and African states. For instance, the question of visas, residence permits and work permits for Western missionaries in India has caused much worry to the missions since the 1950's. The problem of religious freedom is now viewed in a new dimension. The Indian Constitution of 1950 laid down that every citizen should have the right "to profess, preach and propagate" his religion; but according to the Niyogi Report of 1956, from Central India, this right applied only to Indian citizens, and not to foreigners. The right of the Christian Church to mission—that is, to seek to bring men and women to a decision for Christ—is questioned or denied outright by powerful groups in new Asian states, such as India, Ceylon and Burma. Ceylon in particular, with its pro-Buddhist policy in matters of language and religion, has placed great difficulties in the way of mission. However, it should be pointed out with respect to India that Prime Minister Nehru defended Christianity and missionary interests against the findings of the Niyogi Commission. His speech in the Indian Parliament was based on the history of missions and the Church, and claimed that since Christianity had been in India since the very beginning of the Christian era, it had every right to be a missionary religion in his country.

This revolutionary new phase in the East-West relations has placed the missions, both Catholic and Protestant, in an entirely new position. It cannot be stressed too highly that it is now the national Church—not the Western missionary organization—which has to meet and negotiate with the political leaders of the Asian or African State. It will be clear that one of the most important of present-day tasks for the Church as a whole is that of leading the young Churches into conscious political responsibility.

The national loyalties and at the same time the supranational callings of the missionary stood out in a new and clearer light after the Second World War. The 1947 international missionary conference in Whitby, Canada, issued a manifesto on the supra-nationality of mission. The Protestant mission, which for the most part had originated in Pietistic groups, with their characteristic avoidance of all political "involvement", had now reached a deeper consciousness of the political responsibility of the Christian in "the responsible society" (the phrase is J. H. Oldham's). As the ambassadors of Christ, the missionaries' task is to bear witness to a fellowship which is raised high above national and racial boundaries, a fellowship in which there is neither Jew nor Greek, neither German nor Englishman, neither European, Asian nor African. Their task is to show that "our primary loyalty is to Christ, and that our responsibility as servants of the Church universal must dominate not merely a part, but the whole of our thought and action".

CHAPTER 9

SLAVERY AND THE RACE PROBLEM

O UR RAPID SKETCH OF THE RELATIONS OF MISSIONS
and colonial politics has given us a glimpse of one
aspect of our overall problem. Now we must turn to another aspect, which has come to play a prominent, and
even a fatal, role in the present world political situation.
The race problem is one of the burning questions of the
day, and the attitude of missions to race is one which must
not be passed by. However, the race problem in Africa and
America cannot be judged without reference to slavery and
"the negro question" in the history of the respective
countries.

The production of white sugar led to millions of black
slaves being shipped across the Atlantic from Africa to
America. As has well been said, "Sugar was the slaves'
worst enemy." The Spanish emigrants in the north of
South America and the British farmers in the West Indies
and the south of North America supplied Europe with
sugar. And negro slaves were a cheap labour force. The
sugar farmers were the greatest capitalists of the mercan-
tile era. William Carey was one of those who advocated
sanctions against the sugar-producers of the West Indies—
an action which invites comparison with the present-day
boycott of South African fruit and wines. William Carey
wrote in his *Enquiry* (1792):

> Many persons have of late left off the use of West-India
> sugar, on account of the iniquitous manner in which it is
> obtained. Those families who have done so, and have not

substituted anything else in its place, have not only cleansed their hands of blood, but have made a saving to their families, some of six-pence, and some of a shilling a week. If this, or a part of this were appropriated to the uses before-mentioned, it would abundantly suffice. We have only to keep the end in view, and have our hearts thoroughly engaged in the pursuit of it, and means will not be very difficult.[1]

Negro slavery of course dates back far beyond the West Indies slave traffic. Arabs had been carrying slaves eastward from time immemorial. In A.D. 976 a sensation was caused when the crew of an Arab dhow brought a Negro slave to the court of the Emperor of China. The Portuguese found that their new colony of Angola was a valuable base from which to export black labour to Brazil. By 1585 there were already 10,000 negro slaves in the Pernambuco province of Brazil.

But the great epoch of slavery was in the seventeenth and eighteenth centuries; this development culminated in the period between 1750 and 1800, when some years saw the export of over 100,000 negro slaves. And from 1680 to 1786 more than 2 million slaves were imported into British colonies in America and the West Indies. It has been estimated that the total number of slaves sold to European colonies amounted to between 20 and 40 millions. Add to that the number of those killed by the Arab slave-traders, and the vast loss of life incurred in the course of transport from the African villages to the Americas, and it is no longer surprising that Africa should be such a relatively sparsely populated continent. It is claimed that as many perished *en route* as reached the plantations.

There were large sums of money involved. Between 1783 and 1793 880 slave-ships left Liverpool, carrying over 300,000 slaves worth more than £15 million. The annual net profits of the slave trade were 30 per cent.

[1] Carey, *Enquiry* (facsimile ed. 1942), p. 86.

Agents in West African ports contacted unscrupulous chiefs in the interior of the country, who agreed to deliver the requisite number of slaves in exchange for cloth, weapons and spirits. The slave caravans followed well-marked routes through the jungles and across the plains to the coast and the slave-ships. Escape was wellnigh impossible, since the slaves were normally fastened by the neck to a long pole. The slave-ships set out from Lagos and other West African harbours. A 150-tonner could take about 600 slaves, if they were well packed in. The hold was divided horizontally by decks, or shelves, set at about 3 ft. intervals. In these the "cargo" was placed—slaves chained together in pairs. A certain amount of communication was possible along a central corridor. The men at least were treated in this way, though women appear to have been spared this treatment. Heat and disease decimated the slaves' numbers, but a certain amount of selection had already taken place at the port of embarkation. The young and strong were taken on board; the old and weak were disposed of. That is why no more than a sixth of the average "cargo" is believed to have died actually on board ship on "the Middle Passage". On arrival the slaves were auctioned. In the eighteenth century healthy slaves fetched up to £60 a head. The process of breaking in the slaves to their work on the sugar plantation was brutal, and often fatal; the only teaching aid was the whip. A third of all slaves are believed to have succumbed to the brutal treatment they received. Those who survived became slaves in Aristotle's sense, "living tools". Coupland is right when he says, "It is difficult not to regard this treatment of Africa, meted out by Christian Europe in the train of Muslim Africa, as the greatest crime in history."

We must remember that at this time sincere Christians, from Anglicans to Quakers, accepted the slave trade as an economic necessity, and were themselves involved in the traffic. But its abolition came as a result of a protest movement inspired by an awakened Christian conscience. Already in 1671 George Fox had raised his voice against the slave-trade: indeed the Quakers were in the van of abolitionism. In 1774 John Wesley wrote his tract *Thoughts on Slavery*, and in 1780 the Bishop of London exhorted the SPG to take part in the campaign. In the event, it was the Evangelical "Clapham Sect", led by William Wilberforce, which brought about what had seemed to be the impossible. British opinion was aroused. Parliament abolished the slave-trade throughout the British Empire in 1807, and slavery as such in all British territories in 1833. But Wilberforce and his friends were not content with recording their protest; they put forward constructive suggestions for resettling freed slaves in Africa. Africa, they firmly believed, was going to be saved by a combination of civilization, commerce and Christianity. An interesting experiment was carried out by Wilberforce's colleague Granville Sharp, who in 1787 was responsible for founding a colony of freed slaves, Sierra Leone, in West Africa. Here, and in Liberia (a similar enterprise, begun in the 1820's), mission and Christian philanthropy attempted to make some measure of reparation for the previous conduct of the white race. Fourah Bay College, in Freetown, Sierra Leone, founded in 1827, was an early expression of the desire of the mission to serve West Africa. A large number of West Africans later prominent in the Church and the administration received their education at this college.

Wilberforce's struggle, and the decision of the British Parliament, had profound consequences in the Southern States of the U.S.A. and in South Africa (see below, pp. 152–6). During the American Civil War of 1861–65 Abraham Lincoln was campaigning for the abolition of slavery; the actual abolition took place in both North and South States in 1863, at the cost of Abraham Lincoln's life. The negro population of America, which was about 1 million in 1800, had by 1914 grown to 10 million, and to 19 million in 1960. These millions of men and women had been wrenched from their homes in Africa and transported under vile conditions to America and the West Indies. In their new countries millions of Africans and their descendants were brought into the fellowship of the Christian Church, where services in chapel were the brightest events life could afford, and where their longing after rest and peace "across the Jordan" spontaneously gave rise to a body of music and poetry of great beauty, "negro spirituals". Frederick Douglas, one of the negroes' leaders in the nineteenth century, has related how as a slave he first came into contact with Christianity. Oppressed and sorrowful, a Christian negro advised him to cast his burden upon the Lord. He did so; "My heart became light, and I loved the whole of mankind, even the slave-owner." More than 90 per cent of Christian negroes belonged to segregated Baptist or Methodist Churches, such as the African Methodist Episcopal Church, with a full hierarchy of negro bishops.

The decision of the British Parliament in 1833 aroused echoes throughout the world, but meant less than nothing to the Arab slave-traders in East Africa. For centuries there had been a traffic in negro slaves via the Nile to Cairo and in light Arab dhows over the sea to Arabia, Persia and India. The one responsible for putting a stop to this traffic was a missionary, and we claim that that missionary was the greatest man of the nineteenth century. On his tombstone in Westminster Abbey are inscribed the words "Missionary, Traveller, Philanthropist".

David Livingstone was born in Blantyre, Scotland, in 1813, and died in Chitambo, now in Northern Rhodesia, in 1873. In 1840 he arrived in South Africa as a missionary of the London Missionary Society, having qualified as a doctor at Glasgow University. He had been much impressed by Gützlaff's reports from China, and would have liked to have gone to the Far East, but was prevented by the Opium War, and was sent to South Africa instead. His explorations began in 1849, and it was in the course of these journeys across the African continent that he was confronted with the Arab slave-trade in its most abominable forms. Livingstone dedicated his life to healing "the world's running sore". In Bechuanaland he had seen what the LMS could do to help spread civilization, and he wanted to widen this kind of Christian influence to the rest of the African continent. He set greater store by the indirect method of "spreading better principles" than by the direct seeking after conversions. He also had a plan for providing help for helpless Africans—a plan which is doubly interesting, viewed in its historical perspective.

Hitherto commerce and the trading companies had been resolutely opposed to the missions. Livingstone's aim was a synthesis of the two. "Commerce and Christianity" was his motto, and thus he carried on ideas launched by the Clapham Sect more than a half-century earlier. The cause of missions would best be served by practical action. This involved a break with some of his contemporaries' ideas as to what a missionary should be and do: "My views of what is missionary duty are not so contracted as those whose ideal is a dumpty sort of man with a Bible under his arm." His idea was to start growing cotton in the flood areas of the Zambezi and around Lake Nyasa.

If agricultural and industrial enterprises could be set up under Christian auspices, and be made to pay, the economic and social conditions of the Africans would be considerably bettered. As Livingstone said, "If we can introduce a system of free labour into Africa, it will exercise a decisive influence on slavery the world over."

In the course of his famous address to the students at Cambridge in 1857 he said, "I beg to direct your attention to Africa. I know that in a few years I shall be cut off in that country which is now open; do not let it be shut again. I go back to Africa to try to make an open path for commerce and Christianity. Do you carry out the work which I have begun. I leave it with you." Livingstone's contribution in the realm of geographical discovery was epoch-making. Not until his time was the interior of

Africa known to the world. And the venture to the interior which was his struggle against the slave-trade is one of the most notable chapters in the history of missions.

Livingstone died in 1873; in that same year the Sultan of Zanzibar signed the treaty putting an end to Arab slave-trading. His work was carried on by many individuals and groups, among them the Anglo-Catholic Universities' Mission (UMCA) in Tanganyika and Nyasaland, and the missions of the Church of Scotland and the Free Church of Scotland in Nyasaland, who endeavoured to put into practice the ideals of Livingstone. The UMCA aimed at founding "centres of Christianity and civilization for the furtherance of true religion, agriculture and lawful commerce"—modern Central African equivalents of the Benedictine monasteries of medieval Europe.

The journey and reports of Livingstone and Henry Stanley also inspired the Roman Catholic Church to found missions in Africa, with the object of combating the slave-trade. In 1888 the great Cardinal Lavigerie exhorted Western Europe to undertake a crusade against the slave-trade in Africa. He estimated that Africa was being depopulated at the rate of 400,000 persons a year, and begged the Pope and the Catholic rulers for support. An interesting proposal came from King Leopold II of Belgium, who had considerable sums of money invested in the Congo. King Leopold proposed to the Pope, Leo XIII, that he should set up a "pontifical colony" in Central Africa. But the Pope and the Cardinal were too to wise accept any such suggestion: they knew that the problem of missions and colonial politics was not to be solved along those lines.

Racial Discrimination and the Churches

The discussion of the slavery question in the British Parliament was followed with interest in Cape Province, which had been a British colony since 1795. In the later part of the seventeenth century a few slaves had been imported into the Cape mainly from Angola and Madagascar.

In the eighteenth century a larger number were brought from the east coast (now Mozambique) to the western part of Cape Colony. At the same time when Britain took over the colony there were almost 17,000 slaves there, and about 14,000 European colonists. When slavery was abolished in 1834 this was regarded by the Boer farmers as an unjust interference with their rights, and a threat to their economy. Among representatives of British liberalism in Cape Colony the most outstanding figure was that of John Philip (b. 1774, to South Africa 1818, d. 1851), who with his liberalism combined evangelical piety and philanthropy: a man of the Wilberforce and Granville Sharp cast. Like Livingstone he was a Scotsman and a Congregationalist; like Livingstone he was in the service of the London Missionary Society.

In South Africa Philip was drawn into a political struggle with far-reaching implications. His conduct in the 1820's and 1830's set in motion a chain of events, the effects of which can still be observed—not least in our own day. It led to one of the most important events in the history of South Africa: "the great trek". The Boer farmers' dislike of England, the English language and English politics came to be concentrated in their hate of the "foreigner" and missionary John Philip. Between 1835 and 1838 about 10,000 Boers trekked out of Cape Colony to the north, where they set up the independent republics of the Orange Free State and Transvaal. There they would be safe from British liberalism and its reforms; and they would ensure that no British missionaries disturbed them. These words were written into the Transvaal Constitution of 1858: "The people admit no equality (*geenegelijkstelling*) between coloured and white in church or state." The importance of the great trek in the history of South Africa is far more than the story of a great migration. The trek northward has been transposed to the area of folk mythology; it has become a dynamic historical myth, and as such is constantly being re-enacted—*vide* most recently the action of the

Union of South Africa in leaving the British Commonwealth of Nations. But the original trek took place as a reaction against John Philip and all he stood for; in the myth, the missionary is the enemy.

We cannot here deal with the whole of South Africa's later political history, in which the Boer War (1899–1902) and the establishment of the Union (1910) are of especial importance. It will suffice if we point out that the legislation laying down the policy of segregation dates essentially from 1913, and the Natives Land Act. This Act was complemented in 1936 by a territorial law which was aimed at extending the "reservations" allocated to the African population by the purchase from the Boer farmers of certain wide areas of country. But even with these extensions, Africans have only been allocated 13 per cent of the territory of South Africa to live in. Since 1913 Africans have been prohibited from buying or selling land.

In 1948 the Nationalist Party came into power, since when the earlier policy of segregation has been implemented by a steady flow of legislation confirming the policy of *apartheid*. The theory behind the legislation is that racial groups should be completely separated from each other. The Africans have their "countries"—in the reserves. In principle, and as far as possible in practice, they are to stay there. There are seven or eight of these reserves, which have been given the name of "Bantustan".

Of particular significance for the work of Christian missions in the country is the Bantu Education Act of 1953. The Africans' educational organization was separated from the country's department of education, and the missionaries' direct influence over the schools disappeared. Toward the end of the 1950's practically total *apartheid* was enforced in the universities.

The Native Laws Amendment Bill of 1957 was intended to limit, as far as possible, all contact between the races. But at the same time economic necessity is driving a growing number of Africans to the cities and the rapidly expanding industries—a fact which is taken into account by the official forecast of population. It is estimated that by 2000 there will be a Bantu population of 21 millions, of which 6 millions (three times more than at present!) will be working in the towns. The tragic dilemma of the South African situation is to be seen in this tension, between economic necessity and utopian planning, a tension which is becoming total.

Leaders of the Church's opposition to *apartheid* have been among the Anglicans, two Archbishops of Capetown, Geoffrey Clayton (d. 1957) and Joost de Blank, Ambrose Reeves (Bishop of Johannesburg in the 1950's) and Trevor Huddleston (from 1960 Bishop in Tanzania), Alan Paton, the author, and Edgar Brookes, the politician. Among Roman Catholics must be mentioned Archbishop Joseph P. Hurley of Durban. African leaders include the leader of the African National Congress, Albert Luthuli, who is a deposed Christian chief, a member of the Congregational Church. In 1961 Chief Luthuli was awarded the Nobel Peace Prize. The churches and missions in South Africa are in a very difficult position. They have succeeded only in part in retaining the confidence of the African masses. In the Dutch Reformed Church an *élite* opposition has emerged, led by three professors of theology, B. B. Keet, Ben Marais and A. S. Geyser. Their joint work, *Delayed Action*, was published in 1960 in connexion with a contact conference called by the World Council of Churches for consultation between the Dutch Reformed Church, the Anglicans and others.

A remarkable manifestation of African self-consciousness is the "Ethiopian movement" which, coming originally from America, has spread across the greater part of South and East Central Africa, leading to the founding of great numbers of separatist churches and sects. In South Africa alone it is estimated that there are at present some 1,500 such groups.

The problem of segregation in the Southern States of

America has assumed alarming proportions this century. The negro question has been called "the American dilemma" (the term is Myrdal's), the dilemma being between liberal ideals and illiberal practices. At present, taking the long-term view, it is hoped that the question is on its way toward being solved, particularly since President Johnson's signing of the Civil Rights Bill in June 1964. The turning-point was reached on May 17, 1954, when the Supreme Court decided unanimously that segregation in schools was in conflict with the United States Constitution. Ever since 1896 there had been legalized segregation, thanks to an elastic formula assuring negroes of "separate but equal facilities". This, too, was declared unconstitutional. It is true that the Civil Rights movement has been bitterly opposed by most whites in the South. But the battle has now been won in principle. The passing in 1964 of the Civil Rights Bill means that the principle of equal civil rights has now been accepted, and waits only to be implemented—though this may take some time. Among the new generation of fighters for an integrated society is the Rev. Martin Luther King; while on the other side a powerful negro movement styling themselves the Black Muslims is pledged to fight for black supremacy.

PART THREE

CHURCH AND MILIEU

In our account of "Church and Empire" we attempted to give, in broad outline, an account of the relation between missions and politics. We saw how the missionary Church lives and serves "in the world", how she is affected by its political changes and conditions, and how she is confronted by the totality of its cultures and religions. Now we take the term "milieu" as referring to these totalities—cultures, religions and systems of thought. The Church is set in a "milieu".

The problem of Church and milieu is not altogether straightforward. It is important, from the point of view of the missionary Church, to stress two aspects: on the one hand, the relationship between mission and culture, and on the other the interaction of the Church and its setting. One of the most characteristic contributions made by Western missions to the Orient and Africa, particularly during the "epoch of world missions", 1800–1960, has been made in the realm of culture. Missionaries discovered that their commission to translate could not be carried out in a relevant manner without the ABC, first aid and the plough.

We must therefore consider the cultural contribution of the Christian mission, remembering that a typical feature of the young churches is their reaction to, and relations with, their milieu. Church and milieu affect each other, both positively and negatively, in a complex interplay of forces, and one of the tasks confronting missiology is that of understanding and interpreting this interplay.

CHAPTER 10

MISSION AND CULTURE

"CULTURE IS NOT THE AIM OF MISSION."
In 1906, Professor (later Archbishop) Nathan
Söderblom gave a lecture on the subject of "Mission and
the History of Culture", in which he reviewed the cultural contribution of missions to date, and the work of
missionaries in bringing to light knowledge of the cultures
of Asia and Africa. He began with the words quoted above.
Missionaries, he pointed out, were not sent out for the sake
of Western culture, but for the sake of the Kingdom of
God. But at the same time, the work of evangelization had
certain cultural and social consequences. It has been said
that the British Empire originated "in a fit of absence of
mind". Be that as it may, his words might well be applied
to missions: the Christian mission created culture "in a
fit of absence of mind"—as a consequence, however necessary, of its primary task of making disciples of all nations.
But this is a superficial judgment; we cannot distinguish
between "primary" and "secondary" in this mechanical
way. In the religion of the Incarnation the proclamation
of the message of salvation is constantly being associated
with new cultural forms and cultural expressions, and
there are certain cultural factors implied in the very work
of evangelization.

In our present context we have to deal with two separate
and distinct cultural spheres. On the one hand, Western
culture, which to some extent, but by no means entirely,
coincides with what we normally call Western civilization.
And on the other, the totality of the political, social and

religious life of the Asian, African or other people. Note that we refer to a "totality" here; this word, when used in connexion with the Afro-Asian cultures, indicates one of the basic problems facing missions. For it was characteristic of these tribal and national cultures that they were total—that they embraced and integrated the life of the group, and the life of the individual within the group. Compared with their wholeness, Western civilization appeared to be divided, broken, and even schizophrenic, and the conquests of Western technology and civilization were not altogether calculated to benefit those cultures: indeed, they resisted—with varying degrees of success— what they regarded as a threat to their continued existence.

The cultural contribution of the missions—and this brings us to the heart of our problem—was however virtually inseparable from the overall civilizing effect of the West, in education, in medicine and in social service. It became a wedge driven deep into the ancient integrated tribal and national cultures. We must remember, though, that in many cases these totalities had begun to disintegrate before ever missions came on the scene: for a number of reasons—inward decline on the one hand; the influence of Western economics, social methods and politics on the other. But this gives the missionary Church yet another reason to approach the exotic cultural milieu with care, humility and the desire to understand, for it is in this milieu she must work and witness.

The young churches, too, have become increasingly aware of their own cultural task. In the tribal milieu, the little group of the first Christian converts has frequently become the focus of a far-reaching cultural contribution. We may take an example from Nyasaland, where, as we saw, the Scottish Church sent a mission on Livingstone's request in the 1870's. The missionaries first of all came into contact with the Thonga tribe, but that meant that other tribes, whose relations with the Thongas were none of the best, refused even to consider the message of the White Christ. The Thongas accepted churches and schools, and during the British colonial period they were far in advance of other Bantu tribes in the territory: a cultural *élite*, in fact. But churches and schools inspired their critical faculties—and in time a spirit of political protest. Now, in the latest period of Nyasaland's history (or Malawi, as it is now called, after independence), the Thonga are the political leaders who have made Malawi free, under the leadership of Dr. Hastings Banda, himself a doctor and Presbyterian elder. There could scarcely be a better example of the long-term effects of bringing Christian schools to the jungle villages.

It was a matter of concern that the missions should reach the "whole" nation, the "whole" tribe. But at the same time it is evident that the cultural contribution of the Church in Asia, Africa and elsewhere has had an effect on two levels: as a ferment in the betterment of the Afro-Asian masses, and as a source of power for a small but qualitatively *élite* group. T. S. Eliot, in his book *The Idea of a Christian Society*, has drawn a distinction between "Christian society" and "the Christian fellowship". The latter is the fellowship of those devoted church members who, combining faith and education, Christianity and culture, are able as a group to influence society as a whole. It is precisely such groups as these, made up of spiritually and culturally active Christians, who form the backbone of the Christian Church in Nyasaland, Nias and Nicaragua. Of course they are subject to the pressures of modern secularization: as in the West, so in Ghana, Guam and Guatemala. It is part of the cultural task of the Church to increase the numbers of such Christians, by making it possible to keep open the lines of communication between culture and worship, between work and prayer.

We now pass on to some of the more important of the cultural contributions made by Christian missions in recent decades. We shall pay particular attention to the new problems facing missions as a result of the world situation since the end of the Second World War.

Education

Already in the eighteenth century the Danish-Halle mission set up schools for training missionary workers. The nineteenth century in India was dominated by the name and the influence of a Scotsman, Alexander Duff. Duff believed that higher education in English would eventually undermine and destroy Hinduism. It is characteristic of Duff's era that there took place a high degree of co-operation between Duff himself and Ram Mohan Roy, the first, and perhaps the greatest, of Indian reformers, and founder of the Brāhma Samāj. It was thanks to Ram Mohan Roy's help that Duff's first school was opened in Calcutta. In Africa and Indonesia, too, education was regarded as a powerful instrument of evangelization. Here the driving force was the great missiologist, Gustav Warneck: the school was regarded as "a means of education tending in the direction of future conversions". British and American missions in Asia (particularly the latter) before the 1930's laid so much emphasis on education and the colleges and schools that a Roman Catholic critic, J. Schmidlin, was able to talk of "Protestant missionary practice which often becomes indistinguishable from cultural involvement". However, Roman Catholic missions have at present, especially in Africa, far more schools than the Protestants. They have made a remarkable contribution in the field of higher education, up to university standard (e.g. Roma in Basutoland and Louvanium near Leopoldville).

In India, Duff's hopes were never realized. The important Lindsay Commission on Christian Higher Education in India (1929) was able to state that Western education was far from having been a *praeparatio evangelica*. It had led instead to the strengthening of Hinduism. After 1932 Continental missions came out in opposition to the pragmatic and humanistic attitude of British and American missions.

We may take a couple of examples to illustrate the extensive work which the missions have done—and are still doing—for the education of Africa. At the end of the 1950's every child receiving primary education in the Belgian Congo did so at a mission school; in Kenya the figure was 90 per cent; in Tanganyika 86 per cent and in Ghana 78 per cent. According to official figures, there were in 1957 55,000 Protestant mission schools, on various levels. It is now clearer than ever before what an extraordinarily important role the mission school has played. The teaching of women and girls in Asia and Africa was largely carried out by the missions. In the 1950's it was being said that that half of the population of the world which consists of women had undergone a more rapid social change than any other human group—and part of the credit belongs to the missions' girls' schools. Since the Second World War, a new middle class, consisting of teachers, hospital staffs, minor civil servants, secretaries, businessmen and transport officials, has grown up in Africa. This modern middle class is very largely a product of the Christian school.

The new States of Asia and Africa are at present faced with enormous educational problems, for instance in the gigantic universities (the University of Calcutta has some 115,000 students). And in the new African States there are being planned, as far as the available resources permit, far-reaching extensions of both primary education and higher education.

In 1960 a government commission in Nigeria (Africa's largest country, with a *c.* 50 million population) launched a ten-year plan of educational expansion called "Investing in Education". Some figures will indicate the kind of problem waiting to be tackled. The system of primary schools has already been extended fairly satisfactorily, much better than in most other African countries. Of an estimated 800,000 children of primary school age, 640,000 a

163

year attend school. The secondary schools take 12,000 children a year, but 30,000 more places are needed. The local universities have 200 graduates a year; 800 a year come from universities in Europe and America. All these figures require to be doubled. Here, as elsewhere in Africa, teacher training is a great problem. 90 per cent of primary school teachers and 50 per cent of secondary school teachers have failed to reach the minimum standard originally laid down.

There are two factors which have altered the relative status of mission schools in Asia and Africa, particularly since the Second World War. First, the new States in Asia and Africa are becoming more and more interested in their schools, and assuming responsibility for an increasingly large sector of the educational system. A peculiar problem in this connexion is the Bantu education project in South Africa, which dates from 1953. There the missions were relieved of responsibility for teaching, and the State took over, being represented locally by education committees. In general the State schools in these countries observe a policy of religious neutrality, and the teaching of Christian "religious knowledge" has been conditioned by the introduction of the so-called "conscience clause". A second factor is the work of UNESCO on behalf of underdeveloped countries, which has greatly stimulated the interest of the countries themselves in education, and particularly in the literacy of the masses. But it has been an American missionary, Frank Laubach, who has done most to further literacy by his simplified phonetic system of spelling. A Chinese Christian, Dr. James Yen, chose a thousand common Chinese ideograms, on which he based a programme of teaching which has meant literacy for millions of Chinese. In 1956, however, there was officially introduced a Western alphabet with thirty letters.

The problems facing Christian education in Africa are influenced by political aspirations and by the influence of party interests over against the churches and their educational work; by "Africanization"; by administrative appointments in church and school; and by the demand for comprehensive popular education.

"Africa for the Africans!" was the motto of the African nationalist movement. The administration of the State must rest in the hands of Africans. But this would not have been possible apart from the work of the Christian schools. Most of the leaders who are at present standing in the front line of African politics were educated at mission schools.

One result of the rapid expansion of the African educational system has been that many missionaries and African ministers have found the bulk of their time taken up by teaching and educational matters generally. State subsidies to mission schools, in Zambia and Southern Rhodesia, for example, were made dependent on first the missionary and now the African minister carrying out a regular inspection of a large number of schools in his district. In extreme cases more than 75 per cent of his actual working time could be spent on this task. However, the present phase of development is one in which the State considers that it ought to take over all educational responsibility, and relations between the Christian Church and the African State are causing increasing concern. The main question for the churches now is whether they have made sufficiently plain what must have priority in their work. Church and mission are more and more coming to realize that they must concentrate on a limited number of tasks, and a limited number of centres, in which an adequate staff are able to demonstrate what a Christian school is.

Literature

We have already indicated that the question of the literacy of the masses is one part of the Christian mission's commission to "translate". But the problem is not merely one of philology and teaching method! There are at least three separate fields of missionary activity involved: Bible translation, literary evangelism and theological education.

The first translation of the Gospel of Matthew is made, and printed on the mission's first primitive handpress. This press, and its remarkable products, create a hunger for reading material, for books, education and culture. The Christian mission has played its part in one of the most important single factors of the Afro-Asian revolution: literacy. It started on the mission station and in the catechist's infants' school in the jungle. But it grew to be a spiritual revolution. Frank C. Laubach, the missionary who in our day has made the greatest individual contribution in this area, has called one of his books *The Silent Billion Speak*. The illiterate billion are now being given the opportunity to read books and newspapers, to come into contact with the civilization of the world; in short, to begin to "speak". Of course, the missions are not alone in this field. The young Afro-Asian States themselves have often, with great energy and at great cost, carried on the work begun by the missions. UNESCO's programme of "fundamental education", begun in the 1950's, has been of great significance. But the responsibility of the missions and the churches has not ceased. On the contrary, this is one of the most striking dimensions of modern missionary work, a new and vast opportunity for the widening of Christian culture. The goal is twofold: literacy and literature.

Soviet Russia began her gigantic literacy campaign in the 1920's. The numbers of those being taught amounted in 1927 to 1,300,000; in 1928 to 2,700,000; in 1929 to 10,500,000; and in 1930 to 22,000,000. According to the official statistics, 100,000,000 people learned to read and write in 15 years. Before the 1917 Revolution only 32 per cent of the population were literate; now the figure is 98 per cent.

We have already mentioned the name of Frank C. Laubach; it may be of value to take a closer look at his characteristic method. Laubach, an American Methodist

166

missionary, began his missionary career in 1915 in the Philippines, working along traditional lines. In 1929 he came into contact with the Muslim Moro tribe, and began to study their language. He found that this language had twelve consonants and four vowels, and that three words, each of four syllables, together contained all these consonants. *Malabanga*, *karatasa* and *paganada* were the name of a town, the word for "paper" (an Arabic loan-word), and the verb "to study" or "to read". These three words could be divided into syllables thus:

ma	la	ba	nga
ka	ra	ta	sa
pa	ga	na	da

The vowel *a* could be replaced by any of the other four vowels, *o*, *e*, *i* and *u*, giving a wide range of possible combinations. This formed the basis of the first Moro reading exercise, and Laubach began his work as an "apostle of literacy".

ma ma (man)	a ma (father)	a la (god)
mi mi (girl)	a mi (our)	li li (name)

Laubach has succeeded in reducing even highly complicated languages to their basic syllabic components; he has worked out interesting reading exercises, and has organized armies of volunteers in Africa, Asia and Latin America, whose motto is "each one teach one". His work, and the work of his team, has been received very positively by many governments. The Madras director of education knew what was wanted: "An enthusiasm verging on madness, such as we see in certain missionaries, is necessary if anything lasting is to be achieved in this area."

A billion literates. Yes, but what are they to read? The production of literature is now of absolutely vital importance for any party, religion, interest or ideology wishing to influence Africa, Asia or Latin America. The com-

167

munists in these countries are producing and distributing vast quantities of literature. Among religious groups from the West, Jehovah's Witnesses seem to have taken this lesson most to heart. They have long been investing large sums of money in the production of propaganda literature, in many languages.

The Evangelical missions were helped at an early stage in their literary work by "tract societies". In Britain, the SPCK was, from 1698 on, both an active missionary society and a tract society. The Bible societies were of especial significance. The British and Foreign Bible Society, founded in 1804, distributed more than 600,000,000 portions of the Bible in 150 years; now the Society distributes some 30,000,000 Bible portions annually, including 3,000,000 complete Bibles and rather more than the same number of New Testaments. The national organizations came together in 1946 to form the United Bible Societies. The IMC (now the DWME of the WCC) has paid particular attention to the production of literature in Afro-Asian and other countries, by setting up special international Christian literature committees for Africa, Latin America, China, India and the Islamic world, and from 1965 a comprehensive Christian Literature Fund operating on a world scale. Characteristic of this programme is the discovery and training of indigenous authors and providing them with the chance to work —a policy attempted, though without any great measure of success, by the Indian YMCA under J. N. Farquhar in the years after the First World War. The problem, now as then, is to create a high-class Christian press, and to set up centres for the distribution of Christian literature in various parts of Africa and Asia. The problem of distribution is especially pressing. The business of "Colportage" demands time and ingenuity. In this particular field the Seventh-Day Adventists have emerged as the clear leaders. We may sum up by saying that while "devolution" from mission to church may perhaps have rendered the Wes-

terner less necessary for the carrying out of certain traditional missionary tasks, literature and the press are making
new and important demands on the missionary.

Linguistic work was thus one of the main areas of the
Evangelical missions' cultural contribution. Its primary
goal was the translation of the Bible into the vernaculars—
difficult enough in itself, but complicated in certain areas
by the fact that great care had first to be exercised in order
to decide exactly which vernacular to choose in a given
area. For instance, in the Cameroons and West Africa the
Christian mission has actually created nations by creating
a national language for them: by (at least partly) con-
founding Babel. The Ibo people of Eastern Nigeria
numbers some 6 millions; here there are 30 linguistic sub-
divisions, and each of these languages is further divided
into a mass of different dialects. A missionary, T. J. Dennis
of the CMS, succeeded, despite much initial opposition
from the tribal groups, in uniting these languages and dialects into a common Ibo, which became a living culture
language. The first book in this language comprised the
four Gospels (1893). Today the political parties use it in
their newspapers as a matter of course, as a means of communication with the people. In a thousand languages the
first printed book was an ABC, a catechism or a St. Matthew's Gospel—the result of an enormously demanding
work, yet no more than a first attempt, an interim solution, awaiting the day when the people, with the help of
church, school and college, would produce their own
translators.

India has 225 languages, of which sixteen Indo-Euro-
pean and six Dravidian languages are spoken by more
than a million people. There are about 250 Bantu languages. The language of the Sudan negroes has 42 sub-
groups. Some portion of the Bible has been translated into
about 1,200 languages to date. The entire Bible exists in
more than 200 languages; the entire New Testament in a
further 250 or more.

There are Westerners who imagine that (particularly) African languages are simple and straightforward, with a minimal vocabulary. This is a total misapprehension. The Greek New Testament has about 5,000 different words; a modern Bantu dictionary (such as C. M. Doke's Zulu-English Dictionary) contains 30,000 entries, organized according to roots. But since a number of forms can be constructed on each such root, Doke's dictionary in fact contains some 90,000 Zulu words. Dr. Eugene Nida, General Secretary of the United Bible Societies, has said, "No known 'primitive' language has less than 10,000 words." Some Bantu languages permit great subtlety in expression: Zulu is said to have 120 different words for "walk"; Malangasy, on Madagascar, has 200 words describing different sounds, and can distinguish 100 different colours and shades.

The languages of negro Africa are commonly divided into the Bantu languages and the Sudan or West African languages, together with small groups of Hamitic and Nilotic languages. The boundary between the Bantu and the Sudan languages passes from Calabar in Nigeria to the north shore of Lake Victoria, and thence to Zanzibar. Characteristic of the Bantu languages is the substantival prefix; the noun consists of an indeclinable root, preceded by various prefixes. Further, nouns are divided into classes, in most languages about eight in number, each with its special prefix. Thus, to take one example, the Zulu root *ntu* differs in meaning, according to its prefix. *Umu-ntu* (plural *aba-ntu*) is personal class, meaning "man" (when the Africans call themselves bantu, this is to say that they are "people", strangers are not). *Isi-ntu* means "human language"; *ubu-ntu* means "mankind" or "humanity".

The would-be translator is faced with wholly unexpected grammatical complications. The Polynesian and Malayan languages have a dual case, as well as the normal singular and plural. A French missionary published a translation of the New Testament in one of the languages of New

California. Not until much later did he realize that Matt. 6: 6–13 had been made to read, "Thou who are the Father of both of us. . . . Give us both our daily bread; and forgive both of us our trespasses. . . ." In Liberia, a translation of the same passage included a combination of words which in point of fact meant, "Do not come upon us when we sin." Generally speaking, many of these languages are shot through and through with legalism; and so the translator of the New Testament, and particularly the Pauline Epistles, is faced with very great difficulties. The language cannot be understood without intimate knowledge of the structure and culture of the people, their beliefs and customs.

We cannot here stop to give examples from that most fascinating enterprise of Bible translation. But a few words must be said about the problems attending the translation of certain terms. Is the Divine Name to be rendered into Chinese by *Shang-ti*, or *T'ien*, or something entirely different? Fabricus' Tamil translation from the eighteenth century calls God *Parabaran*, "the Most High and Wholly Other". Bower used the common Indian word *Deva*, but this is Sanskrit and therefore unsuitable for nationalist-minded South Indians. L. P. Larsen preferred *Jehovah* in the Old Testament. In the most recent translations, however, the name *Kadavul* has been used, which is pure Tamil. Is the Name of God in Zulu to be *uNkulunkúlu* ("the Great Great One" or "the Old Old One") or *uTixo*, a Xhosa loan-word which, just because it is a loan-word, seems to be more "sacred" than anything in Zulu. Bishop J. W. Colenso proposed in the 1870's a Latinization *uDio*, but this was unacceptable to the Zulu missions. Words for such basic Christian concepts as "sin", "grace", "salvation", "faith" and "conscience" all represent vast problems, theological as well as philological. Advances in theological and philological studies may make it necessary to bring in new verbal equivalents. But at the same time it must be remembered that even words having markedly

171

legalistic overtones can take on new meanings simply by their use in Evangelical proclamation; such new meanings subsist alongside the traditional sense.

We have already had occasion to mention some of the great names in the world of Bible translation by Evangelicals: for instance, the Serampore trio of Carey, Marshman and Ward. We may mention some others. Henry Martyn (1782–1812) arrived in India in 1806 at the age of 24, after a thorough training as a linguist at Cambridge. Although severely hampered by ill-health, he succeeded in a period of six years in translating the New Testament into Hindustani and Urdu, Persian and Arabic. S. Schereschewsky (known as "Brother Sherry"), was born a Jew in Russian Lithuania, converted to Christianity in America, and went to China in 1858; in 1877 he became Bishop of Shanghai, and died in 1906. He translated the Bible into both Mandarin and Wen-li Chinese; in the latter case he was able to build on the Wen-li translation of the great pioneer Robert Morrison of the LMS, completed in 1819. George Pilkington (b. 1865) spent six years, from 1891 to 1897, in Uganda, where he was murdered in a rebellion. During these years he suceeded, with the help of his Ganda colleague, H. W. Duta, in translating the whole of the Bible into Luganda—a translation which has never been bettered. Two German missionaries, J. Spieth and D. Westermann (who later became Professor of African Studies in Berlin) made notable contributions to language studies in West Africa.

Theological Education

The training of men for the ministry in Asia and Africa created a relative *élite*. The minister or pastor often came to be both a spiritual and social leader in his village. In the early generations he was the best educated, and it was he who mediated not only between the white mission and the Asian or African church, but between Western civilization and traditional tribal culture. If it be true, as we have claimed, that mission is translation, then it is also truc to say that the main object of theological education is the training of "translators". But at the same time it is vital that these "translators" should not merely confine themselves to the mechanical transmission of a message which has come to them via the West; they must be sufficiently well trained to be theologically independent, and perhaps ultimately creative. Theological education is of fundamental importance for the creation of autonomous churches in Asia and Africa. It is the quality and nature of theological education which decides whether or not the church has a group of leaders capable of independent thought and action.

The priority of theological education in the missionary Church has come to receive especial emphasis since the Second World War. At the Tambaram Conference of 1938 it was pointed out that the state of theological education was one of the greatest weaknesses in the whole Christian enterprise. In the 1940's and 1950's, on the initiative of the International Missionary Council, a number of comprehensive regional investigations were carried out, the object being to raise the standard of teaching by means of an adequate staff, including well-trained Asian and African theological teachers. The international Theological Education Fund has since 1959 aimed at bringing about inter-denominational co-operation in this field, as well as improving the library resources of the theological schools and colleges. But most important has been the asking of searching questions about the nature and aims of theological education. To what extent are traditional Western forms of theological education relevant to the needs of the Asian and African churches? One radical question was asked by Roland Allen: "Why should the young churches take over the traditional Western system of a paid full-time ministry?" The idea of a voluntary ministry, or part-time voluntary pastors, has been discussed and practised, particularly in South India.

173

Among the most important theological centres must be mentioned Serampore College, near Calcutta, and the United Theological College at Bangalore, South India. Gurukul in Madras is of importance for the Lutheran Churches in South India. There is an important college in Batavia, Java. Some of the new African universities, such as the University of Ghana, have either theological faculties or theological teaching incorporated into a faculty of arts.

Medical Missions

If educational concern and linguistic work have marked the wide cultural contribution of missions, it is no less true to take medical missions as representative of their social dimension. Nor is this something belonging solely to the history of missions; it is one of the most challenging fields of present-day missionary work, connected as it is with the wellnigh insoluble demographical problem.

The present annual rate of increase of the world's population is by some 50 millions. During the last 40 years the population of the world has increased by more than 1,000,000,000; by 40 per cent in the last decade. The greater part of this growth—rather more than 23,000,000 —has taken place in Asia, which now has 56 per cent of the world's population. We may also note that 38 of the 73 cities in the world having a population of more than a million are to be found in Asia, Europe coming second with 17.

Statistics have shown that almost four-fifths of these people are living on the verge—or beyond the verge—of starvation. Some medical missionaries are therefore wondering whether their attempts to save lives and stamp out disease may not have the effect of increasing, rather than lessening, the sum total of human misery, since the resources of the world are insufficient to meet the subsequent increase in population. Sceptics have talked about "bad Samaritans"—whose work we nevertheless cannot question; since we are called to help them in the name of Christ. As a Swedish writer, Anne-Marie Thunberg, has put it, "We have used our increased knowledge in obedience to that code of ethics which requires us to save life where life can be saved."

This complex problem (some have called it, not unjustly, "the world's biggest social problem") has forced the Church into a theological debate on the principle of "family responsibility". Expressions like "family planning" and "family responsibility" are coming to be used more and more widely as a positive Christian substitute for the more negative "birth control". It is hoped, by stressing the responsibility of the family for those belonging to its fellowship, to emphasize the role of the parents in God's own creation. And it is further hoped to provide an answer which is in full accordance with the constructive efforts of the medical missions for the good of mankind. The medical missions themselves are at present intensifying their efforts in two main directions.

On the one hand efforts are being made to concentrate all available resources of men and money to certain selected "strategic" points, in order to demonstrate the possibilities of first-class Christian medical care. The modern Asian welfare state is improving its hospitals, and this new departure on the part of the missions is, among other things, to be regarded as an attempt, despite slender resources, to advance the claims of Christian medical care over against the institutionalism and frequent impersonality of the State medical services.

The second line attempts, in close co-operation with the younger churches, to increase the possibility of providing medical care by means of small hospitals and clinics, in which a greater degree of personal contact is possible. Schools of nursing must also be organized, out of consideration for the needs of the mission churches. It is trying, as far as possible, to avoid combining them in large central training colleges, since it is held preferable to keep them to a size more closely corresponding to the church's financial resources.

The rapid social changes of the 1950's and after in Asia and Africa have placed Christian medical services in a new position. In India the process of devolution to Indian staffs of doctors and nurses is practically complete. There is probably not a single mission hospital left in which the director is not an Indian—though a number of Western doctors still serve on the staffs of such hospitals. Africa is as yet some way behind, since there are relatively few African doctors available. The work will remain in the hands of Western doctors and nursing instructors, at least for the foreseeable future.

In Asia and increasingly in Africa, mission hospitals are now in the hands of the indigenous church: this is an important and an entirely laudable tendency, though local churches *can* be distressingly conservative in this, an area demanding mobility and vision. The aim must be the transformation of what was once a Western medical mission into a living instrument of service (*diaconia*) in and through the young churches. An important task in this context is the provision for the spiritual needs of hospital patients and staff. Every effort must be made to create that specific atmosphere which alone enables us to call a hospital a "Christian hospital".

The work of doctors and nurses points, perhaps more clearly than other branches of missionary work, to an essential aspect of the Christian mission: that it is for "all men and the whole man". This view of mission as a totality has been much emphasized in recent debate, particularly by British and American writers. What is needed is a "comprehensive approach" to the whole of society. The contributions which the Christian mission is able to make in the fields of medicine, education, industry and agriculture together form the totality which requires to be mobilized in order to reach man as he is in African or Asian society.

The comprehensiveness of the view that mission is for "all men and the whole man" has brought with it a greater interest, on the part of mission, in the social status of those groups among whom mission is called to serve. The consequence has been a more realistic analysis of the social situation—problems of housing, work, migration and the like—and new and energetic attempts to meet the overall needs of communities and racial groups. One such problem, which has been studied closely by the International Missionary Council, is that of rapid urbanization, with all that that fact means for the Asian and African churches, which are still largely rural. We may sketch the development briefly.

Between 80 and 90 per cent of the population of Asia still lives in the country areas. The same is probably true of Africa, though in either case the process of industrialization is bringing about radical changes in social patterns. The explosive growth of the cities began between the wars, but has become even more dramatic since the 1950's. We may take some examples:

> Calcutta: 1,000,000 in 1920, 5,000,000 in 1960;
> Shanghai: 1,400,000 in 1920, 7,500,000 in 1960;
> Djakarta: 250,000 in 1920, 2,000,000 in 1960;
> Leopoldville: 20,000 in 1920, 100,000 in 1945, 400,000 in 1960;
> Johannesburg: 290,000 in 1920, 1,100,000 in 1960.

The missions have been deeply concerned with these and similar problems, particularly since the 1928 Jerusalem Conference of the IMC. It would be fatal if, in a dynamic process of social development, the missions were to remain static in their attitudes.

Missionary interest in agricultural problems is partly ideological and partly economic. The idea of stewardship —that the earth is the gift of God, to be cared for and used —enables contact to be made with traditional views. The

M   177

care of the land is however becoming a more and more pressing problem, since soil erosion in certain countries of Africa and Asia is reaching alarming proportions. Further, the need of the missionary churches to be financially self-supporting emphasizes the importance of scientific farming. One solution has been the "Lord's Acre" scheme, in which the church sets apart a patch of land, the produce of which goes direct to church funds.

As we have seen, the missions have in recent years advocated a comprehensive approach, and this has been put into practice in many areas of Asia and Africa. For example, there is the Gosaba Settlement in Bengal, created on the initiative of a Christian businessman in Calcutta, Daniel Hamilton, through which 16,000 people (3,000 families) have been given improved living conditions. The entire settlement is divided up into villages, each with its own bank, school, experimental farm, hospital and church. Another example is the Lutheran centre at Arulpuram, among the leather workers of the Coimbatore mass-movement area in South India. The work of the Canadian Kenneth Prior in Nigeria is also deserving of mention. His Asaba Rural Training Centre is designed to help home industries and handicrafts. Missionaries have for this same reason become affiliated to the Food and Agricultural Organization (FAO).

The problem of industrialization in Asia and Africa has also been closely studied by the international missionary movement since the 1920's. In 1930 there was founded in Geneva an IMC department of social and industrial research under the leadership of the American, J. Merle Davis (d. 1960). The progress of communism in Asia since 1945 has further stimulated Protestant missions and the Asian churches to study the conditions of industrial workers and the Eastern industrial and social revolution. The Indian Institute for the Study of Religion and Society, founded in Bangalore in 1952, has played a large part in this programme of research, under the leadership of such outstanding Indian theologians as J. Russel Chandran, the late P. D. Devanandan and M. M. Thomas.

We started by saying that these problems were intimately bound up with the missions' cultural contribution. The missionaries found that their work of translation required their acquaintance with "the 3 R's, first aid and the plough". A concern with school and college, a conscious attempt to come to terms with the problem of poverty and human distress, and a realistic view of the process of social change were an essential part of the world mission of the Church. It must not be supposed, however, that the creation of independent churches "on the mission field" and the taking up of social work by newly independent states means that this is now a closed chapter. On the contrary, it would seem that these tasks are growing ever more urgent. The growing number of literates requiring education; the growing problem of human distress; yet more social changes—these make it imperative that the missions' cultural contribution should continue. But these efforts, already clarified and illustrated, must be seen in the context of the indigenous churches' confrontation with their milieu. Christian education is organically bound up with the educational programme of the young churches, and is often taken into account in the educational planning of the young nations. Theological education is aimed at aiding the progress of self-government in the churches, and fitting them for wider fields of service. The social work done in mission hospitals and on mission farms helps realize this living service in the local churches. The horizon broadens, from mission and culture to Church and milieu.

Church and Milieu

We have seen that the pattern of political events is more than a superficial framework or chance background to the Christian mission; it affects the missions' conditions and sets its mark on the way in which they are able to work.

179

But it is not only the missionary Church that is affected. We have also seen that the Christian mission itself creates culture, that the preaching of the Gospel implies a conscious cultural contribution, and that the Church influences its "milieu". But the relation between Church and milieu is wider than that. The Church's "milieu"—the totality of the cultures, religions and philosophies, the religio-sociological and religio-historical reality with which the Church is confronted daily—suggests wider dimensions. It is particularly essential to keep this in mind when attempting to understand the character and problems of the "young", "independent" churches.

The "young" church is the local manifestation of the universal Church of Christ. In our missiological section (Part One) we saw how the Church is compelled to be a missionary community, active, formative and creative in relation to its old milieu. But the young church is joined to the order and values of traditional society by a thousand invisible bonds. It is this aspect of the relationship between Church and milieu which we shall now consider. We might borrow a term from botany, and say that we shall be concentrating on the missionary churches' "ecology"— their place and their problems in the *oikos*, the "home", and milieu in which they have to work, witness and widen. By concentrating on ecology we shall attempt to do justice to two separate aspects; the active, in which the Word and the Church influence and reshape their milieu; and the passive, in which the Church is itself influenced by the conditions obtaining in its special milieu.

Ecology further gives us a more direct understanding of the actual situation of the world-wide Church of Christ than could be obtained through a historical introduction to the missionary churches, or a country-by-country conducted tour of the missions. This latter method is especially liable to result in a loss of true perspective.

We find when studying the young churches that we are

actually faced, not with a vast diversity of national and religious factors, but with *only two basic situations*—such is the conclusion to which ecology leads us. The problem of Church and milieu can in fact be summarized as being one of the relationship of the Church to *two clearly distinguishable milieus*. The first of these comprises the so-called "illiterate" peoples, or, to use another term, the tribal cultures of Africa, Indonesia, Oceania and the hills of South-East Asia. It is among such peoples as these that Christian missions have had most success. Here we encounter mass movements or group movements, tribal churches and national churches. Of course these differ widely. But it is of much greater importance and interest to note that they nevertheless exhibit a common structure, both in their cultural and religious background and in the type of situation in which the Church is placed. The second type of milieu is that which the Church encounters in those societies which are dominated by the great religions, Islam, Hinduism, Buddhism and Shintoism. Here the Church's situation is entirely different. Here Christians are in the minority; often a microscopic minority, though one exception is provided by Korea, in which great national churches have grown up. Nevertheless, even in such situations as these, the Church is able, thanks to its *élite* groups, or to its efforts among the poverty-stricken masses, to exercise a surprising influence on Asian society.

This impression is confirmed by statistics. The Christian communities in Africa and Asia are now of approximately the same size, 40 millions in Asia (of a total population of some 1,300 millions), and 40 millions in Africa (total population, 220 millions). In Asia, these are divided between 28,000,000 Roman Catholics and 12,000,000 others; in Africa between 28,000,000 Roman Catholics and 15,000,000 others. In Asia, the Christian community is distributed most unequally: almost half the Christian population of Asia is to be found in the Philippines, and 90 per cent of all Asian Roman Catholics are in the Philippines, India and China (though there is now little or no certainty in any Chinese missionary statistics). The non-Roman Catholic Christians are similarly divided. 80 per cent of them belong to India, Indonesia and the Philippines, and we shall find that in Indonesia the Church is concentrated among certain peoples, on Sumatra for example, and that in India the majority of Christians come from the "mass movement" areas, and the lower castes and outcastes of South India. Elsewhere the minority character of the Church is all the more marked—for instance in the Islamic lands, in the ancient Buddhist strongholds, or Hindu North India. The situation of the Church in these countries can also teach us what it means to live as a despised, persecuted minority in a compact non-Christian world. Not until Christian missions are viewed in this perspective can we properly realize that missions in Asia, so far from being a closed chapter, have really only just begun.

We have said that we have to deal with no more than two separate milieus. We turn now to the first of these, to the Church in the tribal cultures.

CHAPTER II

THE CHURCH AND THE TRIBAL CULTURES

THERE IS A SWEDISH PROVERB WHICH SAYS, "A DEAR child has many names." The proverb might well be applied to the search for an adequate name for the tribal religions. Two expressions much used by the (now obsolete) evolutionist school of comparative religion were "animism" and "primitive religion". The former concentrated for the most part on the belief in impersonal spiritual forces and ancestor worship; the latter was based on the assumption that these religions represented the "original" religion of mankind in a "pure" form, and that there has since taken place a process of development to "higher" forms. The word "primitive" was also sometimes used to describe the simple and unsystematic character of certain religious expressions. However, closer study of the myths and rites of the tribal religions shows that these are often highly complex. There might perhaps be some justification for calling these religions and cultures "primal". It is not altogether wrong to speak of "primitive levels" in all religions. In Indonesia there is a saying: "Scratch a Javanese Muslim and you find a Hindu; scratch a Hindu and you find a pagan," i.e. an "animist". It is true that the level of spirit-worship and magic has often been overlaid by a "higher" religious system, but is there nevertheless, often as a most tangible reality. One term which has been suggested, *faute de mieux*, is "illiterate people's religion", the boundary being thus drawn between the culture religions and those in which no use is made of writing in the religious and social life of the people. This definition has however not gone un-opposed.

We do not wish to take sides in this terminological debate; it will suffice to point out once more that we are dealing with common religious traits over wide areas, and that it is in these areas that Christian missions have made most progress. And further, that we are not dealing only with Africa, but with Indonesia, Oceania, the hill peoples of South-East Asia, and to a very great extent the outcaste millions of India. Spirit and ancestor worship, magic and the black arts are found in all these cultures, often within an elaborate system of myth and ritual. All these cultural patterns, too, are "totalitarian" in their nature, having what appears to be complete interdependence in all spheres—social, economic and religious.

The main function of the religious cultures and the practice of magic is that of sustaining and strengthening the harmony and balance of the social organism. Religion serves as the bond or the sociological "cement", holding together not only the different hierarchically differentiated groups, but generations of the living and the dead.

The Christian Church's encounter with these cultures leads to a great number of interesting problems, having to do with the life and work of the Church. In the following pages we shall give an account of some of these characteristic problems, and discuss the attitude of the Church towards the phenomena involved. For purposes of illustration we have chosen an African tribe, the Haya tribe of North-West Tanganyika, which may be taken as representing characteristic tendencies in the traditional African milieu; at the same time it is clear that Papuans and Dayaks, Karens and Santals would feel themselves on familiar ground in most of its features.

Here we can do little more than emphasize the basic role played by the connexion between myth and ritual in these cultures. The intensive debate surrounding these problems (names such as Hocart, Jensen and "the Uppsala School" are deserving of mention) is well known. But the pattern of myth and ritual is of vital importance in the encounter between the Church and the tribal cultures, and we shall have occasion to return to this later, in various contexts.

There are three levels of religion here which can be clearly distinguished. In the tribal religion of Hayaland, such as we encounter at the present day, these three have coalesced to form a closed system, capable of assimilating external influences by a process of syncretism.

First there is belief in a high god or creator god, called *Lugaba* ("the Giver"), who is still considered to have power over life and death, but who is not worshipped in the cultus. Secondly, reverence for the spirits of the departed, an important religious and sociological consequence of which is totemism. And thirdly, worship of the deified spirits of the Hamitic kings. Here we encounter in the religion of the Bantu a newly assimilated system of beliefs, taken over from the Bahinda, a Hamitic people who conquered the area between the great central African lakes, probably about A.D. 1600. Powerful Hamitic kings were deified after death, and came to be assimilated, together with Lugaba beliefs and the ancestral cult, by the Haya. The Bahinda were more powerful than the Haya, and it followed that their gods must be more powerful than those of the Haya people. Thus there arose a dynasty of the gods, a pantheon.

The most important levels of religion in present-day Hayaland are the worship of the deified spirits of the kings and "animism".

Each village has its sacred grove, in which the local deity dwells, served by a priest (*omugulusi*, literally "elder"), who sacrifices and prays to the deity. Should a clan find itself in need of especial help from one of the great spirits, it may set apart one of its own members (commonly a girl) to be the slave of the great spirit. It is not uncommon to meet in the church with women who have had some such experience in the past.

The great spirits, *abachwei*, are worshipped primarily through their priests, whose office is hereditary in a certain group of families. The individual concerned experiences the call to become a spirit-priest as an irresistible sense of possession, mediated mainly in dreams. At the ceremony of consecration two sacrifices are made to the great spirit: a black goat for propitiation and a white goat for purification. The priest has the responsibility of caring for the great spirit's temples—little grass huts in the banana grove. He also receives sacrifices—sheep, goats or, from the poor, bunches of bananas—on behalf of his deity. These are designed to propitiate the deity, and turn aside his wrath, which has been brought upon the individual by something he has done or failed to do.

The creation myths of the "high god" religion and the belief in the "great spirits" has coalesced in Haya religion; similarly, the Hamitic worship of Wamala and other great spirits has been assimilated to animism. The spirits of the dead (*emizimu*) are sometimes called "those who belong to the kingdom of Wamala". These spirits live on or near the house-altar which was formerly to be found in every Haya hut. But only the spirits of departed men lived there; the spirits of departed women and children were believed to flutter around in the banana grove, while the spirit of the dead king stayed in his residence.

However, it was not enough merely to die in order to become an ancestral spirit; it was equally necessary to be properly buried. Burial and the associated rites, the object of which was to "follow" the dead man to his home, were of the utmost importance. Mortuary rites and beliefs within the Christian Church are of greater significance than any missionary realizes.

The spirits reveal themselves mainly in dreams. They bring both accidents, illness, death and material losses as a means of complaining that they have been neglected and that they require a sacrifice in order to be propitiated. The Haya believe that sickness and accidents have two primary causes, and two only: the work of the spirits and sorcery.

The spirits or the great spirits may become irritated because someone in the family has transgressed the laws of the clan; for example, he may have broken some family taboo. Or they are disgusted at not having received the sacrifices they consider that they are entitled to. They thereupon seek vengeance by bringing disease, death or material loss upon the guilty party or upon one or other of his relations.

The other cause is sorcery. The witch-doctor (*omulogi*, "one who practises black magic") works in secret. It is believed that the witch-doctor has it in his power to harm a person by means of corpse-poison, or by sending poisonous toads, which carry the fatal substance. He is also believed to be able to harm a person by means of a bundle of sticks, into which a nail-paring or a fragment of some garment belonging to the victim has been inserted. A Haya woman was absolutely petrified with fear, because she had found that a piece of her husband's shirt had been cut off; she was convinced that this had been done by an enemy, by an *omulogi*, and that something terrible was going to happen to them. For her this was a fearful reality.

When an accident happens, or when someone falls ill, the first thing to be done is to find out what—or rather *who*—has caused it. To have this question answered is really more important than to have matters set to rights. The answer is provided by a diviner, *omulaguzi*. The diviner has a number of methods, the main one being the reading of the liver of a dead hen, by which to discover the nature and cause of the illness.

He may answer that the illness has been caused by a spirit or a great spirit, for example in revenge for some transgression of the taboo laws, such as the eating of fish or hippopotamus meat. If the illness has been caused by some spirit, the next step is that the diviner gives the inquirer the name and the address of the next specialist to whom he must turn: the spirit-priest, *embandwa*, concerned. Here the inquirer is told what kind of sacrifice (cattle, goats, etc.) the spirit requires.

But should the seer find that the illness has been caused by sorcery, then a healer, *omufumu*, is called in. The healer shows what herbs must be used to neutralize the sorcery; or he may himself pronounce spells to drive out the powers of evil from the sick man into a bunch of herbs. These are bound to a hen, which is taken out and buried alive on the plain. This is believed to have the effect of neutralizing and binding the evil forces which have been at work.

Amulets are worn as protection against sorcery. It is characteristic that the Haya word for amulet, *olugisha*, comes from the same root as the word for good fortune and blessing, *omugisha*. The amulet keeps the powers of destruction at a distance, and thus preserves a person's good fortune.

The harmony, light and balance which ought in principle to govern the world in which Lugaba has placed mankind, are transformed into chaos and darkness when the destructive forces of Disease and Death attack man; then the individual lives in a state of fear and anxiety such as we can hardly imagine. Should a disease have been caused by the spirits, it has to be conquered by religious means, i.e. by sacrifice. It is important for our understanding of the awakening faith of the young Haya Church to remember that the word "to heal", *okutamba*, also means "to propitiate, to sacrifice". Here we have a word and a concept stemming from the period when priest and doctor were one and the same. Religion and medicine were basically only two aspects of the same thing, and both served the same purpose: the restoration of *omugisha*, the harmony and blessing of life.

Tribal Law and the Church

The culture and religion of a tribe is a closed, integrated

world with strikingly collective traits. This means that the tribal traditions had the effect of imposing conformity within the tribe, both on an individual and a collective level. At the same time, religious reorientation and the fact of conversion depend upon the individual and the group being able to break with the customs, rites and traditions of the collective. Externally, this integration gave the tribe solidity and unity. The Christian mission has been faced with many unexpected problems in the course of its confrontation with this world, not least in respect of the missions' attitude to tribal traditions and tribal law. A particularly good example of this is to be seen in Indonesia. Nowhere was this tribal order so thoroughly or so well preserved as in the unwritten code of the Bataks of Sumatra: the *adat* law, which from time immemorial had ordered and shaped the life of society, the clan, the family and the individual.

The missions could not overlook this *adat* order, but the first missionaries in the country, the American Congregationalists Munson and Lyman, rejected it as heathen. The Bataks thereupon reacted in a heathen manner: they killed the young missionaries and ate them. This took place in 1834.

Ludvig Nommensen and the German Barmen missionaries who came thirty years later, on the other hand, took the *adat* law and tried to give it a theological interpretation. They rejected what they felt to be anti-Christian in it, but regarded *adat* as a *praeparatio*, or rather as an attempt to interpret the orders of creation and natural law. As Merle Davis has said, "The Rhenish missionaries dug through the surface layer of dirt and superstition down to the granite in the Batak character, and built on the foundation." With patience and persistence *adat* was christianized, with the result that the structure of Batak society could be retained in the Christian Church, thereby facilitating the reception of the masses into the Church. Tribe and Church became one. Church life, too, was organized around a vast number of casuistic rules. Christians of the third generation could see in the new *adat* no distinction between original Batak influence and those rules which were specifically Christian in origin. But this was not without its dangers. Christianity came to be regarded as a new law, *nova lex*, which no longer presupposed a radical change of heart. To dispel this impression was to be the greatest task of coming generations.

Similar problems of legalism are having to be met in Africa and elsewhere. Church discipline plays an important role. The church council has to guard the morals of the congregation. The value of this institution in pastoral care can scarcely be over-emphasized. But it has its weaker sides, too. Church discipline often loses much of its evangelical pastoral function. Meetings of the church council at which cases of church discipline are to be dealt with often appear to be little more than Christian versions of the traditional trial before the tribal chief. Instead of the chief we have the African minister (formerly the missionary) in the chair, the churchwardens as his assistants, and the members of the church council as the jury. Witnesses are called on both sides, and give their evidence. The defendant has to defend himself with the support of his witnesses. More than 90 per cent of all cases have to do with alleged adultery. It was once common to find the practice of magic and the like reported as breaking the first commandment; this often led to punishment.

Africans, Indonesians, Papuans, Indians and others are deeply interested in legal matters, and often have much experience of trials; this training they bring with them into the Christian Church, where the problem of church discipline is pressing. There is however a marked tendency towards legalism. The commonest punishment is exclusion from communion for a definite period: six months to a year or more. There are churches in which delinquents are placed in a "penitents' class" which, under a simple village evangelist, is little more than a catechetical exercise. There are also "penitent forms", which the sinner must occupy when in church, placed at the front of the church or chapel.

It has been asked in a Lutheran theological college in South Africa why the Lutheran Church does not have a collection of detailed rules for moral behaviour and conduct in various situations. We see how easy it is for the emphasis to shift from the free grace of the Gospel to the merits of observing the law.

This same problem comes up in connexion with the delicate task of translation, for certain languages are legalistic through and through. "Sin" may come to be no more than a technical error, the breaking of certain rules; not until misfortune comes can there be any question of real sin. In Kruyt's phrase, "Sin looks out of the punishment." But on the other hand these churches have known many wonderful examples of a deep and central Christian experience, both of the guilt of sin and of the certainty of divine grace.

Five Missionaries

There are a number of individual missionaries who are deserving of special mention in connexion with the missions' and the churches' attempts to preserve and use tribal structures in Indonesia and Africa. Among these are two German Lutheran missionaries, Keysser and Gutmann; the Dutchmen, Kruyt and Adriani, in the Celebes; and the Anglo-Catholic Bishop, Vincent Lucas in Tanganyika.

Christian Keysser (1877–1962) was brought up in that atmosphere of Lutheran confessionalism and missionary concern which centred upon Neuendettelsau, and spent the first two decades of the present century in New Guinea, among the Papuans. He has written of his experiences in e.g. *Anutu im Papualande* (1929). His objective was essentially Pietist, that of "founding churches of real, serious, believing Christians" among the Papuans.

He preached *miti*, the Gospel, to the people, but the people were not impressed. "Why," they asked, "should we come and listen? Your *Anutu* (God) speaks our language so badly that we understand nothing in any case. And we should be punished with death if we came; the spirits of our ancestors would revenge themselves on our disobedience." Finally Keysser, as he himself said, "learned from Scripture that God wishes to save not only individual souls, but whole peoples." Keysser determined to try and gather the people together. He had won a devoted Papuan fellow-worker, Zake, who advised him to invite the people to—a dance. Dancing meant peace; if there were no dancing, those invited would not come, and the whole of his enterprise would be regarded with suspicion. The people of the Kate tribe met together in a clearing in the jungle. When darkness fell, the drums began to sound. According to Papuan custom, only the men danced, each with his long wooden drum, on which he beat time with one hand. The dancing was interrupted for food, and then continued until dawn, when the missionary was able to speak.

"*Kāte*—there is a thing which creates distress and confusion among the people; that is sorcery and the fear of sorcery. It is a festering sore on the body of the people, which must be lanced if the body is to be healthy." Zake took over, confessing that he was a murderer, having murdered Moga a year before. The chief rose up in defence, denying the existence of sorcery. But the murmurings of the crowd compelled him to change his tone, and he at length confessed to having commanded sorcerers to bewitch others; he had even tried to murder a neighbouring chief by means of sorcery, but his sorcery had not been strong enough that time, and he had failed. A number of other men spoke up, confessing that they had been guilty of sorcery. The meeting ended with an exhortation to abandon sorcery and keep to the truth of *Anutu*.

Keysser was finally able, thanks to a number of other

dramatic meetings and challenges, to reach the people as a whole. His aim was the building of a Papuan national church. One important question which had to be dealt with *en route* was that of language. The smaller tribes were persuaded to give up their dialects. Keysser's view was that a united Papuan people and a united Papuan church could only be created if there were unity in language. Characteristic of later development was the missionary enthusiasm of the young church; Papuan Christians went out in groups to neighbouring tribes (frequently their deadly enemies) with *miti*—the joyful news. Keysser's experience in Papua, in which the actual missionary situation brought about a re-expression of missionary principles, and in which the foundation of a missionary national church was the objective, was of considerable importance in the German missionary debate. Gustav Warneck in particular was responsible for the systematization of its results, notably in respect of the relations between church and people.

The christianization of the Papuans invites comparison with the acceptance of the new faith in the Celebes. N. Adriani was a Dutch philologist, sent out to Indonesia by the Netherlands' Bible Society. A. C. Kruyt, a Dutch minister with some medical training, was a missionary of the Dutch Missionary Society. In the 1890's they came to Lake Posso in the Celebes, the first Europeans to visit what had hitherto been the wholly isolated Toradja tribe. The "primal" Toradja culture was characterized by faith in "the Kneader"—their name for the creator, or high god— by ancestor-worship, and by tribal solidarity extending over all areas of life. Kruyt's medical work brought him into contact with individuals, and he was soon able to start an elementary school, but when he referred to the God of the Bible by the name of "the Kneader" his listeners answered, "Listen, white man. You are still young, but when you have been with us longer you will realize who the

Kneader is, and what he is like. For he is not at all like your description." In the first years he could have persuaded individuals to be baptized, but the collective character of the tribe and the people's fear of the vengeance of the ancestors and neighbouring tribes, should they join the White Christ, counselled extreme care. So instead of proselytism he in fact advised enthusiastic individuals not to join the Christian community, though more and more were attending his school and listening to his preaching. At the same time the Dutch administration in the Celebes had succeeded in establishing law and order, and peace between the tribes. The Toradja tribe as a whole began to realize that collective acceptance of the new faith could no longer be postponed.

In 1908, after seventeen years' unbroken missionary work, a great festival was held in honour of the ancestors. It took the form of a farewell feast, in which the tribe together bade farewell to their hereditary faith. At a great service on Sunday, July 4, 1909, the supreme chief Papa in Wunte issued a proclamation: "Clan chiefs and village head men, gather together all your groups and speak to them about the word of the Christians. Then we shall be able to arrive at a decision together." On Christmas Day of the same year hundreds were baptized, the supreme chief first of all. It was a decisive breakthrough, since when the tribe has become wholly Christian. The Posso Church, which has been independent since 1947, now has more than 50,000 baptized members.

Another striking profile in the German missionary debate was that of Bruno Gutmann (b. 1877), a missionary of the Leipzig Missionary Society to the Chagga people on the slopes of Mount Kilimanjaro. Gutmann's main sociological interest was in the interplay of man and milieu—of the African man in his traditional family and village milieu. For him, the great enemy was modern Western civilization, and his aim was through the Church to protect the African from the influence of civilization. Gutmann's sociological theories have an important theological dimension. He held that the forms of fellowship practised in the tribe corresponded to the will of the Creator: they were *urtümliche Bindungen*, rules laid down from the beginning, having lasting validity. Among these were the clan, the neighbourhood and the age-group. The whole of the Kilimanjaro area is criss-crossed by a complex system of canals, which lead water from the eternal snows through the intensive green fields on the slopes of the mountain. Each canal has its own overseer. Gutmann's idea was to make the canal overseers and elders of the clans into the Church's elders, and to make use of the age-groups in the Church's youth work. "Both the church and the original social order are divine creations", and must therefore condition and influence each other.

The development of the Chagga Church, like that of German missions generally, has been profoundly affected by two world wars. Gutmann was forbidden to return to Africa, and his plans were gradually abandoned. There is nevertheless still a growing affinity between tribe and church. The most influential chiefs in the area, all of them members of the church, have played the part of "defenders of the faith"—at least until about 1960. The supreme chief Eliufoo (appointed in 1960, and minister of education since 1962) is a faithful son of the Lutheran Church, formerly a teacher in a church school, where he was a colleague of the present leader of the Church, Stefano Moshi, who was appointed bishop in 1960. In the 1940's and 1950's a powerful mass movement took place in this church, which now has some 200,000 members.

A comparable contribution, this time in South Tanganyika, was made by an Englishman, William Vincent Lucas (1883–1945) of the UMCA, the first bishop of the Diocese of Masasi. He was more closely concerned than any of the other missionaries we have discussed with the christianization of the sacral tradition; his inspiration came more from the early history of the Church than from sociology. In fact one source of inspiration for the building of a church in twentieth-century Tanganyika was the letter written in A.D. 601 by Pope Gregory the Great to Mellitus.

One of the corner-stones in the society in which Lucas worked (the Yao and Makua tribes) was the rite of initiation, *lupanda*, by which boys were transformed into men, and without which no boy could be treated as a man. *Lupanda* was really the name of the bare trunk of a tree which stood outside the chief's residence. Here flour was offered to the spirits of the ancestors; here the young men were brought after circumcision; here they were taught the tribe's code of honour.

Instead of condemning or ignoring what was a basic social custom in the life of the tribe, Lucas endeavoured to christianize it. Instead of the *lupanda* tree a cross has now been set up; instead of the spirits of the ancestors, prayer is offered to the saints of the Church. At night there is drumming and dancing—though the dances are chosen from a list prepared by the bishop. And on the following day, circumcision is carried out at a camp in the forest by an African nurse or doctor. Then comes a dance of joy, while the boys stay in their camp, and for six weeks attend confirmation classes; Christians teach the elements of the faith, while a village chief instructs them in the tribe's code of honour. At the end of this period each of the boys goes to confession (also a part of the pre-Christian ceremony). Their heads are shaved, they are given new clothes and their old belongings are burned. On the last Sunday all are assembled early for a thanksgiving mass in the cathedral, after which the priest leads the young people to the west door of the church, where he gives back to their expectant parents the boys who, in the shadow of the Church, have become men.

Thus, under skilled leadership, the Church has been able to make use of customs and institutions which an-

196

swered to a real social need, and to incorporate them into the new Christian fellowship.

King and Church

It is not only the priests and witch-doctors who have an important sacral role to play in the religious and social structure of the tribe. In most cases the king, too, fills a sacral function. He is the one who sums up in his own person the legal and sacral traditions of the tribe; he it is who guarantees the strength of the tribe, and his authority depends on the tribesmen's need to participate in the source of strength. The problem of the relationship between king and Church has been a source of much concern in the encounter of the Church with African tribal culture.

One of the first missionaries to appreciate the connexion between king, tribe and Church was Charles de Lavigerie (1825–92); originally a professor of church history, he later became Cardinal and Primate of all Africa, and was one of the Roman Catholic Church's seminal thinkers in the field of African missions. Like Lucas, Lavigerie drew on church history for his missionary principles. As professor, he had had occasion to reflect on the role of kings and chieftains in the christianization of North and Central Europe, and he endeavoured to apply the principles of medieval church history in the strategy of African missions. In Ruanda-Urundi his plan was dramatically successful, but at the same time created problems which were not fully appreciated until the 1960's. African society in Ruanda-Urundi consists of two ethnic groups: the Watutsi, the traditional rulers, who are of Hamitic stock, and the remainder of the population, who are Bantu. Concentration on the chiefs led to the reception of 80 per cent of these into the Roman Catholic Church; in 1947 both the king and queen mother in Ruanda were baptized. The Church in Ruanda-Urundi grew rapidly. However, when Western democratic ideals began to replace Watutsi feudalism in the early 1960's, the essentially royalist church was faced with considerable problems of adaptation. There is no doubt that these will eventually be solved, but it will take time.

The Church Missionary Society similarly attempted to utilize the traditional power of the kings and chiefs in Uganda. Bishop Alfred Tucker, who worked in Uganda from 1890 to 1911, was the great architect of the Uganda Church. In less than a generation he was able to see his church develop from a persecuted minority into a great dominant evangelical national church. Tucker and the CMS, as we have already seen, had played an important role in determining the political future of Uganda. Tucker found that the traditional African society in the real Uganda was based on a hierarchical system, from the king (in Uganda called *kabaka*) down to the village chief, and he adapted the administrative machinery of the church to this traditional structure. The political and church hierarchies in Uganda now correspond closely, on the following scheme:

Kabaka	Bishop
Saza chief	Rural dean
Gombolola chief	Priest
Muroka chief	Deacon
Mutongole chief	Catechist

The African rural dean usually lives near the residence of the *saza* chief, and the two have much in common; they can eat together, thus demonstrating that they are of equal rank. It has been justly remarked that "the rural dean is the Church's *saza* chief". This system works admirably as long as the king is a loyal supporter of the church. But it is not inconceivable that this support may vanish, placing the church in a difficult position.

Tribal churches were founded by missions which originally had not the slightest intention of supporting such a development. But once more the history of missions shows that missionary principles may well be modified in the light of practical experience. British Congregationalists of the London Missionary Society were individualist in principle; their ideal, both in the West and on the mission field, was the establishment of independent local churches. But in Bechuanaland they built a national Church nevertheless. In 1872 the Bamangwato tribe chose Khama as their king; and Khama was a Christian, a purposeful Christian leader, whose object was the establishment of an African theocracy. He built churches and schools, and instructed his chiefs to do all in their power to further the civilizing work of the missions. He introduced the plough, and succeeded in persuading his men to drive it—a veritable revolution in a culture in which women had previously done all the agricultural work. And he set a stop to the sale of liquor, which was threatening to corrupt the whole people.

The LMS were able to build a similar tribal church in Tahiti, once the missionaries, after much heart-searching, had agreed in 1819 to baptize King Pomare II, "the Clovis of Oceania". Pomare was a member of an ambitious aristocratic family who had for some years been attempting to play off pagan and Christian group interests against one another. In 1815 the influential high priest Patii gave up his opposition to the White Christ: he burned his idols and became a catechumen. When the king claimed the right to be the first to be baptized, difficulties at once arose, largely on account of his attitude to alcohol, which was not exactly that of his African colleague Khama; rather the reverse. Finally, however, he was baptized together with his entire court. He built an enormous church, and introduced Christian laws, against murder, adultery, robbery and the breaking of the Sabbath. Once the king had been baptized, his people soon followed his example, and Tahiti was rapidly christianized.

In 1820 the LMS had founded a church in Madagascar; a period of persecution followed, but in the 1870's, due in part to the influence of the new queen Ranavalona II (1868–83), the Church grew rapidly. The queen was baptized, together with her prime minister (whom she later married) by a Malagasy Congregationalist minister. This was the sign for general acceptance of "the queen's religion". The Congregational Church in Madagascar grew from a membership of 20,000 in 1867 to almost 300,000 in 1895. British Dissenters, bitterly opposed in principle to establishment, had founded a national Church.

In much of Africa, however, the chiefs were tenaciously opposed to the Church. As guarantors of the unity and ritual life of their tribes, they were in no position to be able to abandon their traditional religion. Polygamy was a further hindrance. There are cases on record of chiefs attempting to stop their people from joining the white men in their religious fellowship. In the circumstances, there was little the missionaries, Catholic and Protestant alike, could do except advise their converts to leave their tribes and form "Christian villages". This method was applied by the Roman Catholic Church in both East and West Africa by F. M. Libermann and his Fathers of the Holy Spirit, partly inspired by the example of the Jesuit "reductions" in Paraguay. In Africa, Catholic villages were founded in particular by groups of freed slaves. The Christian village as such became a new sociological phenomenon, led first by the white missionary, and later by an African minister. An agreement was commonly arrived at by which the people did a certain amount of work for the mission; otherwise the connexion between the village and the mission was close. But this form of organization was not without its risks; it had a tendency to give rise to "greenhouse" congregations, without missionary initiative and without contact with the tribe as a whole. It was therefore abandoned in 1933 on the recommendation of the Belgian Congo bishops' conference.

Protestant "Christian villages" are by no means unusual. Occasionally the very name of the mission station was enough to indicate its purpose—as a refuge from tribal paganism. The name of the Berlin Mission's great Botshabelo station in the Transvaal, "Refuge", may serve as an example of the tendency to regard the mission station as a sanctuary to which the Christian convert could come, out of reach of chiefs and tribesmen. Mission farms, too, frequently served this kind of purpose. In Tanganyika, the main Christian villages are to be found in Usambara (Bethel Mission) and Bena (Berlin Mission). It is therefore possible in the Usambara mountains to study topographical aspects of the sociology of religion. We often find three villages facing one another on opposite hillsides: the original "pagan village" with its grass huts on one side; the Christian village, made up of modern limestone buildings with windows and corrugated iron roofs clustering around the church and the school on another; and a Muslim colony around its minaret on a third hillside. Here too it is generally recognized that "Christian villages" are no real solution of the problem of evangelization: the church should be a centre of spiritual power in the midst of society, not a closed community on its own.

Mass and Group Movements

We have so far viewed the encounter between Church and tribe mainly in terms of the more or less conscious planning and strategy of the mission in question. We must now widen our horizons to take in mass and group movements, which have for the most part been determined by quite other factors. It seems in many cases as though the way has been prepared for the coming of the mission. These movements illustrate an aspect of the encounter which must not be overlooked—the intrinsic links between Church and tribe in the tribe itself. We may take examples from Burma and India.

Adoniram Judson was one of the most capable of nineteenth-century American missionaries, well prepared for the demanding task of evangelizing Burmese Buddhists. He studied the Pali scriptures, translated the Bible into Burmese, and held learned discourses for small but patient groups of listeners. The result was however far from encouraging. After a hundred years of tenacious missionary work, the American Baptist mission to which he belonged had won only 4,000 Buddhists.

But as it happened, Judson had engaged as one of his servants a rough and suspect individual called Ko Tha Byu. He was not a Burmese, but a Karen, and the Burmese agreed that the Karens, a race of mountain people from the far north of Burma, were despicable and stupid. The Burmese had a saying to the effect that "you can teach a buffalo, but not a Karen", and Judson was tempted to agree in the six months during which, in his spare time, he was preparing Ko Tha Byu for baptism. But he succeeded eventually, and Ko Tha Byu was determined not to keep the message to himself. He asked nothing better than to bring the Gospel to his own people. As Judson's servant he was able to travel far and wide in Burma and, while his white master preached to the learned Burmese, to visit the Karen quarters. He started a chain reaction of dynamic spiritual influence the effects of which are still being felt today. The Karens were a "primal", South-East Asian mountain people, who had been pushed into the mountains of the north by the more powerful Burmese. Their religion was "animist"; their organization collective. To them the White Christ came as a liberator not only from magic and superstition, but also from Burmese oppression. Ko Tha Byu reached all his relations, and these in turn passed the message on. Families, clans and even whole districts were baptized. A rapidly expanding group movement began, and while there are still very few Burmese Baptists, the Karen Church now has half a million members, and is influencing the neighbouring Kachin and other similar hill peoples.

Also deserving of mention in this context is the Batak Church in Sumatra, which we have already discussed, since it[1] has a largely similar structure and has grown rapidly into a vast folk church, with about 700,000 members.

A similar course of events can be recorded in respect of the Kols of Chhota Nagpur, south-west of Calcutta. J. E. Gossner's young German missionaries came in 1845 to Calcutta, with every intention of preaching to Hindus. To that end they had been instructed, before leaving Berlin, in the complicated religious philosophy of classical Hinduism, and they hoped either to enter into learned disputation with the *gurus* and *sadhus* of Bengal, or alternatively to penetrate into the unknown interior of Tibet. But they could not ignore the street-sweepers outside their door. These were neither Hindus nor Bengalis, they were of another race, and they had another religion. They were Kols from the distant and inaccessible Chhota Nagpur ("the little town of the snakes"). The Gossner missionaries now made their way there. The Kols (the word *Kol*, like *Bantu*, means simply "people") proved to consist of a number of distinct tribes of hill and forest-dwellers: Mundari, Uraon, Ito, Santals and others. Together they numbered more than a million and a half, remnants of the aborigines, *adibasi*, who had been pushed into the hills by invaders coming from the north and north-west. The Kols were tamers of tigers and bears in the jungle, as well as an active agricultural people who had learned to construct artificial terraces for their rice. Their religion was "primal", with a tribal and social structure reminiscent of Africa.

The Gossner missionaries founded a church which grew rapidly. Rejected and despised by Hindus, these tribes were offered a new future by the Christian mission. Schools, medical care, improved agricultural methods, and a new sense of community in all reaches of life—all these were factors which accelerated the mass movement into the Lutheran Church, particularly towards the end of

[1] Above, pp. 189f.

the nineteenth century and in the twentieth century. The coming of the First World War hastened church independence, which was proclaimed in 1919. However, since then it has not been possible to avoid tensions in the church, due to tribal conflicts and the desire in some quarters for personal prestige. Anglican and Roman Catholic missions have reaped a considerable harvest in this area. Of the present population of 6,000,000 about 760,000 are Christians (Roman Catholics 360,000, Lutherans 200,000, Anglicans 200,000), and these set the tone of tribal life.

This applies equally to Santalistan, whose population is closely related to the *adibasi* of Chhota Nagpur; to Assam, where mass movements have led in some districts to a Christian population of 80 per cent; to the Karens and Kachins of North Burma; and to the aborigines of Taiwan (Formosa), where there has also been witnessed a striking Christian mass movement.

One author who has emphasized the responsibilities of Christian missions among the hitherto isolated hill peoples of South-East Asia is the American, D. A. McGavran. In his book *The Bridges of God: A Study in the Strategy of Missions* (1955) he draws a striking contrast between the nineteenth-century mission station and Christian colony or village, gathered around the person of the missionary, and the spontaneously expanding "People Movements" among these tribes and peoples. The "Mission Station Approach" leads to dependence upon the missionary and prevents healthy growth; the Christian People Movements, on the other hand, are expansive and often show dramatic results. McGavran, with an American's sense for the concrete, has found that these churches are on the average able to reckon with a rate of growth of at least 5 per cent per decennium. This is clearly of the greatest importance for missionary strategy.

Something of the spiritual struggle which lies behind this development can be seen in a Christian name popular in Chhota Nagpur: "Christ-Hardugan". The meaning of the word *Hardugan* is best expressed by a picture. A tiger gets into the sheepfold, and begins to drag away a sheep. The neighbour of the man who owns the sheep sees what is happening, rushes up and manages to save the sheep. It is now his property by law. He puts it on his shoulder, takes it to the owner and says, "*Hardugan*". That means, "I have saved it, and therefore it is mine." The man who, on baptism, chooses to be called "Christ-Hardugan" has certainly understood one of the basic doctrines of Christianity.

The Christian mission did not come in order to pull up these tribes by the roots; rather the opposite: Christianity came to strengthen and confirm them in their own milieu.

Problems essentially similar to those facing the Church in the tribal milieu are also to be seen in the Christian mass movements in India, and particularly in South India. It would have been quite possible to discuss them here, together with our account of the churches which have grown up among the hill-people of India. A further relevant factor is the close similarity in social structure between the lowest social groups of South India and the hill tribes. Nevertheless, we have chosen to discuss the South Indian movements in the context of the Church in the Hindu milieu, since these groups now belong to Indian churches whose "milieu" is largely Hindu.

The Word and the Church

The aim of the Evangelical missions was the building up of churches in accordance with the word of Scripture, and the method they used was individual and collective instruction in the elements of Christianity by means of Bible and catechism; their ideal was a church in which the preached and taught word occupied a position of pre-eminence. Catechetical interests were dominant. It is characteristic that the Zulu term for "church" is *isikole*, "school", and that the word for "Christian" in Luganda is *omushọmi*, "reader"—i.e. someone who can read a book. Protestant missions, faithful to their traditions, planted in Africa and Asia a verbal culture, a form of religion which was primarily auditive.

The question of the meaning of the biblical message for men and women in the tribal context prompts a further question, which is commonly ignored. What part is played by the Bible and Bible study in these young churches? No one answer is possible; nor has the question been fully answered when we have drawn up our statistics of the various languages into which the New Testament has been translated. In the East African *abalokole* revival movement from *c.* 1935 and later, regular and systematic Bible study has evidently been both one of the conditions for the movement's origin and rapid growth, and a source of missionary inspiration in the subsequent life of the young church. But there are other areas in which we are faced with newly christianized groups made up for the most part of illiterates. That the attention of Protestant missions has been drawn to this problem is due in large measure to H. R. Weber, a former missionary in the Celebes. In his book, *The Communication of the Gospel to Illiterates* (1956), he has pointed out that the Bible is still a closed book for more than half of the total population of the world, illiterates and semi-literates, and has suggested new ways of communicating the biblical drama of salvation for such groups.

One fact which has frequently been observed and commented upon is that the preacher in Africa, Papua or Santalistan seems to prefer the Old Testament—and especially Genesis—to the New. The traditional myths reach back to "the beginning", and must therefore be confronted with the witness of Genesis. Also fundamental to the traditional interpretation of reality is the concept of "the first man" and the origin of mankind. The Christian preacher, too, is deeply concerned with the Beginning.

This raises the question of the role of the Pentateuch in

the young church. It has been said that the African mind is generally "more Hebrew than Greek"—an explanation which can scarcely be called satisfactory. Of more direct interest is the fact that the great Hebrew narratives have been shown to have parallels in African mythology: so with the Creation, Cain and Abel, the Flood and the crossing of the Red Sea. This provides at least one reason for the pleasant surprise with which the young African church recognizes the Old Testament. As a pastor from the Cameroons has said, "We recognize ourselves and our own history in the Pentateuch."

The biblical drama of salvation, rooted in history, provides a sense of purpose which the cyclical pattern of thought, mystical and naturalistic in essence, lacks. The interest shown by so many of these preachers in the Old Testament is an expression of their desire to confront the mythological cycle with the drama of salvation, stretching from the Creation and the Fall to the final summing up of all things in Christ.

The African preacher's theological confrontation with his own religious past may be viewed as an ellipse, one of the foci of which is "the Beginning". The other is the corporate life of the tribe—the tribe also serving as a link between present and past generations. The question of the nature and meaning of death is central to this interpretation of Christianity. In the words of Dr. C. G. Baeta of Ghana, "whatever others may do in their own countries, our people *live* with their dead". It would seem that we can look forward to interesting theological developments in these young churches, not least in the interpretation of that neglected phrase in the Apostles' Creed, "He descended into Hell." But the most prominent role in preaching and faith is occupied by the Resurrection of Christ and the resurrection of the dead; this is a distinctive feature of African Christian piety. Vicedom comments, with reference this time to New Guinea, "Their greatest comfort was that in the Resurrection the soul puts on immortality and lives on. At the end there stands, not absorption into the Infinite, as Mbowamb believes, but God, who bestows eternal life."

The encounter with the Risen and Living Lord is mediated by His word in the New Testament. Special significance is attached in Papuan or African preaching to the parables of Jesus. And it is easy to see why: because the proclamation of the Gospel must try and make contact with that world of ideas and images already current in the tribe. It goes without saying that the preacher draws on his store of vernacular parables and proverbs; among the Dayaks he must even connect up with the sacred secret languages, *Basa Sangiang*, the use of which was formerly the prerogative of the priesthood in the traditional Dayak religion. It goes without saying that sermons must link up with the past in this way—for their constant and overriding concern must be with *translation*. This concern is no less pressing in Africa and Papua than elsewhere in the world.

This is not to say that there is a simple method, applicable in all situations. The task of the preacher in Africa is not to apply a method, but to respond to a call. And in all this he must be aware of the recalcitrance of language. True, he is called to proclaim the simple Gospel; but the preaching of the simple Gospel appears somewhat less simple when it is realized that many of the basic terms have a quite different content, and convey quite different associations, from those to which we are accustomed in the West. The white preacher uses words like "sin", "grace", "salvation" and "faith"; but what the preacher says and what the listener hears are two different things. Tribal languages are full of associations drawn from religions which are not the Christian Gospel. They suggest religious legalism, piety based on achievement, or cosmic harmony in a pantheistic universe, and it is at first simply unavoidable that these are the pictures which traditional Christian language conjures up. At first—until church-people have reached the stage of being able to refill the old words with a new Christian meaning.

Witness to the Holy and Risen Lord in the African or Papuan church is also borne by the Sacraments.

Baptism

The sacrament of Baptism is the great missionary sacrament: the witnessing Church's sacrament. The problem for Evangelical missions is that of the relationship between faith and baptism, or between instruction, faith and baptism. The preparation of catechumens in the village chapel can take from six months to two years. Some missions lay great emphasis on this period of preparation; as the great German missionary leader M. Zahn said as far back as 1893, "Preparation for baptism came to be more important than baptism itself." But Zulus, Papuans and Santals, with their inherent understanding of ritual, soon came to value baptism more highly than the Western missionaries imagined. In Papua, baptism was preceded by private confession, and could be postponed until the catechumen had cleared up what was troubling his newly-awakened conscience—murder, theft, or lesser transgressions.

Baptism in a river, a lake or the sea—"living water"—increased the people's understanding of the total character of the Sacrament: a dying to the old existence and a resurrection to new life. Personal testimony makes it plain that baptism has both a negative and a positive aspect. A *Nyakyusa* in the Moravian Church in Tanzania said of baptism, "It is like throwing away our life"—a drastic image of the absolute break with the customs and beliefs of the tribe. And in a positive sense it means a change of allegiance, the taking of service under a new Lord.

A leading Ghanaian described his baptismal experience in these words: "I felt that I had become a different person." And as different persons—new men and women—Christians belong to a new fellowship, having become members of *Kristofo asafo*, the tribe of Christ. The Ashanti (Ghana) word for baptism is *asubo*, borrowed from the traditional religion and originally denoting the rite of purification. But the *asubo* of baptism takes place in the name of the new king, and that is the important thing. Baptism leads out of the realm of fear into the realm of peace, liberty and joy. To the newly-baptized Christians in Hayaland their day of baptism was "a day of joy"; and the Ghanaian whom we have already quoted exulted: "Now I shall do nothing but beat the drum for days, to tell everybody what God has done with me." The cate-chumen is free to choose his own Christian name. At one time biblical names were the most common, but now, since the growth of nationalism, African or Papuan names have come into wider currency; nevertheless the meaning is the same, and is clear to everyone. It is typical that, in the Chagga church, Christian names usually express something of what God has done in the act of baptism.

A simple Papuan Christian has written a song about the meaning of baptism.

> Come, all people,
> Let us gather to gaze on the jewel
> He has bestowed on us.
> The Almighty changed our hearts,
> The Lord comes down and gives us
> Strengthening water,
> Poured upon our heads,
> Renewing our hearts.

The Eucharist

Fellowship at table is not without religious significance for the African. Real fellowship at the deepest level can-not but be expressed in the act of eating together, sitting (or lying) at table together. The whole of this social and religious background is recognized by communicants in the Haya Church. In receiving the elements and in enjoy-ing table fellowship they are receiving what they hold most important: strength, health of body and soul, joy, "peace". The spiritual is not something forced or intellectualized; it is inextricably bound up with the physical. This is clear from the role played by the Sacrament of the Lord's Supper in this church.

The Eucharist is able to create fellowship deeper than can be reached by words or speculations; and is even able to bring together members of families and tribes which until recently hated each other. It draws in new individuals and new groups, and there are plentiful examples of the concrete link between mass and mission in the front line of the Church's work in Africa, New Guinea and elsewhere.

The Sacrament of the Lord's Supper purifies and renews the fellowship. But it is also a judgment—and for that reason the young churches are particularly concerned to prepare for their communion. It has been known for Papuan Christians in New Guinea to be unable to eat or sleep for a week before communion; the conscience has been stirred, and they do their utmost to banish everything which is not in accordance with the will of Jesus Christ.

Style and Rhythm

The patterns of worship brought with them by the Western missionaries have been of great importance in the history of missions, not least in providing contact and continuity with the Church Universal in space and time. But Africa will not be silenced, and church life has come to be coloured by African, as well as Western patterns. In Africa or Malaya there must be greater freedom for rite, rhythm and movement than has generally been the case in Western Protestantism. But far too little has so far been done to meet the corresponding need in church architecture, where the usual style is Western pastiche.

It must be remembered, however, that it is not easy to determine in advance exactly what is meant by "African church architecture". An interesting attempt to adapt the traditional form of the Congolese royal residence has been made in the Roman Catholic Cathedral of St. Anne in Brazzaville, and there have been similar experiments elsewhere in Africa, on the part of both Catholics and Evangelicals. One problem is that the African congregation actually prefers Western practice, simply because it conveys prestige. Consequently the initiative in launching "the African style" has been taken by non-Africans—the question then being just how African it really is.

The church year and the liturgy are factors which the missionary church ignores at its peril. The threat of syncretism from the sects has prompted churches in Africa to stress the dogmatic and catechetical function of the liturgy: a richly developed Evangelical liturgy is able to convey solid instruction in the biblical drama of salvation.

Dramatic presentation is of particular interest. Africans are by nature richly gifted in this sphere, and the Church must be prepared to take this gift, use it and develop it. John V. Taylor has interpreted this in his book, *The Passion in Africa* (1957).

Another question, the importance of which can scarcely be stressed too highly, is that of music and sacred song. When the Thonga of Northern Rhodesia want to join the Church, they say, "I want to start singing"—an eloquent testimony to the role of music in these churches.

The American negro has in his "negro spirituals" made a powerful and original contribution to the music of the Christian Church. Unfortunately, the Church's song in Africa and Indonesia has for the most part been anything but original. It has usually been borrowed from the West, and set to Western tunes. There are exceptions, however, such as this African hymn from the Bukoba diocese of the Evangelical Lutheran Church in Tanganyika.

> Friends, it is night no more, it is night no more.
> It is the glorious dawn.
> The sun is not yet sharp, does not yet burn;
> May we be borne by the freshness of the dawn.

Let us go out to greet the King,
Let us go out into the beautiful meadow
And dance the spear-dance for Him.
Let us go, let us go. O let us go,
Let us dance the spear-dance for Him.
Let us be strong, strong, we who have been helped;
We are but children.
Let us not be afraid on the path,
But seized by longing,
Let us all say:
The King loves us.
Let us not sleep, it is dawn, it is dawn, it is dawn,
    let us not sleep.

Catholic and Protestant missions alike long refused to have anything to do with African music, which they regarded as heathen and obscene. But in recent years a renewed study of this music has shown the uses to which it may legitimately be put. First, however, it must be "baptized" into the Church. Modified, it is well able to be used in the liturgy and serve the worshipping Church. The Roman Catholic Church has taken the lead in this respect, and there are now a number of examples of African liturgical music, the best known of these being the Congolese *Missa Luba*. A Swedish musician, Dr. Henry Weman, has made an important contribution to the study of African church music in his book *African Music and the Church in Africa* (Uppsala 1960). Dr. Weman has also attained highly encouraging results in adapting African folk music for use in the Evangelical liturgy. We have asked Dr. Wemen to comment on African church music; he writes:

"Musically, there is no reason why African melodies should not be used in Christian worship. They can be used most simply and easily in *psalmody*; they suit this purpose particularly well, since African tunes are often short, having the character of mottoes. The African technique also corresponds to that of psalmody in its repetitive quality.

It is possible to avoid 'heathen' associations altogether

213

by choosing neutral tunes. Nor is there anything to prevent the use in one country of a tune originating in another. We may give some examples of tunes which have proved fully usable in the African churches:

Langa Lashona

This tune, *Langa Lashona*, is sung in Zululand to the text "The sun is setting", and can be used as a psalm-tune as follows:

African Psalm-tune No. 1
A.M., p. 160

This psalm-tune can of course be sung either in unison or in harmony, or in a mixture of the two. It has in fact been sung in South Africa, Southern Rhodesia and Tanganyika, thus proving that there is a certain body of melodic material common to African music as a whole.

Instrumental melodies without texts are even more "neutral". Another melody from Zululand, *Inyoni Emaqhanda*, is played on the one-stringed fiddle:

Inyoni Emaqhanda
A.M., p. 160

This was used for a psalm-tune of more serious character, suitable for the penitential psalms or during Lent.

African Psalm-tune No. 2
A.M., p. 160

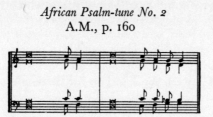

Psalm-tune No. 2 came into wide use in Southern Rhodesia, both as the basis of a litany and for the melodies of the Introit during Lent.[1]

A similar procedure can be used in the composition of African hymns: starting with an African melody, it is not difficult to produce new hymn-tunes in which African vocal techniques (parallel fifths, parallel fourths, choruses, etc.) may be used.

This technique (a compromise between Western and African) may serve as an interim measure, the primary object of which is to show Africans themselves how to make use of their own melodies. The ultimate objective is obviously new African composition, settings of new African texts. The role of improvisation is important in this context."

Finally in this chapter brief mention must be made of the modern messianic movements which have arisen in Africa and Oceania as a consequence of, and in competition with, the preaching of the Western missionaries. Racial discrimination in South Africa has influenced not only the concept of man but also the concept of God. The African has felt himself justified in asking whether the White Christ may not be a Christ for the white man only. The Bantu prophet assumes the mantle of the Messiah.

[1] Cf. *African Music and the Church in Africa*, pp. 250–53.

Similar manifestations are to be seen in the Cargo cults of New Guinea.

The patterns and colours and rhythms of the African or Papuan tribal culture have not been crowded out by the Church. In some cases missions have been alive to their importance, and far-seeing enough to incorporate worthy elements from the traditional cultures into the ritual and life of the Church. We stand on the threshold of a new era. These churches are under indigenous leadership to an extent never before seen. It may be that the Church in the tribal cultures of Africa and Asia will help the Church Universal to reach a deeper understanding of certain vital elements in the Christian message of salvation.

CHAPTER 12

THE CHURCH AND THE GREAT RELIGIONS

IN OUR LAST CHAPTER WE SAW SOMETHING OF THE Church in the tribal milieu, that milieu in which the Church has had its most notable successes, numerically speaking. Here have been established vital autonomous churches, local manifestations of the Universal Church of Christ.

The second main type of milieu with which the missionary Church has been confronted consists, as we have already indicated, of communities and peoples dominated by the great religions—Islam, Hinduism, Buddhism and Shinto. The situation of the Church in these areas differs radically from that of the Church in the tribal milieu. Here Christians are very definitely in the minority, and are often a near-microscopic group. The Gospel "makes an impression" only with the greatest difficulty; the task of translation is vastly complicated. Nevertheless, the Church of Christ is there, as a living community, and we shall see what it means to be a church in such surroundings.

When studying the Church and the great religions we have strictly only one type of milieu to deal with. However, we shall for the sake of clarity divide this long chapter into three main sections. First we shall consider the Church and Islam; secondly the Church in India; and finally the Church in the Far East. Each of these has its own special contribution to make to our understanding of the situation —and the possibilities—of the missionary Church in the world.

Dr. Samuel Zwemer, the American missionary, once called Islam "the immovable block". Zwemer had travelled widely in the East, and had encountered the same problem everywhere. The "block" extends from Senegal in West Africa to the provinces on China's western frontier: from town to town, from country to country, the *muezzin* calls the faithful to prayer: *la Ilaha illa' llah*, "there is no God but Allah". And he does not call in vain, for he calls to what Pope Pius XI called *Oriens orans*, "the praying Orient".

But the adjective "immovable" is perhaps not altogether accurate. It fits somewhat the dogmatic structure of Islam; for as Lord Cromer observed, "Islam cannot be reformed; a reformed Islam would no longer be Islam." Or it seemed to fit until recently when we should now refer to "renascent" Islam. The Christian missionary, however, sees Islam as impregnable, impassable, inaccessible: here the Christian mission meets its most difficult task, the decisive test of its faith. But Islam is certainly not static, having no missionary will of its own—least of all in these days. The "immovable block" is on the move, in the whole of Africa and Indonesia; at the same time Islam is at present experiencing a mighty ideological renaissance. Its leaders now look upon Islam as a world religion, a faith, too, for what they are convinced is the irreligious West.

The problem of the missionary Church's encounter with Islam is rendered all the more acute by the fact that Islam is a post-Christian religion. In its anti-Christian propaganda Islam claims that Judaism and Christianity are no more than a *praeparatio* for the final revelation through the prophet Muhammad. On this view "after Christ" is synonymous with "superior to Christ" or "in opposition to Christ"; consequently, no religion is so effectively immunized, historically and ideologically, against Christianity.

The person who turns to the history of missions with a

view to strengthening his faith with the record of rapid results and victorious progress would be well advised to avoid the chapter dealing with Christian missions to Islam. For there is little enough of victory in that particular chapter. Its sign is the sign of the cross—the cross of failure. Pascal observed that Islam desired to *"réussir humainement au lieu de périr"*. But for Christian missionaries to Islam exactly the opposite is true. They come with the paradoxical claim of Christianity, that God, the King, the Merciful Judge, has become man in Him whom the Quran calls the prophet Isa; this they have to preach in a milieu which is always unfriendly and often bitterly opposed to what they are doing. Humanly speaking they succeed not at all; they must accustom themselves to what Zwemer called "the patience of unanswered prayer". But in that very fact missions to Islam have a precious lesson to teach the Church in the world.

The only possibility for the survival of the Church in this kind of milieu is to live in an eschatological dimension.

What, then, is Islam? D. C. Mulder, an expert on Indonesian Islam, answers simply, "Islam is Islam. As far as the Christian mission is concerned this means that Islam today is still that religion which from the first rejected the central message of the Gospel; the incarnation, the cross, the resurrection of Christ."

The goal of Islam is, in obedience to the will of Allah, to bring peace to the world. This peace is made up of three elements. First the struggle against *Shirk*, which is the attribution to other than Allah of that which properly belongs to Allah alone; secondly, the propagation of *Islam*, the true order; and thirdly, *Ummah*, or fellowship. The strength of Islam's conviction and of its position to Christianity, is scarcely imaginable, save against the background of its utter abhorrence of *Shirk*. *Shirk* is the root of all evil, against which the Prophet thundered. It is idolatry, and worse; it is man's vain attempt to place something—or someone—on a par with the One True God.

Hence the great assertion, "There is no God but Allah." The foundation of Islam is the unity of God. And anyone who worships another God—for example, anyone who believes that God sent His Son into the world—is a *Mushrik*, i.e. one who commits *Shirk*. Islam is the positive aspect of religion, standing on five pillars. Of these, three are ritual demands, *Salāt* (prayer), *Ramadān* (fasting) and *Hajj* (pilgrimage); the remaining two are religious and social, *Shahādah* (confession) and *Zakāt* (the giving of alms).

On these five pillars rests "the house of Islam", the fellowship of Muslims, elect according to the free choice and eternal decree of God. Remembering this decree, the Muslim theologian says, not "I am a Muslim", but "I am a Muslim, if God has willed it". Hence, too, the oft-repeated, not seldom anxious prayer, "Oh God, let me die a Muslim."

But Islam is more than a religion. It is a socio-political order based on religion, an absolute theocracy shaping both the life of the individual and every function of society. There is no dichotomy here between secular society and the religious community, for these are but two sides of the same coin.

What does it mean to be a church in these surroundings? The situation of the Christian Church is determined by three separate types of Islamic milieu. First we have the milieu in which Islam is dominant, and in which the ancient Islamic penal code is still applied (e.g. Arabia and Afghanistan), leading to death for apostasy from Islam. Secondly, there are those countries in which Islam, though it still has a superficial authority, seems to have stagnated. And thirdly, there are areas in which Islam and Christianity are in conscious or unconscious competition. The boundaries between the second and third of these are, however, flexible, and we shall therefore treat them as being basically the same situation.

In the Islamic countries of the Middle East and North

Africa, the Church has been forced to take the fatal step of withdrawing into the *Millet*—the Islamic equivalent of the Jewish ghetto. Non-Muslim religious groups are tolerated only if they keep within their own churches and avoid crossing the frontiers of their own particular enclave. These frontiers were laid down 1,300 years ago, when the Muslim wave rolled across North Africa and the Middle East, sweeping away the greater part of what had once been flourishing Christian communities. The tiny groups that are left, together with such new groups as have been formed, are now barely tolerated; the atmosphere is one of uneasy co-existence.

It is a tragic fact that converts from Islam are seldom made to feel at home in any of the many Christian denominations. Bishop H. B. Dehqani-Tafti, himself an Iranian convert, has said, "In most Middle Eastern churches a Muslim convert feels himself to be a stranger, and he is sometimes made to understand that he has committed a crime!" This applies especially to the ancient Eastern churches; it is still said—and justly so—that these Eastern churches are themselves the greatest obstacles in the way of their neighbours' conversion to Christianity. Nor have the Evangelical churches any cause for complacency. Dr. L. Levonian of the Lebanon, a devoted Christian scholar, wrote in 1955: "The Evangelical denominations in the Near East differ from the other churches there in their Protestant faith, their forms of worship and their knowledge of the Bible, but not in their attitude to the Muslims." However, there has in recent years been some change for the better, and some slight sign of a new missionary enthusiasm.

The old-established Middle Eastern churches are small, and have shown little concern for missionary work among Muslims. In Syria there are Jacobites, Orthodox and Uniate churches in communion with Rome; in the Lebanon notably Maronites; in Egypt an important Coptic church, numbering a million and a half.

The church leader who played the most important role in the activization of the Uniate churches was Cardinal Lavigerie, whom we have already had occasion to mention (above, p. 125). As Archbishop of Algiers he was responsible for the laying down of a generous programme for these churches' attitude to Middle Eastern culture and religion. "The latinization of the Orientals is one of the Latin Oriental missionaries' most deplorable mistakes. The true method of the Oriental missionary is to become an Oriental himself, and adopt these churches' dress, language and liturgy." In accordance with this view the Church of Rome has stressed the importance of theological training for Melchites, Maronites and the other Uniate churches, while at the same time insisting that these should retain their Eastern rites; in this way it is hoped that a realistic approach to Islam will be evolved.

Another prominent Roman Catholic missionary to the Arab lands was Charles de Foucauld (b. 1858, French officer in North Africa and the Sahara 1881–86, converted 1886, Trappist monk in France 1890, in Nazareth 1897, in the Sahara from 1901 to his death in 1916). De Foucauld built his "mission station", after long years of caravan wandering, in Tamanrasset, among the superficially Islamic Tuaregs. This was an oblong building, 12 metres by 3, only 2½ metres high, with clay walls and a roof of palm-leaves, a high threshold to keep out the snakes and two tiny windows. An iron cross was erected on the roof to show that this was a chapel. Inside, it was like a long corridor, divided into two by curtains; one half was a chapel, scarcely big enough to hold four people, with an altar knocked together out of packing-cases, and round the walls a little series of Stations of the Cross, painted by the monk himself. In the other half of the house de Foucauld lived: a tiny kitchen, a bookshelf and a packing-case to serve as a writing-desk. There he received visitors and studied the Scriptures. In the chapel he celebrated Mass and meditated.

And outside: "Wherever I look I see nothing but the endless desert, merging into the sky, the beautiful sky of the Sahara, compelling one to think of eternity, of God— *Allah akbar!*" The nearest priest was sixty days' journey away. The house he called *Kaua*, "Brotherhood"; he wished himself to be known as Brother Charles, *Khuia Carlo*, or "the brother of all", "*le frère universel*". He took as his sign *Christus Caritas*; and he had two mottoes: "To live this day as though I were to be martyred before the evening comes," and, "To be all things to all men that I might win all men for Jesus." All men? He baptized two persons: one boy, a freed negro slave, Abd-Jesu, and an old and blind negro woman, Maria, *in extremis*. In his diary for May 5, 1903 we read: "The old catechumen Maria is very ill. There is no doctor. Since I was afraid that she was going to die, I baptized her after she had clearly asked for baptism. I let her say Our Father, Credo and prayers for faith, hope, mercy and penitence in Arabic. Then, after she had once more asked for the Sacrament, I baptized her."

Brother Charles was once visited by a French Protestant doctor, Dr. Hérisson. "How do you reach the Tuaregs?" he asked. "You must not be a district medical officer, or even a doctor with them," he was told. "You must not be shocked by anything. Be human, merciful and always happy. You must laugh all the time, even when they say the most commonplace things. As you see, I am always laughing and showing my bad teeth. People come closer to one another when they laugh, they understand one another better. Among the Tuaregs you must always laugh."

Brother Charles was killed during the First World War, in the course of a Tuareg rebellion. He was dragged out of his hut, bound and shot. He wrote of himself in a letter: "I am no apostle. I am not a sower—all I do is break up the ground a little; others will come and sow; and others again will reap."

The life and example of Charles de Foucauld led to the

setting up of two orders, the "Little Brothers of Jesus" and the "Little Sisters of Jesus", both working also in Islamic countries, and both expressions of great Christian devotion, mercy and faith.

There are Evangelical missions at work in Syria, Egypt, Aden and elsewhere. In Syria a Syrian Evangelical Church has been founded, mainly as a result of educational and medical work. Most of its members are, however, converts from the Greek Orthodox Church, thus raising the question of proselytism. There is a theological faculty in the University of Beirut, at which the Evangelical Church trains its pastors, and which forms a nucleus for the small Evangelical groups in the country as a whole.

In Arabia there are practically no Christians. The British colony and protectorate of Aden, with its 800,000 inhabitants, has a little handful. The pioneer work was done by such outstanding English and Scottish figures as Henry Martyn (cf. p. 172), General F. T. Haig and a Cambridge Professor of Arabic, Ion Keith-Falconer. Martyn and Keith-Falconer both died at the early age of 32.

At present there are three Evangelical missions at work in Aden: the Danish Missionary Society, the Church of Scotland Mission and the Sudan Interior Mission. They have been there for at least half a century, and have sent men and money into the area. And the result? The Evangelical Christian group in Aden comprises fifteen persons, of whom five are Somalis. The Christian Somalis have founded their own church, with a Somali pastor, while the Arabic Christians, who have contacts with Danish and Scottish missions, agreed in 1960 to form their own church, "The Church of Christ in Southern Arabia", with its own simple constitution. This church was started with ten baptized members: seven men and three women, together with some children. Of these, one man and two women were born, not in Aden, but in Palestine. The Roman Catholic Church in Aden has 6,800 members, practically all of whom are foreigners: Indians, Americans and Italians.

What it is to be the Church in Arabia was forcefully described by Dr. Paul W. Harrison, an American missionary doctor, in the course of the 1938 Tambaram conference. He there painted a picture of what he called "the Church which is in Arabia"—a handful of four or five Arabs, men and women, who have held on to their convictions despite terrible opposition and suffering.

The missionary situation in Egypt is characterized rather by the Coptic Church's existence than by its missionary enthusiasm. With its one and a half million members it represents the largest Christian denomination in the Arab lands. Traditionally it lives in its *Millet*. The Anglican missionary, Temple Gairdner, found that the Copts preferred to hand over possible converts from Islam to the Anglican diocese, purely in order to avoid irritating their Muslim neighbours. But the risk was in any case slight. Social contacts, marriage and the like, ensure that such conversions as take place are usually in the opposite direction, from the Coptic Church to the house of Islam.

During the first decade of the present century the Anglican Church in Egypt had a number of exceptionally well-equipped missionaries, who were able to make a relevant contribution to the encounter of the Church with Islam. The two outstanding names here are Douglas Thornton and Temple Gairdner, the latter of whom was an outstanding figure in the international missionary movement from Edinburgh 1910 to Jerusalem 1928. Both were first-class linguists, and well acquainted with the Arabic language in both its classical and its modern vernacular forms. They published a journal, *Orient and Occident*, aimed mainly at meeting the interests and needs of intellectual Muslims. Gairdner was also highly musical, and experimented with the use of Near Eastern music in Christian worship; to this end he collected some three hundred folk melodies, from Muslim dervishes, from boatmen on the

Nile and from Syrian peasants. One of the best teachers in this field was a blind *arif*, a Coptic choirmaster. Gairdner was also convinced of the importance of religious drama as a "method of evangelization", and more, as a means of translating the Gospel of salvation into a language the Muslim could understand. He wrote, and performed, a number of dramas on biblical themes. When asked whether these were to be played in church, he answered that they were to be played nowhere but in church. Both Gairdner and Thornton were deeply concerned to rouse the Coptic Church to a sense of its own missionary responsibility, and therefore did their best to cultivate their contacts with the Copts.

In Cairo, Thornton and Gairdner worked with a missionary we have previously named, Dr. Samuel Zwemer (1867–1953), an American Presbyterian of Dutch extraction. Someone has justly said of Zwemer's background: "I think that God has given only the Dutch the divine stubbornness that is needed to be a missionary in Arabia." After twenty-two years of itineracy in Arabia (1890–1912) he spent the years from 1913 to 1930 in Cairo, where he founded the Nile Mission Press, the provision of high-class Christian literature being of great importance for missions in this area. But Zwemer's great passion was for itinerant preaching.

In this connexion we may draw attention to the work of a number of Danes, who have made what is unquestionably the main Scandinavian contribution to missions in Islamic countries. Their organization, founded in 1898, is the Danish Orient Mission (*Dansk Österlandsmission*). One of their missionaries, Alfred Nielsen, began in 1922 to work in Damascus, where he distributed tracts, established a reading room, and incidentally acquired an extraordinary knowledge of Arabic. He later became head of the Evangelical missions' joint language school in Damascus, which was removed to Jerusalem in 1929.

One of the most interesting of Scandinavian missions is

to be found at work in North Pakistan, in the corner between Afghanistan and Kashmir, among the fanatical
Muslim Pathans. This work was begun by a Danish
woman doctor, Dr. Marie Holst (1866–1917), in conditions which forced missionaries to live in tents for years on
end, and was later extended by her successor, Dr. Anna
Bramsen (d. 1962). The difficult situation in which this
mission was placed led to the setting up of an ideal similar
to that formulated many years before by one of the
Church's greatest missionaries to Islam, St. Francis of
Assisi. Dr. Bramsen, inspired by the Franciscan ideal, proposed the formation of a Pathan order of "Little Sisters".
The theologians in Copenhagen were horrified, decreed
that the whole enterprise was un-Lutheran, and demanded
the resignation of Dr. Bramsen. In the following crisis—
one of many in the little Pathan mission—an important
part was played by Jens Christensen. Christensen is from
the theological point of view the most interesting of modern
Scandinavian missionaries—a Lutheran who has been
deeply influenced by Karl Barth, and who makes wide use
of paradoxical ideas and statements calculated to shock
the missionary *bourgeoisie*. One of his books bears the
characteristic title of *Forargelsens Gud*, which we might perhaps translate "The Troublesome God". As a Barthian he
strongly criticized the conventional reasons put forward
for carrying on medical missions. He felt that to use
philanthropic work in order to demonstrate Christ's
"spirit of service" was purely human self-exaltation, binding others to the good works the Christian does, though
the intention may be to show them the way to Christ. "The
unfortunate word 'witness' has been so terribly misused
that one is almost ashamed to use it. . . . The witness of the
Church is one thing, and one thing only: the Apostolic
witness." This theological position naturally led him to
criticize "institutions"—which meant the greater part of
the Protestant missionary enterprise in the Islamic lands.
But this has not prevented the mission in Mardan from

227

running schools for Christians. The church, which now has some 400 members, became independent in 1955, with Jens Christensen as its first bishop.

An entirely different situation—though one which is equally serious for the Christian mission—is that found in connexion with Islam in Negro Africa and Indonesia. The rapid advance of Islam in Africa is one of the most important missionary facts of the present day. Up to the outbreak of the Second World War the situation was roughly as follows: Islam was a religion which appealed only to the peoples of the desert and the plains, to Hausa merchants and a few ethnic groups which had come from the north and settled on the Guinea coast. Christianity had come by sea; missionaries, voyaging in the ship of the Church, had founded churches along the coasts. The two religions were separated by mighty areas of tropical forest, and there was very little real encounter between the two.

By the middle of the present century, however, messengers from the coast had reached the savannahs, and some missionaries had penetrated far into the compact Muslim areas—the CMS in Northern Nigeria, for instance. And at the same time Islam had begun to move southward on a wide front: solid, ponderous and to all appearances irresistible. It was principally a spontaneous collective movement, facilitated especially by the local Muslim brotherhood groups. But at the same time it must be viewed in the context of Islam's new political ambition to become the ideological ruler of all Africa. With headquarters in the Al-Azhar University in Cairo and political centres both in North Africa and Pakistan, the Muslim organizations began a great missionary movement. When we come across organized Muslim mission in these areas it often proves to be inspired and supported by the Aga Khan's Ishmaelite sect. This group played an important role in an important teaching conference held in Dar-es-Salaam in 1958, with delegates from the whole of Muslim

Africa. The main topics discussed on this occasion included the extension of Islamic teaching in the schools and colleges, and the improvement of Islamic literature. Another sect notable for its missionary enterprise and strategy is the Ahmadiyya sect, whose books, pamphlets and newspapers in the African vernaculars are a constant challenge to the Christian missions. Ahmadiyya opposition to Christianity has a particular logical motivation in that the founder of the sect, who died in 1908, is held to be a reincarnation of Jesus.

J. S. Trimingham (*The Christian Church and Islam in West Africa*, 1955) stresses that there is no Christian Church among Muslims in West Africa. Christianity, being Western, is too "foreign" to be able to compete with Islam, "the religion of the Blacks", which has penetrated deep into the popular consciousness in some parts of West Africa. Islam provides the African or Indonesian "animist" with a good alternative to the Christian Church's uncompromising demand for conversion and baptism. Within the fellowship of Islam he can keep most of his old religion, including ancestor-worship and magic, but at the same time set it in a wider and more powerful context, in harmony with the modern age. It has been estimated that in Ibadan, Nigeria, the largest city in West Africa, Islam is at present gaining twenty times more converts than Christianity.

The same problem is now being experienced in East Africa; not, it is true, to the same extent as in West Africa, but disturbing nevertheless. This applies particularly to the coastal belts of Kenya and Tanganyika. There were living Christian churches here in the second and third decades of the present century, but these have now been reduced to miserable little enclaves surrounded by Islam. Trimingham has well said, on the subject of Islamic expansion in Africa: "Naturally the converts and the majority of their sons and grandsons have but a superficial knowledge of Islam. Missionaries everywhere mentioned this as though it were very significant. Yet simple adherence to Islam is usually permanent, and, in spite of their retention of pagan motives and practices, Islam gradually gains a real hold upon them and effects a radical change."[1] An important initiative was taken towards the end of the 1950's by the International Missionary Council. Trimingham and Pierre Bénignus of France had in their reports stressed the seriousness of the situation from the point of view of Christian missions to Africa. Christian missionaries with experience of Islam have accordingly been placed at strategic points in East and West Africa, with two tasks; on the one hand they have to study the confrontation of Christianity and Islam, and on the other to provide the local churches and missions with information and advice. Here and there the Church has succeeded in winning individuals and groups from Islam. The situation is still fluid in Southern Nigeria and North-East Tanganyika—to name only two areas in which the struggle is especially pronounced.

Baptism is a distinct problem in the Islamic milieu. It is by no means out of the question for a person to show some interest, and a certain amount of sympathy, for the white man's religion, without forfeiting his place in the house of Islam. But baptism is another matter. Here is where the dividing line has to be drawn.

The "how" and "where" of baptism are in themselves problematic. This may be illustrated by a concrete example. Some Christian missionaries went to work in a Muslim village, near which was a pool of mud which they called a lake. Years of prayer and work were finally crowned with success; two persons declared that they were willing to become Christians, and to witness to their conversion in public, by being baptized. Their baptism took place in the village pool. How these two managed to survive the hate of the rest of the village is not known, but the

[1] *Ibid.*, p. 23.

230

public ceremony made it impossible for Christian work to continue in that particular place. Experienced missionaries in a Muslim milieu of this kind prefer that baptisms should take place quietly, in the presence of a little group of Christians only—a significant action, when it is remembered that baptism is an incorporation into the Christian congregation.

Sometimes the problem is to decide whether baptism should take place at all. A woman belonging to the Druze sect in the Lebanon witnessed openly to her faith and was said to have been a blessing to many. Should she be baptized? She knew that if she did, she would certainly be killed. Her brother had gone the same way; he had read the New Testament, declared that he wished to belong to Jesus Christ, and was baptized. There were no dramatic repercussions—then; but a few days later he was found murdered. It is not merely a question of personal security: it is more a question of how the convert shall best be enabled to win others for the Christian faith. However, the Asmara conference of 1959 declared that secret baptism was not to be recommended, and that baptism should as a rule take place in the presence of the members of the church. Further, that in situations where baptism might be expected to result in persecution and physical danger, both the church and the convert ought to seek the guidance of the Holy Spirit as to the right course to be followed.

In those areas in which the Evangelical churches have managed to establish their right to exist, increased autonomy had led to a richer liturgy and a deeper ecumenical interpretation of the nature of the Church. Charles Malik, one of the most influential of Lebanon's Christian laymen, came from an Orthodox family, but like many others became an Evangelical Christian as a result of his experiences in school and at the university. He writes: "My deepest prayer is for the unity of the Church of Christ. Missionaries must love and seek this unity with all their heart. A great deal in fact took place between the death of the Apostle Paul and the birth of John Knox in the history of the Church, and particularly in the Eastern Church. This mighty tradition must not be overlooked by the missionaries. In worship and ritual, in faith and doctrine, and in the matter of social milieu, this tradition has 'a unique aroma of unity'. We in the Middle East regard John Chrysostom, Ephraim the Syrian and John of Damascus as belonging to the essence of our tradition. Our wonderful liturgy is the fruit of their inspiring genius. Is it right that the missionary should ignore such things?''

It would therefore seem as though a constructive, positive, collective witness on the part of a living Christian church could be of great missionary importance. The liturgy and the message of the Church year are sources of inspiration. Just as the Muslims invite their Christian neighbours to their *Ramadan* celebrations, so it is the concern of the Christian community to invite Muslims to the Church's great festivals. The Indonesian Church in Java, whose surroundings are largely Muslim, lays particular emphasis on Christmas; the celebrations last for several weeks, a number of religious groups taking part in a spirit of neighbourliness. Incidentally, the situation in Java is distinctive in that there is a national Christian church there, in the midst of a Muslim milieu. In Africa, Easter and, to a lesser extent, Christmas are important festivals. An African Anglican priest in Tanga, in the largely Islamic coastal belt of Tanganyika, held a service of Benediction for his assembled congregation. The consecrated Host was lifted up in the monstrance by the priest, and shown to the people. The whole of the white-clad church responded by bowing low in silence and reverence, their heads to the ground. They were conscious of a Living Presence, of Holiness, in a manner utterly relevant to their situation.

What is needed is that the Church should open a real dialogue with Islam, on a level which is meaningful to those to whom the message is directed. We once witnessed in East Africa one method of dealing with the situation—a method which is unfortunately not yet a thing of the past. A Scandinavian Pentecostal missionary took us to visit the African quarter. This was in 1955! Turbanned Africans gathered round the Christian missionary, who thereupon started what was supposed to be a religious dialogue. "Who was the greater, the Lord Isa (Jesus) or Muhammad?" The answer came without hesitation: "Muhammad." "No, you have not understood. Who was the greater, Isa or Muhammad?" Answer: "Muhammad." "No, you have not understood. . . ." And so on. That there was *someone* there who had not understood was all too obvious. The conversation, the dialogue, which must be opened will have to be rather more subtle than that. The preaching of the Gospel by means of humble, self-effacing service creates contact and bears its fruit. True, the usual way is to meet the legalism of the Quran with Christian moralism, but that particular way is not quite as effective as some people imagine. Sacramental Christianity, on the other hand, is able to express a more radical theocentricity than any Muslim legalism, particularly when combined with the message of the boundless forgiveness which is in Christ. The encounter with Islam gives the Christian preacher a new joy in forgiveness, and the contrast with Muslim legalism exhibits the breadth and depth and height of the Gospel.

This particular situation has consequences for the missionaries concerned. Missionaries to Islam in Africa might ideally comprise a Third Order, either of unmarried men or of men with sufficient powers of adaptation to be able to marry Africans. The Gospel must be translated into African categories and symbols. The real problem of Christianity in West Africa is its social failure, in the sense that the Church has not always succeeded in forming societies which the African is able to recognize as his own. This problem is not restricted to Africa.

233

The religious history of India is something more than a record of past events. The India of today, like the India of yesterday, regards religion as an omnipresent, all-embracing reality, which none can escape—and which few have any desire to escape. India is *the* land of religion and mysticism. Everywhere the traveller hears the sound of temple bells; missionary or tourist, he cannot avoid seeing that the people of India take their worship very seriously indeed. Should he want to cash some of his travellers' cheques, he finds that he must wait until after 10.30 a.m., until the bank-clerk has completed his *puja*. First the clerk goes to the temple, where he takes his daily bath of purification in the temple pool (which often looks like no more than a slimy mud-hole); then he enters the temple itself, and marks his forehead with three lines of Siva's holy ashes. The traveller by train shares a sleeping-compartment with five others, Indian businessmen and civil servants. Early in the morning he is awakened by the sound of these gentlemen, each on his bunk, humming or singing his *puja*, with words from the Vedas. The rector of a world-famous university grants the visitor an interview. He is a professor of medicine and India's representative on the World Health Organization. He wears Western clothes and has had a Western education; but he bears the mark of Vishnu on his forehead.

What, then, is Hinduism? The first thing to be said is that Hinduism resists definition; so much so, that some have even claimed that "there is no such thing as Hinduism". It has so many facets; so many levels; so many tendencies—all of which have their given place in its luxuriant and incredibly complex system of ideas and visions, myths and rites.

There are nevertheless certain fixed points with the help of which the outsider can find his way through the Hindu jungle. One such is *the caste system*: the social pattern in which the Indian lives. Religion in India is not a matter for the private individual; nor for the people as a whole; but for the caste to which the individual belongs. In fact a man who is a member of a caste is a Hindu; a man who is not born into a caste is not, nor can he become, a Hindu. Indians as a rule are more conscious of their caste than of their own individuality. Ask a conservative Hindu his name and he will give the name of his caste first of all; not until the second or third complementary question will he give his own name. The life of the Hindu is bound up with that of his caste, and he lives within its appointed limits. Every caste has its own *karma*, the immutable consequence of the lives of its members in their previous incarnations. To the Hindu it is inconceivable that a person should change caste; and the loss of caste—a necessary consequence of conversion to Christianity—is the equivalent of social death, and must be accompanied by funerary rites.

There are some three thousand castes all told. But alongside and beneath these are those groups which are now officially called "the Scheduled Classes"—the outcastes, now numbering at least 60 millions. These in turn are divided up into vast numbers of sub-groups or "castes", separated from one another by rigid boundaries. Gandhi, himself a high-caste Hindu, modified the caste system in that he gave the outcastes the honorific name of *Harijan*— "the sons of God". In so doing he was bringing to completion an initiative taken by the Christian mission ever since the days of Carey and Duff. India's new constitution of 1950 officially abolished caste for political and social purposes. This is nothing short of a revolution in India's history, but still has to be implemented, at least in the country districts.

A bitter struggle against the Brahmin-controlled caste system and its Indian "colour bar" (the Sanskrit word for caste is *varna*, meaning "colour") has been waged in South India in recent years by the Dravidian movement. South India's population of 60 million is made up of four Dravi-

235

dian races: the Telegu, the Tamil, the Malayalam and the Kanarese (Kannada) peoples. In 1925 there was formed, under the leadership of a former Congress politician, Ramaswamy Naicker, a Dravidian self-respect movement; in 1944 this became the "Dravidian Society" (*Dravida Kazhagam*). A powerful splinter group, led by Annadurai, has great and growing influence. Although the ultimate objective of the movement is the creation of an independent South Indian "Dravidastan", the immediate struggle is with the Brahmins and their caste system: its mottoes are "caste is past" and "one God, one caste". Ideologically it is anti-Hindu and secular, and has as its popular heroes a number of Western "freedom fighters", notably Martin Luther, who is regarded as having fought against sacerdotalism, dogmatic tyranny and the imposition of a foreign language—which in the South Indian situation means the Brahmins, Hinduism and Sanskrit!

Classical Hinduism is monistic, that is to say that it identifies the essence of man and the essence of the divine, *ātman* and *brahman*. Its fundamental Sanskrit term is *advaita* (not-two). There can therefore be no "I-thou relationship" in this form of Hinduism. Insight into the true nature of reality can be gained in a number of ways: knowledge, works and devotion (*bhakti*) among them. All things have their place in the eternally turning wheel of existence. Life, death and all things are ruled by *samsara* and *karma*: the course and the law, the principle of perpetual renewal and the law of exact and merciless retribution. But such knowledge is beyond the reach of the common people. Salvation, *moksha* (which is release from the changes and chances of existence), is attained only by the very few, those who have come to realize the illusion (*māyā*) of the manifold forms of the phenomenal world, and who can therefore reach *sat chit ānanda*, truth, wisdom and love.

The essence of Hinduism is well symbolized by the wheel: which is both a symbol of contact with the greatness of India's past—as in the wheel of Asoka in the flag of the new India—and a symbol of the Hindu interpretation of the nature and destiny of man.

Hinduism is said to have no less than 330 million gods and goddesses. This very plurality of divine images gives us a glimpse of the power of Hinduism. Some of them are more popular than others: Ganesh, with his elephant trunk, and the elegant peacock-form of Subramanyam are the sons of Siva. These images are often stone or wooden statues, or they may be represented by mighty horses, which the gods ride by night. Images are generally placed at the spot on which the god in question is believed to have shown himself, giving a *darshan* (theophany) to men. But this does not mean that each and every idol is able to serve as a vehicle of deity: not until the Brahmin priest has consecrated the image is it holy and an object of worship. In principle the Hindu worships, not the image itself, but the dynamic presence of the deity *in* the image. Once consecrated, it is the duty of the Brahmin priest to take care of the image—and hence the deity in the image—as though it were a living being. It is awakened in the morning, washed, fed and exercised on the occasion of the regular processions through the town. But should an outcaste approach the statue, its deity abandons it, and it reverts to its original nature, mere wood or stone. When in 1939 Gandhi succeeded in having the Madura temple opened to outcastes, one of the leading Indian newspapers, *The Madras Mail*, carried an article entitled, "The deity has left the temple."

The *apologia* of modern India for idols is twofold. First it is pointed out, correctly, that the figures themselves are often of considerable archaeological and artistic interest. But the leaders of the Hindu renaissance since Ramakrishna and Vivekananda have tended rather to explain them in psychological terms, saying that we think in images, and that we therefore need images on which to focus our religious aspirations. According to Vivekananda there are however two categories of men who have no need of images: the perfect man, the *Mahatma*, and "the human animal, i.e. the kind of person who has never had a religious thought".

The nineteenth century saw the rise of a number of important reform movements within Hinduism, the three most notable of which were the Brahma (or Brahmo) Samaj, the Arya Samaj and the Ramakrishna Mission. The dominant personality of this renascent Hinduism was undoubtedly the leader of the Ramakrishna Mission, Swami Vivekananda (d. 1902). It was largely due to Vivekananda, following upon his appearance at the World's Parliament of Religions in Chicago (1893), that Hinduism became conscious of its universal calling and its missionary possibilities, not least in the West. His basic tenets were: (i) That all religions are true and good, and that there is therefore no reason why any man should change his religion. (ii) That God reveals Himself everywhere, in all men, in all gods, and supremely in a number of *avatars* (incarnations); the latter concept has been immeasurably important for Indian syncretism generally. It was of course easy on this view to incorporate Jesuswami into the system. (iii) That the Hindu people are a spiritual people, while the civilizations of the West are materialistic. Hinduism is the most spiritual of all religions. Although it is no part of our purpose to trace the history of the Ramakrishna Mission we may point out that its record of social work among the sick, the poor and refugees is most impressive.

A fascinating figure is Sri Aurobindo Ghose (1872–1950), the militant nationalist journalist whose experiences in prison led him to renounce the world, and led to his becoming one of India's greatest speculative philosophers. Sri Aurobindo had a large part to play in the development of Neo-Hindu universalism. The basis of his thought was Vedic, and unlike Gandhi and Tagore, he was little attracted by the figure of Jesus. But he drew on Western thought (he was educated in England) for the evolutionary theory on which he built his teaching that man was capable of developing to a higher order of consciousness—an Indian form of "superman" speculation.

Rabindranath Tagore (1861–1941) emerged from the Brahmo Samaj. A poet and artist of the first order (he was awarded the Nobel Prize for literature in 1913), he was an outstanding representative of the universalist and syncretist tolerance so characteristic of Neo-Hinduism. In 1901 he founded his school Santineketan at Bolpur, north of Calcutta in an effort to build a bridge over the chasm between East and West, and thereby to create harmony between races and religions. In 1914 he was joined by C. F. Andrews. In his own words: "No religion must dominate over the other. And if ever such a catastrophe should come upon mankind as that one single religion should flood all, then God would have to send a new Noah's Ark to save his creatures from spiritual decay." For Tagore, as for the other Indian leaders we have mentioned, Christian missions were an expression of Western imperialism and proselytism. "Christ," he claimed, "did not preach himself or a new dogma or a new doctrine; he preached only the love of Jesus." He interpreted Christ mainly in aesthetic terms.

Vivekananda and his successors wished to make Hinduism into a religion for the whole world; Mohandas Karamchand Gandhi (1869–1948) aimed at making Hinduism into a religion for the twentieth century. He was a politician and a social reformer, but the deep springs of his action was religious. He is reported as having once said, "Most men of religion are disguised politicians, but I, who wear the mask of a politician, am heart and soul a man of religion." In his generous estimate of the religions he was one with Vivekananda, claiming that all religions were equally true, though Hinduism was nearest his own heart. His philosophy may be summed up in three basic categories: *satyagraha*, soul-force or truth-force, the holding fast to the truth in the teeth of all opposition (*sat*—truth as that which actually exists); *ahimsa*, non-violence, the negative expression of love and humility, as well as political pacifism; and *brahmacharya*, continence and fasting. In his famous autobiography *The Story of my Experiments with Truth*, Gandhi relates how he first met with the Bible and Christianity during his period in South Africa (1894–1914), being particularly impressed by Tolstoy's exposition of the Sermon on the Mount. Here he found confirmation of the ideal of *ahimsa* which he claimed to have derived first of all from the *Bhagavad Gita*, but which was much strengthened by the Sermon on the Mount. These scriptures also inspired him to take the part of the untouchables, the outcastes.

Gandhi's position has been characterized as one of *imitatio Christi*—an ethical interpretation of Christ, where Tagore's interpretation was aesthetic. His example has done much to spread the ideal of "Christ-likeness" in modern Indian culture. The tradition of Jesus filled him with profound respect, though whether or not the tradition was historically true he held to be irrelevant. He regarded the content of Jesus' teaching as existing on a different level from history, embracing eternal truth, the law of vicarious suffering and innocent suffering. But he agreed with the other Hindu reformers in rejecting the Christian missions' "proselytism", since he held (regretfully) that Christianity had become corrupted by its contact with Western culture.

Sarvapalli Radhakrishnan, the present President of India and a former professor of philosophy, is the most outstanding representative of modern Hindu syncretism. He tells adherents of other religions (Buddhism, Christianity, etc.) that what they are seeking in their religion is to be found in Hinduism. We have said that the doctrine of incarnations (*avatars*) is basic to classical Hinduism, the two foremost incarnations being Rama and Krishna. From this point two developments are possible: one universalist, in which Ram is exalted as the Supreme God; another relative, in which all men are able to become *avatars*. Modern Hindus, of whom Radhakrishnan may serve as the typical example, tend to follow the latter interpretation in that they apply the *avatar* idea to the founders of all the great religions, Buddha, Muhammad and Jesus. By virtue of his central position in Indian cultural life Radhakrishnan has been enabled to exert considerable influence on the teaching and practice of religion in schools and universities; it is thanks to his influence that the teaching of religious knowledge has become compulsory at all levels. Each day begins with silent meditation and the study of the leaders of the great religions and their writings. The goal he regards as being the propagation of "universal religion" in which an all-embracing God is preached and in which all religions are harmonized to form a universal synthesis—a view characteristic both of Radhakrishnan himself and of India.

It is well known that Western missions in India have long concentrated on Christian higher education; ever since the 1830's, and Alexander Duff, the provision of an adequate educational system has been regarded as of the utmost importance. Duff's objective was, by the dissemination of Western knowledge in English, to undermine the foundations of traditional Hinduism, and by Scripture teaching to lay a new Christian foundation. Government approval of this scheme, and the making of English compulsory for entry into the civil service, meant that English-language colleges won enormous popularity. In most Christian colleges three-quarters or more of the pupils were Hindus, while it soon became necessary to engage Hindu teachers—a situation which has persisted to the present day. The teaching of the Bible, a subject on which Duff laid great emphasis, is no longer compulsory; a conscience clause gives a pupil the right to absent himself from Scripture classes, though surprisingly few have so far availed themselves of the opportunity. It is not uncommon to find Brahmin youths carrying off the first prizes in the Bible competitions which are so popular a feature of Indian school life.

The Christian Geography of India

Christianity in India is a minority religion; only 3 per cent of the population are Christians, though this is a larger percentage than that of the Sikhs, the Jains or the Buddhists in India. 35 per cent of all Christians live in the provinces of Madras and Kerala; two-thirds of all Christians—Syrian, Roman Catholic, Protestant—live south of latitude 20° S. It is generally true to say that Christianity has become a religion for Dravidians in the south and the hill-peoples (Kols, Santals and Assamites) in the north. Between 80 and 90 per cent of Indian Christians have come into the Church through mass or group movements, particularly among outcastes. Otherwise Christians are only to be found in small groups in and around the great cities, Calcutta, Bombay, Poona and Nagpur. There are great groups of Indians, notably high-caste Hindus, together with Parsees, Jains, Sikhs and Muslims, who have scarcely been reached by the Christian message. The various denominations are of course of various ages; the Syrian Christians of the far south claim their church to have been founded by the Apostle Thomas, and have a history which can be traced back to the fourth century; the Roman Catholic missions began in the sixteenth and seventeenth centuries; while Evangelical missions are of much later date. The Tamil Evangelical Lutheran Church, however, dates its beginnings back 250 years. The traveller in the province of Madras can thus come into contact with some churches of great antiquity, and others founded only a few years ago.

The Christian pattern in South India is characterized by the presence of the Syrian or Jacobite churches alongside the Roman Catholics and Evangelicals, and representatives of these churches are frequently to be found in Indian public life, as doctors, businessmen or scientists. That a man comes from a Syrian group is usually revealed by his biblical or otherwise Christian name—Chakko (Jacob), Pathappan (Peter), Cheriyen (Zechariah), Verghese or Verkey (George), Mathai or Matheu (Matthew), Thomas, etc. Together they form a unique social group who have lived, and survived, in the midst of Hindu syncretism for at least 1,600 years. They have left their mark upon their surroundings, but have themselves been influenced by the Indian national heritage and by Indian social forms.

The Syrian Christians are made up of the following groups:

1. The Malabar Jacobite Church, the original Syrian church, believed to have been founded by the Apostle Thomas; since 1958 autocephalous, historically linked with the Syrian Patriarch of Homs (Syria), and having some 800,000 members. The church suffered for fifty years from a serious schism between those who remained faithful to the Patriarch and a national party under an Indian Metropolitan. The schism was healed in 1958.

2. Syrian Uniate Church, following the Syriac-Malabar rite: 1½ million members, in seven dioceses. These represent the groups who submitted to Rome in the sixteenth century.

3. Syrian Uniate Church, following the Syriac-Malabar rite: 100,000 members, in two dioceses, founded in 1932 after collective submission to Rome under the leadership of two Jacobite prelates.

4. The Mar Thoma Church, a reformed branch of the Syrian family of churches founded in 1889 under Evangelical Anglican missionary influence: about 200,000 members; five bishops; head of the church is at present Metropolitan Johanon Mar Thoma, a former President of the World Council of Churches. This church combines Syrian tradition in the matter of liturgy and the ministry with Evangelical piety. However, schism arose on account

of the revision in 1954 of the *kurbana thaksa*, the eucharistic liturgy.

5. The Evangelical Church of St. Thomas, founded in 1961, holds itself to be more biblical than the Mar Thoma Church, and rejects the 1954 revision of the liturgy. This splinter group is at present in process of consolidation, and has very few members.

6. Anglican missionary work in Travancore, which began in 1816, led to certain groups associating themselves with Anglican dioceses, now incorporated into the Church of South India. There are a number of CSI leaders whose background is "Syrian".

Syrian dioceses were granted land on which to build Syrian communities; the Syrians were often merchants and craftsmen, specializing in carpentry and the blacksmiths' and goldsmiths' trades. Barbers, too, were frequently Christian. The Syrians' corporate sense was marked, and they came more and more to be regarded as a separate caste, the *Nasrani* or Nazarenes, a little lower than the Brahmins but on the same level as the Nayars. The problem for the Nasrani was to come to terms with their Hindu neighbours. Thus it could happen that a Christian was made caretaker of a Hindu temple, while a Hindu looked after a church. On special occasions Christians made sacrifices in the temple, but on St. George's Day the Hindus came to church, bringing with them hens as an offertory. On the great Church festivals, Christians at Palayur, like the Brahmins on the occasion of their festivals, bathed in the sea. One consequence of the Christians' caste-consciousness was that they were forbidden to come into contact with the untouchables, the outcastes; should they, despite all precautions, touch an untouchable, they were forced to take a bath of purification, not necessarily because they believed themselves to have been polluted, but because if they did not, they would be cut off from all social intercourse with their equals in the Nayar caste. The closely-defined group character of the Syrian Christians was further emphasized by their marriage rules, which were strictly observed. Here, too, there were affinities with Hindu practice; for instance, it was common to consult an astrologer (*kanniyān*) before fixing the wedding-day.

We must not leave this subject without mentioning the personal devotion and piety in which this church is so rich. The main source is the *kurbana*, the Lord's Day liturgy of the Syriac rite. This is the event on which the Church's life is focussed, the dramatic representation and proclamation of the death, resurrection and glorification of the Saviour of Mankind. It is this event which has throughout the centuries preserved the Syrian group as a true fellowship of Christians, despite the fact that they understood but little of the prayers and readings, that sermons were seldom preached, and that the Bible was a closed book. The rich biblical content and the pure poetry of expression of the Syriac liturgy are able to convey a sense of the mystery and joy of worship even in the midst of temporal poverty; some of its features have been incorporated into the famous liturgy of the Church of South India.

The Roman Catholic Church's main centres in India are, apart from the hill-tribes of Chhota Nagpur and elsewhere, Bombay and Goa, and of course South India. Indianization of the church has been the great concern of the twentieth century. The first Indian bishop was consecrated in 1923 to exercise oversight over the diocese of Tuticorin, within which are to be found the fisher population (Paravas) who have been Roman Catholic since the days of Francis Xavier. Today practically all South Indian dioceses have Indian bishops, under whom European missionaries serve. Here the organization of the church gives the impression of being wholly Indian. Such is however far from being the case in Central and North India. Taking the country as a whole, more than thirty of the Indian church's seventy or so archbishops and bishops are Indians.

In 1952 Archbishop Gracias of Bombay was elected to the college of cardinals. A great impression is made by the church's liturgy, the rhythm of the church's year and the colourful processions through the crowded Indian streets. Considerable influence is also exercised by the Roman Catholic Church's educational system. Roman bishops and educationalists were able to play a prominent part in the educational crisis which arose in the 1950's in Kerala, during that State's short period of communist rule.

The focus of India's Evangelical churches is also in the South. It is there that the greatest numerical accessions have taken place. At the same time, it must not be forgotten that a missionary contribution of the highest quality has been made in North India, beginning with William Carey and Alexander Duff and continuing down to the present day. The characteristic emphasis in the North has been on missionary higher education, and though there have been no spectacular results numerically, there can be no question of the important cultural contribution made by the missions in this area. The Anglican cathedrals of North India, built while the British Empire was at its zenith, no longer play the same part in Indian religious life since independence. There are fewer and fewer Britons in India, and Anglican services according to the Book of Common Prayer now attract no more than a handful of worshippers. These cathedrals and churches have in some cases degenerated into "national monuments", the fabric of which is cared for by the Indian Government.

But this is not the whole of the picture. Missions and churches in North India have made an invaluable contribution in many fields, notably the field of literature (though here the peak was reached between the wars) and theological education. Among the most prominent of the North Indian theological colleges are Serampore, north of Calcutta, and the Methodist Church's Jubbulpore; while in South India there is the Union Theological College in Bangalore (indisputably the finest on the subcontinent), of which the great Danish missionary, L. P. Larsen, was once Principal. There is also a Lutheran theological college, Gurukul, in Madras. The Evangelical churches of India now have some 10,000 ministers and pastors; the Roman Catholic Church is said to have more than 3,000 Indian priests (while 1,000 Indian men and 16,300 Indian women are at present members of religious orders).

The Indian National Christian Council was founded in 1923, and has its centre in Nagpur; it has been responsible for a number of far-sighted moves, particularly in the field of ecumenical relations. The question of union has occupied the minds of the Evangelical churches of India since the early 1920's, not without tangible result. The impression is inescapable, that the pattern of the Indian churches is being reshaped into constellations, whether these take the form of denominational federations or united regional churches with episcopal constitution.

In India, as elsewhere, attempts were made to carry out the Protestant "three-self" programme—of a self-governing, self-supporting and self-propagating church—formulated in the mid-nineteenth century by the Anglican, Henry Venn, and the American Congregationalist, Rufus Anderson. Both of these men were able to build on the experience of their respective missions in South India when developing their programme; and it was not long before Protestant missions as a whole came to concentrate on the building of autonomous Indian churches.

An indication of what might be expected was given in 1912, when V. S. Azariah was consecrated Bishop of Dornakal, north of Madras: it was clear that Indians had to be admitted into the leadership of the Church, though some felt that the scheme was fraught with danger. Bishop Henry Whitehead of Madras calmed the more nervous of his colleagues by pointing out that Dornakal was only a small area, and that should Azariah fail, he would have done no great damage! But the small area grew into one of India's largest dioceses.

In 1912–13 John R. Mott paid his third visit to India, and advocated energetically the idea of independent Indian churches which should be able to co-operate within an Indian national council. The process was accelerated after the First World War. The Lutheran Gossner Church in Chhota Nagpur and the Lutheran Tamil Church became autonomous in 1919, and their development set a pattern for other churches to follow. Two years later, in 1921, the Tamil Church became episcopal—its leader taking the official title "Bishop of Tranquebar"—as a result of Swedish influence. Two stages can be discerned in the Anglican development: first the integration of the missionary societies into dioceses, "diocesanization"; and secondly, in 1927, the formation of an ecclesiastical province, independent in relation to Canterbury, and covering India, Burma, Ceylon and (after 1947) Pakistan.

Anglican missionary work in India has for the most part been shared between the two great societies, the Evangelical CMS and the Anglo-Catholic SPG. Originally their work was directed, despite the establishment of Anglican dioceses, from London. Diocesan integration in the 1920's brought the two traditions together under bishops and cathedral chapters, and at the same time incorporated the dioceses into the new Province of India, the constitution of which was passed in 1930; the Bishop of Calcutta is now Archbishop and Metropolitan. In 1950 the Province received its first Indian Archbishop, A. N. Mukerjee, who was succeeded in 1962 by a Ceylonese, Lakdasa de Mel.

Episcopal and non-episcopal Methodists; Presbyterians; Baptists—all were faced with substantially the same kind of problem: how to integrate Western mission into the Indian Church, and how to ensure that the administration of the church was made the responsibility of Indians?

248

From the point of view of organization, the development of the Tamil Evangelical Lutheran Church was typical of what was happening in most Indian Evangelical churches at this time. We shall therefore pause to consider this in a little more detail.

The vital period was one of thirty years, from 1920 to 1950. It began with a view of mission and church which regarded the two as separate entities, continued with an attempt to determine the relation between them, and culminated in 1950 in the union of church and mission.

A document from 1921 laid down a twofold scheme: on the one hand the mission, with a "missionary council" on the field; on the other the Indian "daughter church" under a church council. The bishop, appointed from Uppsala after consultation with the missionary authorities in Leipzig, was chairman of both. Further, there was a "joint council", the task of which was to deal with questions of concern to both parties. This arrangement led in practice to a dualism between mission and church; tensions were unavoidable, both here and in similar situations in India. The church's own leaders were energetic in their demands for a "merger" of the mission and the church—tones echoed by other Indian churches. In 1944 the National Christian Council issued a statement which had the effect of accelerating the process, not least in the Tamil Church.

By 1950 it was generally agreed that the time had arrived for positive measures. Accordingly, the whole of the work was placed under the jurisdiction of the bishop (since 1956 an Indian, Rajah B. Manikam) and his chapter. In the chapter laymen, and especially two Indian doctors, play a prominent role. The missionaries are now directly responsible to the church, and their work is mapped out by the church. The property of the mission (with the exception of the missionaries' own residences) has been transferred to the church. The missionary council has been abolished as an instrument of administration: instead a

249

missionary has been appointed "field secretary"; his responsibility is to deal with questions concerning the Western missionaries' stationing, accommodation, furlough and the like. The missionaries work "in, with and under", the Tamil Church (the expression, taken from Luther, was coined by Bishop Rajah B. Manikam). At the same time the Swedish and German committees fulfil their missionary obligation by making annual grants and by sending out missionaries at the request of, and in answer to, the call of the church.

The Church of Sweden Mission Board no longer has the automatic right to appoint the bishop of the Tamil Church. It is true that the 1950 document states that the actual appointment is made from Sweden, after due consultation with Leipzig; but this takes place "on the request of the Tamil Church" and "until further notice".

The Tamil Church has a special "pioneer committee" responsible for the extension of work in the mass movement areas. This committee has a somewhat more flexible relation to the chapter than the mission's original "institutions"—hospitals, colleges and the like—which are entirely controlled by the church.

The Tamil Evangelical Lutheran Church, with its 60,600 baptized members (at the end of 1962), is a relatively small body; nevertheless, most of the points we have touched upon in this sketch are to be found elsewhere in India, and not only in India, in the history of the past sixty or so years. Of particular significance is the changing status of the missionary, illustrating what we have earlier said on the subject of the relationship between mission, missionaries and church.[1]

The Castes and the Church

Very few Indian Christians come from Brahmin families. This is not for want of energetic evangelistic effort from the side of the missions. For instance, ever since Robert de

[1] Above, pp. 40–44.

Nobili's day the Roman Catholic Church has been particularly concerned to try and win individuals from this group. The methods used, however, led to the Roman Church adopting an attitude to caste rather different from that of other churches. In 1923, when the Indian Jesuit, T. Roche, a member of the Parava caste, was appointed bishop, Catholics of the Nadar caste protested to Rome. In 1945, the ordination of the first outcaste priest in Travancore led to disturbances. But church leaders have done their utmost to overcome these difficulties, and the Roman Catholic Church in the new India has at last come to terms—in theory and very largely in practice—with its traditional problem.

The Roman Catholic attitude to caste, unlike the Evangelical attitude, has always been generous. A Jesuit missionary, H. Staffner, has written expressing the wish that the Church should teach that it is not necessary to repudiate caste on becoming a Catholic. With goodwill it is possible to interpret the practical demands of Hinduism in purely social terms, and thus to ignore their religious aspect: the daily ritual bath; endogamy (marriage only within the caste); the prohibition of beef and pork; and certain rites of initiation and remembrance (*upanayana* and *śraddha*). Experience has shown that Hindus recognize those Catholics who perform these ceremonies, and retain their caste, thereby remaining within Hinduism. The Hindu *dharma* and the Catholic faith should not be regarded as mutually exclusive. The *dharma*, claims Staffner, is a high ethical ideal, which the Catholic cannot simply dismiss; he ought rather to accept "the good in Hinduism".

We have mentioned Christian higher education as a means of reaching Hindus of the highest castes with the Gospel. The number of Brahmin converts has never been large, though individual converts have often been of outstanding quality, intellectually and spiritually. Prominent Christian educationalists of the past included Duff in Calcutta, John Wilson in Bombay, Robert Noble in Masulipatam and William Miller in Madras, while a twentieth-century educationalist whose influence has been extensive was the Scotsman, A. G. Hogg (d. 1954), Principal of Madras Christian College to 1938.

One of the best-known Brahmin converts in the history of Protestant missions was Theophilus Subramaniam. He first received a strict traditional education , after which he was given Western education at a Methodist college. The faith, the example and the teaching of the missionaries made a lasting impression upon him; the missionaries gave him his first copy of the New Testament, and the book did even more than the men to capture his mind and heart. But he had determined to be a *sannyasi*, a holy man, and so went to live with a *rishi*, a hermit, in his cave. One day he heard a voice calling, "Follow me!" He ran out of the cave, and across the hills, looking for the one who had called him, and whose voice he could still hear. He heard other voices, and saw visions, and finally was convinced that he was called to follow Jesus Christ. He wrote of one of his visions that the rising sun in all its glory could not compare with the wonderful light that filled his room. In the vision he saw a group of Brahmins and a group of outcastes; then he saw a hand, shining like fire. The hand placed him among the *pisachas*, the wretched outcastes. It rested upon his head and once more the voice said, "Follow me!" He went to a Methodist Church and told them about his vision and his wish to learn more about Christianity. When he told his family about his plans, he was subjected to torture from his closest relatives, and his mother died of sorrow over her son's apostasy. After his baptism they made a "corpse" of reeds, representing the apostate; the funeral ceremonies went on for ten days, Theophilus being once and for all excluded from his family, his caste and his religion. But he became a fine minister in his own country and in South Africa.

This story is fairly typical of the high-caste Hindu in

relation to Christianity. A prominent Indian Anglican, E. Sambayya, has pointed out that no one ever becomes a Christian in India for any other reason than that Christ exercises an irresistible attraction for him. Everything— common sense, feelings, public opinion, Indian philosophy —says that this is *not* the way to follow. Subramaniam's visions are, of course, the expression of his own particular form of piety, but can be paralleled in other conversions in India; similarly his photisms and "voices" agree—often in remarkable detail—with the experience of African Christian "prophets".

Often the decisive impulse which convinces the high-caste Hindu comes from Christian work among the poor: service becomes witness. Such was the case which Christopher Mayhew records in his book *Men Seeking God*.

An Indian pastor speaks of his father in these words:

My father came from the Brahmin Sect. And he was one of those very orthodox types of Brahmin. He was very hostile to the Christian missionaries. He couldn't stand them going about preaching the Gospel. That worried him very much. . . . Then once, when there was an epidemic of cholera in the city, and hundreds of our poor, sweeper-class community were dying, he was greatly struck by the service which the two church missionaries at Bankura—Mr. and Mrs. Hanbury-Smith they were—rendered to these untouchable sweepers. My father used to persecute them, along with their Indian workers. But he was struck by their service, and that has drawn him in, and at last made him a servant of Christ. I am a born Christian, and it has become so real to me. And it has been so real in my work—that overflowing love that my father saw and which I see, and which I want to practise, which is compelling me in this work; and it is so in the work itself. Everybody finds this thing in it. . . .

I have never seen God—I can't say ever I have felt a time when I can say I have seen God, or have got His touch; but it is service—I mean, look at the leprosy asylum you have

253

seen [this was in the course of an interview], those poor patients. What I do for them is something that I feel God calling me to do. When I pick up a patient, even with big maggots all over his body, and take him in my car, and lift him, and take him right into the hospital for treatment, this is something I feel God has asked me to do.[1]

Another who wore the sacred thread was Narayan Waman Tilak, who was early recognized as one of Hinduism's leading poets and intellectuals, but who became less popular among the high-caste Hindus when he tried to improve the conditions of outcaste labourers. He studied English literature, and found his way to the Bible, which he read with avidity, being particularly impressed by the Sermon on the Mount. He also read the lives of Indian Christians, but was at first opposed to the idea of becoming a Christian. Instead he wanted to found his own rationalistic religion, in which faith in the Creator should replace the doctrine of transmigration. His personal religion was based on the complementary ideas of the Fatherhood of God and the brotherhood of man. In 1893 Tilak was travelling by train, and shared a compartment with a European, who, when he heard of Tilak's new religion, prophesied that he would be a Christian within two years. Tilak wrote, "I felt his prophecy was nothing short of lunacy." In the following year, November 1894, three nights running he heard a voice which said to him in his sleep, "Follow me. Do not be afraid." Again in Tilak's own words:

"Then could I restrain myself no more; though there were so many difficulties in the way of my baptism, I was resolved to make it known at once to the world that I was a Christian, and thereupon requested Dr. J. E. Abbott of the American Board of Foreign Missions to publish this fact. He announced it in the *Dnyanodaya*, Indian Christian magazine, and my greatest desire was fulfilled. May God be praised, I was baptized on 10 February, 1895, in Bom-

[1] Christopher Mayhew, *Men Seeking God* (London 1955), p. 81 f.

bay in the American Mission Church. The prophecy made two years earlier in the train by that stranger had come true."[1]

N. W. Tilak now has his own place in the church history of India as the one who gave the church songs of Christ in the Marathi language, and as a Christian patriot. There has probably been no convert in less danger of Westernization than Tilak.

The great barrier for the high-caste Indian was a water-barrier: the rite of baptism. But was baptism really necessary? Syncretistic Hinduism, which was able without difficulty to assimilate the figure of Christ, devotion to Jesus, the Sermon on the Mount, and its own interpretation of the Gospel of John, made it possible to have such a tolerant view of "the religion of Jesus" that there was no difficulty in remaining an anonymous disciple. Friso Melzer, a German authority on India's church, tells of the man who went down to the river at dawn one day and baptized himself. No one had seen him; but that did not matter, since religion was purely a matter between himself and God. However, the situation at length became impossible; he was forced to make a real decision and be baptized publicly according to the rites of the Church.

But this is not to say that anonymous Christianity is not a power in India. It is to be seen even among the leaders of the nation, but is always disposed to deny the need for conversion and church membership. It has had impressive historical manifestations: for instance in the Brahmo Samaj and its great nineteenth-century leader, Keshub Chunder Sen. It is to be seen in the common present-day Indian assertion that Christ was an Asian. It influences those seekers who find temporary refuge in a Christian *ashram*, and who then come into close contact with Christian social workers. This, however, is a frontier territory, a

[1] L. Tilak, *From Brahma to Christ* (World Christian Books No. 9, 1956), p. 39.

watershed on which the stream can easily flow in the other direction, when the Western missionary, gripped by Hinduism, or Buddhism, leaves Christianity. We have a number of examples: W. Hauer, who began as a Basel missionary, then became a "German Christian" (in the 30's), and finally devoted himself to Yoga; K. J. Saunders of the CMS and the YMCA who was deeply influenced by Buddhism, without, however, becoming a Buddhist; and Verrier Elwin, an Anglo-Catholic member of the Christo Seva Sangha in Poona, and a colleague of the well-known Anglican missionary, Jack Winslow, who became, like C. F. Andrews, a disciple of Gandhi. Unlike Andrews, Elwin turned from Christianity to the preaching of Hindu vitalism.

But for many an Indian, baptism was the gateway to a new life. The taking of a new name meant the making of a decision to follow Christ. The history of baptismal names in the Indian Church provides a most interesting chapter, as we have already seen in the case of the Syrian tradition. Biblical and European names, of course, occur very frequently, but the Indian names which the Christian chooses may reveal an important tendency. Jesudasen means "the servant of Jesus" (an Indian doctor, leader of the famous Tirupputtur Ashram); Jesumithram, "the friend of Jesus"; Christianatham, "Christian teacher"; Devadas, Devanandan, Devanesan, "the servant of God, the love of God, the lover of God".

Unlike the situation of the Church among the higher castes, the Church is often able to muster large numbers of low-caste Indians. Bishop J. W. Pickett, the author of the standard work on mass movement in India (*Christian Mass Movements in India*, 1933), estimates that some 85 per cent of the total membership of the Evangelical churches in India has come into the Church by this means; mass movements have, as is well known, led to rapid growth in the Church in many areas. The membership of the American Methodist Episcopal Church in the Punjab increased in thirty years from a mere handful to 350,000. Similar results were to be seen in Lutheran and Anglican missions among the Telegu people of Andhra (the province north of Madras). The American Baptist mission in Andhra, whose centre is at Ongole, after forty years of what appeared to be utterly fruitless work, which had resulted in only a minute number of baptisms, experienced a break-through in 1878. This church has now grown to a membership of almost 300,000. One of their leading missionaries, John Clough, laid down three simple commandments for Christians of the outcaste Madia group: the keeping of the Sabbath; the prohibition of Christian participation in heathen ceremonies; and the prohibition of eating the flesh of animals which had died a natural death. His rules were in fact such as to threaten the whole structure of Madiga society; nevertheless a mass movement took place, resulting in the great Telegu Baptist churches. (An even larger Baptist mass movement took place in Assam, which now numbers three-quarters of a million members.) The Madigas became Baptists; their traditional enemies in the State of Hyderabad, the Malas, also an outcaste group, became Anglicans, Lutherans or Wesleyans. Church members in Bishop Azariah's famous Anglican-CSI diocese of Dornakal are for the most part Malas.

The Church of Sweden mission encountered the movement in the district of Coimbatore in south-west India. At Dharapuram a Methodist mass movement took place among the Adi-Dravidas (the "original" Dravidians); members of the same racial group in the Coimbatore district came during the 1920's into contact with these recent converts, partly by way of marriage. There was a vague rumour going around in the outcastes' villages that something unusual was happening: that there was a new religion being preached, the religion of a god they called Jesuswami. There were already a number of Christian families in three Adi-Dravida villages, when an Indian pastor, the Rev. G. Stephen (formerly a member of a higher caste) came to Karunagarapuri in 1934. Stephen invited the entire population of these villages to colourful Christian festivals, at Christmas and at Easter; his first attempt drew 350 participants, but there were soon five times as many. A Christian procession, with Indian music and Indian songs, passed through the village; Dravida songs were sung, and pupils in the newly-founded schools took part in a Bible competition. Adi-Dravida people in village after village came expressing their wish to receive Christian teaching, and were baptized. The entire ethnic group in the district of Palladan is now Christian. Twenty years later a similar movement took place among the lowest of all outcaste groups, the Madaris, the leather-workers, the most despised of all, the people whom all castes, and even other outcastes, regarded as polluted. (The cow is of course a holy animal, and anyone who demeans himself so far as to prepare the hide of a dead cow is especially polluted.)

We have already pointed out that the social structure of low-caste groups of South India closely resembles that of the "animistic" tribes; at the same time we stressed that the mass movements could be dealt with to the greatest advantage in the context of Hindu influence. We must now pause to consider the nature of the change which takes place when these low-caste groups join the Church.

1. The Western observer's first questions when faced with the fact of the mass movements are, "Why did they become Christian? How did they come to become converted? Are they Christians at all?" Pickett's answer is realistic: "When a Hindu comes to Christ, he comes as a Hindu, not as a Christian." And the correctness of this observation, though all too seldom recognized, becomes perfectly clear after a little thought. The starting-point is simply human misery. One day an individual, or several individuals, may come to realize that there is something

more to life than a perpetual dull ache, and they begin to seek that which they had hoped that Mariamman or some other god might have given them, but did not. They know of people in another village who have begun to worship Jesuswami. "Why should we not follow them?" they ask one another on their way home from the rice-fields. One of the village girls has just contracted marriage with a Madari in a nearby Christian village, and this brings the whole question of the people's religion up once more. They wonder whether the Church might not help them to get a little patch of land, or even some food. They know of a village in which the ministers of this Jesuswami have taught new methods of tanning. They say that the Church takes care of the sick, and that children are taught things that only a few high-caste people know, like reading, writing and arithmetic. Imagine—that they care about the Madaris: for everyone else hates us. Who is this Jesuswami, who seems to have started it all?

The minister invites them to attend a service in his church. After a few visits, they want to show that their decision is a serious one, and so each man signs with his thumb-print a written declaration that he and his family wish to become Christians, and that they are taking this step together, after serious consideration and of their own free will. They leave a small gift, one rupee per family, as a sign that the village knows what it is doing. Women and children come too: the entire village comes, and a service is held for the village as a whole. It is necessary that the villagers should come together, for should some of the families in the village be left out, these might well be used by the Hindus as propaganda material for a return to Hinduism, should there be an epidemic or some similar crisis. The village teacher teaches them all a simple prayer, Jesuswami's own prayer.

2. Preparation for baptism takes from four months to a year. Young people learn the four main parts of the catechism, while old people may have to be content with

stumbling through the Lord's Prayer. The day of baptism is a day of rejoicing, a festival for the whole village. The catechumens' relations from nearby villages are invited; the village chapel is decorated. Family after family—man, wife and children—are called to the font, where water is poured on their heads. "I baptize thee in the name of the Father, and of the Son, and of the Holy Ghost." The minister makes the sign of the cross on each forehead and breast.

Bishop Azariah of Dornakal elaborated the baptismal ritual. After the act has taken place, the newly-baptized Christian, whether old or young, places his hand on his head and says, "Woe is me if I do not preach the Gospel." (After 1 Cor. 9: 16.) The rite is now turned outwards; its function and its meaning are now evangelistic. The Church of the despised now bears its witness before the rich, the proud and the mighty of the high castes. Sometimes these have been profoundly influenced by what they have seen of the power of the Gospel to change men's lives. Individual *sudras* in the Telegu area and landowners in the Tamil district have followed the path pointed out to them by men and women who were once the dregs of Indian society.

3. Few of the baptized reach confirmation. Nevertheless, solid confirmation classes, co-ordinated as far as possible with the schools, mean a vast improvement in the whole existence of the congregation. In these classes Christian knowledge is extended so as to cover the fifth part of the catechism, and instruction is given in the meaning of the Eucharist and of the liturgy as a whole.

Communion is not something which takes place once and once only. The Eucharist is celebrated at least once a month. Participation in the holy mysteries has an observable effect, both on the individual and on the village as a whole. In Vicedom's words, "The Sacrament meets man in his psycho-somatic totality." It lifts the group to a new quality of life, expressed in a new sense of order and decency at home. Compare two Madari villages, one of which has not yet been reached by the message of the Gospel, while the other has been influenced by five years of church fellowship around the Word and the Sacraments. The difference is striking: it is to be seen in men's faces, and in their conduct towards others who are not members of their immediate group. The apologetic demeanour of the outcaste has given way to a certain degree of confidence; there is a shy assurance that things *can* be improved; and there is something very like thankfulness for the strange discovery that Jesuswami is interested in the outcastes, and wants to help them.

4. It is important that the village congregation should function as a missionary unit in the whole of its new life. Worship is especially important. The liturgy is sung to Indian settings; the hymns are frequently *kirtans*, also with their characteristic Indian tunes. The church year is emphasized as much as possible, particular emphasis being placed on Christmas and Easter. On these occasions colourful and joyful processions serve to intensify the festal atmosphere, as well as providing a tangible Christian witness to outsiders. The whole of the congregation processes through the village after the cross, from house to house and finally back again to the church. This is not to say that Indian liturgical tradition is already fixed; on the contrary, it is continually being enriched. As an example, we may mention the wedding service, at which the bridegroom places an ornament of gold or silver round the neck of the bride, after which the bridal pair turn to the altar in prayer to Christ.

5. Here the Word and the Sacrament are communicated to leather-workers. At the same time the total life of the group is improved by the initiative which mission and church have taken in such matters as improved methods of tanning and collective distribution of the finished products. In some cases this has increased the total income of the average leather-worker by three times, and it ought to

be capable of being increased still further. The school and clinic in Arulpuram would seem to have great possibilities for future development.

But the low-caste Christian village in India must not be regarded as being a protected reserve, sealed off from its Hindu surroundings. The old faith continues to exert its powers of attraction, particularly in crisis situations, such as epidemics and prolonged periods of drought. The Madaris are economically dependent on the Gond caste, and one of their minor duties is to beat the drums at Gond Hindu festivals. They have no choice; this is a social function, though of course with religious overtones. But where is the dividing line between God and Satan? The young Christian church has to make up its own mind on this and similar questions; it must itself draw the dividing line. To be a musician in a situation like this is merely part of the Madari's work. But when the members of the caste tell newly-baptized Christians that they are to be permitted as a special favour to make a mark on their foreheads with the sacred ashes, then they refuse. For this is the mark of Siva, and the Christian already bears in his body the mark of Another Lord.

The caste system came to an end—officially—in 1955 with the passing of the Temple Entry Act, but the system lives on, virtually unaltered, in the villages. Extensive financial aid goes to "Harijan uplift", that is, to help these groups—provided that they are not Christians. The Christians are considered to have received sufficient help from church and mission to enable them to set up their own schools, hospitals and industries. This may, of course, be a certain form of discrimination. And at the same time there are Hindu organizations—the Arya Samaj is one—which are doing their best to attract these outcastes who have become Christians back into the Hindu fold. Hindu propaganda has a great deal to say about their "re-incorporation", but tends to overlook the small fact that these

Harijans have always been outside the caste system, traditionally forbidden all access to Hindu religion and society.

What, then, of quality? Are these Christians of the mass movements to be regarded as "Christians in the full sense of the word"? Have they been "converted"? An English missionary leader with years of experience in Hyderabad has given a Christian answer to these ultimately unchristian questions: "Was every individual 'really converted'? I am content to leave the answering of that question to God. But I know one thing, if I should ever have to undergo the trial of my faith in Jesus and my obedience to him that some of my old friends in Hyderabad have been through, I should thank God if I could pass the test as well as they have done." The same missionary has given an example of the kind of trials involved. There was once an illiterate Indian peasant, who was to all intents and purposes the slave of the village headman, from whom he was paid for his labours with a daily portion of rice for himself and his family, and a piece of cloth or a blanket now and then. One day the headman told Daniel to bear false witness in court, where a question of property was soon to be decided. In this way, by committing perjury, he would be helping his master to retain the piece of ground in question. But Daniel refused, politely but firmly. He could not tell a lie. The Lord Jesus Christ would suffer if he did so, and Daniel would do anything in his power to prevent his Lord suffering. Daniel's courage cost him dearly. The next time he appeared, both his hands were quite useless. He had been hanged by the wrists from a beam and whipped; the damage to his tendons and muscles was permanent, and he was crippled for life.

At the same time it must be pointed out that it is by no means taken for granted in the older and better-off churches, the members of which are normally drawn from the higher castes, that so much time and money should be spent on the outcastes. Unfortunately there is often opposition to work among the outcastes from these quarters.

When an Indian becomes a member of the Church, he has to leave his caste, and is often torn away from his own surroundings. It was therefore unavoidable that many of the first Christian congregations in India consisted mainly of people whose daily bread came entirely from the mission—tenants of land belonging to the mission and workers in industries organized by the mission. Sometimes the nucleus of the congregation today consists of men and women who have lived most of their lives in the church, beginning in the missionary kindergarten, and later educated in missionary schools and colleges. A good example of this pattern is to be seen in the case of the Dohnavur Settlement, within the diocese of Tirunelveli, in the extreme south of India. An Englishwoman, Amy Carmichael, who worked in India from 1910 to 1951, together with her colleagues, saved literally hundreds of thousands of children from temple prostitution and its modern equivalent, and brought them to the beautiful surroundings of Dohnavur, where they were able to grow up in an atmosphere of evangelical piety. But it is often difficult for young people brought up at Dohnavur (they can stay there until they reach the age of 18–20) to adapt themselves once more to life in Indian society; this does not of course detract in any way from the value of Amy Carmichael's contribution.

The Western atmosphere and colour of the Christian Church is particularly noticeable in some parts of India in the matter of church architecture, worship, and the structure and administration of church affairs. But the problem is not one which is easily solved. The growth of Indian nationalism from 1905 to 1947 was a phenomenon which was not always wholly acceptable to missionaries and Indian Church leaders; the result was that many nationalists regarded the Christian Church as a tool in the hand of Western imperialism, and no fit home for the patriotic Indian. At the same time, energetic attempts

264

were made to dispel this impression, though not with any great success.

The Western stamp of Christianity is perhaps most noticeable in the difficult and yet vitally important area of theological translation and semantics; the main reason for this is perhaps to be found in the understandable and largely praiseworthy attempts to "preserve the purity of the Evangelical message". But allowing that the message *was* preserved, was it ever communicated, and is there any real reason why it has to be transmitted in Western terms and no others? Is it quite out of the question for the missionary Church to take hold of, and baptize, the true religious language of India? Is the true goal not rather to bring about a genuine encounter with Hindu philosophy and Hindu mysticism, to the end that the message of the Gospel may be communicated in its fulness—and its purity? There is no doubt that this is to take a risk, but is there really any alternative?

As far as the Roman Catholic Church is concerned, the most comprehensive and daring attempt at "accommodation" was made in the seventeenth century, by the Italian nobleman and Jesuit priest Robert de Nobili. Among South Indian Brahmins he introduced himself as a Roman *rajah* belonging to the highest class of society, and as a *sannyasi* (holy man). He wore the yellow robe of a monk, with a white cloak over his shoulders and a turban, and appeared to be an Oriental. The thread he wore over one shoulder was like the sacred thread of the Brahmin, but instead of ten knots he had only five, three of gold and two of silver, with a cross in the middle. The three knots of gold represented the Holy Trinity; the two silver knots the passion and death of the Saviour. The young *sannyasi* from the West was as ascetic in his way of life as any Indian *rishi* or any modern vegetarian. He ate only once a day, and then only rice, vegetables, milk and water. But more important, he succeeded in surrounding himself with the numinous atmosphere of the Indian *sannyasi*, keeping himself for the most part hidden in meditation in his little chapel. When he appeared in public in order to converse or teach, he sat cross-legged, while his teaching constantly drew parallels with the Bramins' own four Vedas. But de Nobili had a fifth Veda, which he called the Esur Veda, and which was in reality the Holy Bible of the Christians. Robert de Nobili's opponents in the Roman Catholic Church—and they were many—stigmatized his evangelistic methods as "the Madura scandal". Conservatives within the Church did their utmost to discredit him in the eyes of Rome, and while the retrenchment and final abolition of the Society of Jesus in the eighteenth century meant the end of de Nobili's attempt, there were others at a later date who were to try and follow in his footsteps. Dom Bede Griffith had observed ruefully that, "One feels that the Indian Church is not yet ready for an encounter at the deepest level with Hinduism." Attempts were however made.

Upadhyaya Brahmabandhav (1861–1907) attempted to fulfil de Nobili's intentions. His ideal was to baptize Hindu philosophy and make of it a stepping-stone to the Catholic faith. But he was before his time; he was condemned by the hierarchy, whose members as late as at the beginning of the twentieth century were anxious lest there should be a new Madura scandal. The boldest initiative in this present century has been taken by a Belgian Jesuit, whose theological support came from the great Jesuit theologian, Pierre Charles, in Louvain. The journal *Light from the East*, published by the Belgian Jesuits and Sanskritists Dandoy and Johanns, exercised considerable influence. Johanns also published a book, *Through Vedanta to Christ*. Another Jesuit, the Indologist Joh. Neuner, has a correspondence course on Hinduism for Roman Catholic priests and laymen.

We might also mention in this context two notable practical contributions by French Benedictine monks. L'Abbé Jules Monchanin (d. 1957) came from France to Tiruchirapalli in 1932. After seventeen years of work in isolation, he joined in 1949 with a younger French Benedictine, Henri Lesaux, to found an *ashram* on the banks of the sacred River Kavery near Tiruchirapalli. Their *ashram*, which they called Shantivanam (the dwelling of peace), consists of the simplest possible unfurnished brick huts, and a little chapel in Dravidian style. They both lived with the greatest simplicity, dressed in the sannyasi's saffron-yellow *kavi*, and always travelled barefoot. They knew that the encounter with Hinduism would take place not primarily in the realm of thought, but in the realm of contemplation. "Contemplation is the most important calling of India and the Indian Church." Their contemplation takes place in the chapel or on the banks of the river. The Hindu *sannyasi* meditates continually on the sacred symbol of reality, *aum* (or *om*); so does the Christian *sannyasi*. But the three sacred letters are for the Christian the three Persons of the Holy Trinity. The well-known Hindu formula *sat chit ananda* (truth, wisdom, love) is also taken as an expression of faith in the Father, the Son and the Holy Ghost.

A similar attempt has been made in Kurisumala in Kerala by a Belgian Cistercian. In 1959 he came to Shantivanam, where he spent a year, after which he founded his own *ashram*, in which the Syriac rite was followed. Otherwise the life and worship of the *ashram* has the same ascetic and evangelical simplicity as that which is so much a feature of Shantivanam.

The most characteristic Indian expression which is to be seen in the Evangelical churches is also the *ashram*, or retreat-house. The Tirupputtur Ashram, near Madras, is built in Dravidian style, with a church of South Indian *mandapam* type, and a *gopuram* or tower; but its most noteworthy achievement is on another level: its open-air meditation at dusk and by moonlight; simple and even ascetic forms of fellowship; devoted service among the poor and sick. Another Christian *ashram* which became important as a place in which high-caste Hindus and Christians could meet together was that founded by the Methodist missionary, E. Stanley Jones, the Sattal Ashram at the foot of the Himalaya. There are now more than twenty Evangelical *ashrams* in all.

Indian music now plays a large, and increasing, part in Christian worship in India. Exotic and unwonted Western melodies have been replaced by their vastly better Indian equivalents. We may quote an example of this kind of Indian Church music.[1]

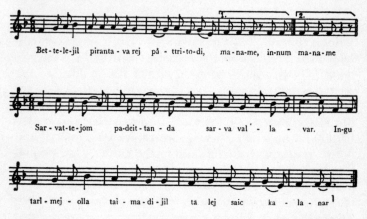

Bet-te-le-jil piranta - va rej pâ - ttri-to-di, ma-na-me, in-num ma-na-me

Sar - vat-te-jom pa-deit - tan - da sar - va val' - la - var. In-gu

tarl - mej - olla tai - ma-di-jil ta lej saic ka - la - nar [1]

In the 1930's a group of prominent Indian Christians attempted to reach an interpretation of Christianity which made the fullest possible use of the Hindu philosophical and religious background. This was particularly characteristic of the Christo Samaj, the headquarters of which were in Madras. The leaders of this group were two lawyers, P. Chenchiah and V. Chakkarai, and A. J.

[1] Translation:

> He who created the whole world
> And governs it by His law:
> Him behold we now in lowliness,
> Of a poor woman born.
> *To Him who was born in Bethlehem*
> *Give praise and worship today.*

Appasamy, Bishop of Coimbatore. Chenchiah's message was that Christianity is new creation. The birth of Jesus is the good news of the Gospel, the task of the individual Christian is in his life and work to realize anew the life of Jesus. Bishop Appasamy wrote a number of books in which he expounds the idea that the sacred traditions of Hinduism are a *praeparatio evangelica*, a school of Christ; the Hindu Scriptures cannot replace the Old Testament, but are to be regarded as a complement.[1]

Chakkarai's contribution is of particular interest in this context. In 1930 he wrote a book which he entitled *Jesus the Avatar*, and in which he interprets the incarnation of Jesus as the tenth avatar (Hinduism having nine avatars). However, he is concerned to point out that the concept must be given a new content, drawn from the New Testament: the Hindu avatars are transient, but Jesus is with us always. Hindu avatars do not return, but Christ has sent the Holy Spirit as our helper and comforter. Otherwise Chakkarai finds no difficulty in making use of the idea.

He has of course not gone unopposed. The Indian Church has in general rejected the *avatar* concept as impracticable and misleading in a Christian context. The idea was also rejected by Indian Christians like N. W. Tilak and Sadhu Sundar Singh. One exception is however the Kanarese translation of the New Testament, which is well known for the bold use it makes of Hindu terms, and which speaks of *nara-avataara*, "human avatar", in John 1:14.

The most serious objection to the use of the *avatar* idea to describe Jesus Christ is that it fails altogether to do justice to the fact of God's intervention in history through Jesus Christ, born when Augustus was Emperor and when Quirinius was governor of Syria, and who suffered under Pontius Pilate. Here we have the profound difference between Eastern and Western interpretations of Christianity

[1] Cf. A. J. Appasamy, *Temple Bells: Readings from Hindu Religious Literature* (Calcutta 1930).

The rationalism of the West has no difficulty in accepting the fact that Jesus was a figure in history, a Jewish prophet; what is difficult and disturbing is that he is said to be the Son of God, and even God Himself. Indian mysticism accepts without question the fact that Jesus was God; difficulty arises in the claim that he was a historical figure; Galilee and Calvary are not mythical lands, wrapped in the veil of *Maya*, glimpsed through a mist of unreality, but topographical facts; the cross was raised in the midst of man's everyday life. Indian philosophy has always looked upon history as an inferior form of reality: hence its instinctive opposition to biblical realism, based as it is on the assertion *ephapax* (Heb. 7), the revelation and the atonement made once and for all, at a point in time.

Here, in the missionary message, is a veritable line of demarcation, an issue in comparison with which all else is of secondary importance. It is not without significance that the Syrian Church was monophysite, having rejected the doctrine of the Council of Chalcedon (A.D. 451) that Christ was true God *and true man*. Here, too, we may discern the supreme task of the missionary church amid Indian syncretism: to proclaim in Indian terms and with the fullest possible use of Indian forms of expression, the Triune God.[1]

Mission-Church-Unity-Mission

The most noteworthy contribution which the evangelical churches in India have made to the Church Universal in recent years has been in the field of church union. It began with the realization of the weakness which attends disunity. In India, as elsewhere, an attempt to deal with the problem had been made along the lines of comity: according to this principle a certain geographical area was allocated to a particular mission, while a nearby area was left to the care of another mission. This system proved

[1] On this important theme, see Leslie Newbigin's recent study *The Significance of Trinitarian Doctrine for Today's Mission* (London, 1964).

reasonably successful in the nineteenth-century world. But the limits and weaknesses of denominationalism were clearly seen, both by the Church and by individual Christians, in the intensifying pattern of urbanization, migration and more efficient communications. Bishop V. S. Azariah, who was born in Vellalanvillai and brought up in a classical Anglican missionary area, Tirunelveli (Tinnevelly), and who was far from being unaware of the value of the Anglican Church, once remarked jokingly: "I am an Anglican, not because of theology, but because of geography." Indians from all parts of the country were agreed that radical measures were necessary in order to secure the unity of the Church, and at the same time it was recognized that the process would not be an easy one. As Father Goreh once pointed out, the difference between a cow-worshipping Hindu and a Christian is so great that theological disagreements between Christian churches make little or no impression on Indian Christians.

In South India, words gave place to action. In 1947 there was founded the Church of South India, in which for the first time episcopal and non-episcopal churches entered into full organic unity. The Churches concerned were the Anglicans, the Methodists, the Presbyterians and the Congregationalists, representing fifteen different missions in all. On its foundation the CSI had over a million members. It is necessary to say something about the presuppositions of church union in South India.

1. A measure of racial unity, the majority of South Indian Christians being Dravidians. Christians of the Nadar caste, from the Anglican Tirunelveli area, had an important part to play; Nadar Christians had migrated to different parts of South India where, adaptable as always, they had joined other South Indian Churches. These were from the very first supporters of the idea of union. The Indian Christian minority as a whole was deeply concerned that the Church should live and work as a unity, though it would be unrealistic to suppose that this was

271

unanimous: there were of course Indians who regarded their own particular denomination as the best possible, and who considered it wrong to associate with other denominations.

2. An enormous missionary task, which could not be adequately dealt with without joining forces. Millions of outcastes at the door of the church—that was a missionary commission with which a divided Church was wholly incompetent to deal.

3. The missionary situation had changed the original structure of many of the denominations, and, in South India at least, had led to a close approximation between them. The demands of the mission-field had led Anglicans to build up a synodal diocesan structure which had close affinities with Presbyterian forms of church organization. Congregationalists, who brought with them the ideal of independent churches, had discovered that a higher degree of central leadership was desirable; why should it not be episcopal?

4. The Faith and Order debate in the West had in a sense begun in the East. Bishop C. H. Brent, who was one of the foremost advocates of theological church union after Edinburgh 1910, had been bishop in the Philippines. The Faith and Order movement was in close touch with developments in South India.

5. Leading personalities in the Church embraced the cause of church union. The best theologian among them was Bishop E. J. Palmer of Bombay (in India to 1929, d. 1954). The man around whom the movement centred was Bishop Azariah of Dornakal. He had said, in words which had made a profound impression, "Unity may be theoretically a desirable ideal in Europe and America, but it is vital to the life of the Church in the mission field. The divisions of Christendom may be a source of weakness in Christian countries, but in non-Christian lands they are a sin and scandal."

Other names which must be mentioned are those of the

Congregationalists, J. J. Banninga and C. B. Firth; the Methodist, J. S. M. Hooper; and, among the younger generation, the Presbyterian, L. Newbigin, and the Anglicans, A. M. Hollis and S. C. Neill.

There began a long and difficult theological debate, which lasted for nearly thirty years, from 1919 to 1947. It was finally decided to apply a method of union which has since become classical in ecumenical discussion as "the South India method". The most difficult theological problem connected with union was that of the ministry, and here the South Indian method has four elements. (i) All members and pastors in the different uniting denominations were to be recognized as members and presbyters in the united church. (ii) In the united church ordination would be carried out only by bishops. (iii) The "thirty-year clause", in which a transition period was reckoned as lasting for one generation after the foundation of the church (thus from 1947 to 1977). The problem here was to know how to regard those Western missionaries who were sent out during this period by the non-episcopal missionary societies which had begun the missionary work from which about half the united church had derived. It was necessary to have a transition period, it was felt. The negotiators did not want to demand that these "free-church" non-episcopal missionaries should unconditionally be episcopally ordained during this period; however, after 1977 the question would come up for further consideration. (iv) A solemn pledge. Church union is a matter of spiritual reality, and therefore cannot be wholly regulated by legal formulae. A mutual pledge was given by all parties concerned to respect the consciences and distinctive traditions of the individuals and local churches concerned; there was to be no ecclesiastical interference with the worship and rights of the local churches.

The act of union was twofold. On the one hand, a declaration was made that the churches had become one, "the Church of South India", and on the other, nine new bishops were consecrated. The Church was divided into fourteen dioceses, each with its own bishop. Before 1947 there had been Anglican bishops in the area; these were placed in charge of certain dioceses of the Church as constituted in 1947. The consecrations were carried out by three of these bishops, assisted by six presbyters, whose participation was derived from the Swedish tradition of consecration, in which two or more priests from the bishop's new diocese take part in the act of consecration. The consecrating bishop was an Anglican, C. K. Jacob of Kottayam, who himself had come from a Syrian background.

Indianization in the Church of South India has proceeded apace. The South Indian liturgy is justly famed for its beauty; it is noteworthy that this liturgy includes ancient elements, drawn from the Syrian tradition. At union six of the Church's fourteen bishops were Indians; the figures are now eleven out of fifteen. The name, "the Church of South India", indicates the goal aimed at—the incorporation into one body of the whole of South Indian Christendom. Further union negotiations have taken place in recent years, particularly with the Lutherans, though these have not as yet led to any concrete result. Union negotiations are also taking place elsewhere in India, notably in North India, and Ceylon, and it will be of value to compare these briefly with the constitution of the Church of South India. The picture which is gained is at one and the same time simpler and more complex.

The Ceylonese and North Indian schemes have attracted a larger variety of traditions than was the case in South India. In the former case, there is the additional problem of uniting different episcopal traditions, the Anglican and the American Methodist; there is further the question of baptism, its theology and practice, since Baptists are taking part in the union discussions.

However, the method in which the united church is to

be inaugurated on the completion of negotiations seems simpler and more direct. This we shall call the "Ceylon method".

First, a preliminary observation. The Churches in Ceylon comprise a very small minority of the population: in a population of some 10,000,000 their total membership is little more than 1 per cent, *c.* 110,000, of whom *c.* 60,000 are Anglicans. Thus apart from the primary theological reason for church union there is the further pressing reason that the Churches, surrounded as they are by Buddhism, feel the need of mutual support and real unity. The Church of Ceylon (Lanka), which already has two Anglican bishops, will when it is united have six dioceses, and it is intended that three or four of these will be under bishops elected from non-Anglican churches (Methodists, Baptists, etc.).

The act of church union in the Ceylon method will take place as follows:

(*a*) The new bishops of the united Church will first be consecrated by at least three other bishops. (*b*) Presbyters from all the Churches of Ceylon will, by prayer and the laying-on of hands, express the fact that the office of these six bishops is an office in the whole of the united Church. It is regarded as essential that the bishop should not represent merely the separate tradition to which he has previously belonged, but should represent the totality of the united Church. (*c*) Each of the six bishops now goes to his new diocese, assembles the presbyters of the various traditions who are to serve with him, and in his turn inducts them into their offices in the new Church; the meaning here is to emphasize that the local presbyter is responsible for the whole of the Church of Christ in his area, and not merely to those who, prior to the union, were Anglicans or Baptists or Methodists. At the same time the bishop makes a declaration to the effect that this is not tantamount to denying the reality of the ordination which the presbyter in question has previously received.

In theory these three separate actions can take place on the same day, but in practice it seems likely that the ceremony by which the new bishop enters his diocese will take place some days later. This is regarded as being one point at which the Ceylon and North India method is superior to that of South India: the latter presupposes a thirty-year transition period, while the three basic elements in the former can take place at once, thereby constituting the united Church of Ceylon with the minimum of delay.

As far as baptism is concerned, the presence of a double baptismal tradition will be recognized in the Church, but in the case of infant baptism it is assumed that the act will lead to confirmation, and in the case of believers, or adult baptism, an act of blessing the child will take place. At the same time, representatives of both traditions are concerned to stress that baptism takes place once and for all, and that it may not be repeated, whichever of the two methods has been followed.

Indian Christians have furthered the cause of the wider fellowship of the churches in the East in other ways besides direct Church union. Bishop Rajah B. Manikam was during the early 1950's East Asian general secretary of both the International Missionary Council and the World Council of Churches. The first Eastern Asia Christian Conference met at Bangkok in December 1949, and took permanent form in 1957 as the East Asia Christian Conference, the leaders of which were D. T. Niles, a Methodist from Ceylon and one of the great names of the modern ecumenical movement, and a Burmese Baptist, U Kyaw Than. There was a time years ago when ecumenical relations were mainly in the hands of the missions, but now Asian Church leaders meet in their own right to discuss an Asian programme. They regard it as of the utmost importance to intensify the dialogue with the non-Christian religions; the Church, they hold, must not become a ghetto. The Church, too, must be a missionary Church. Bishop Manikam feels that the time will come when Asia can only be evangelized by Asiatic Christians; this is already true of China. The Church of South India and the Mar Thoma Church already have overseas missionaries; the Tamil Evangelical Lutheran Church has missionaries in Central India, working under the auspices of the National Missionary Society (founded in 1905). We have already discussed the question of Asian missions in Asia, a new factor which illustrates the change which has taken place in recent years in the missionary situation. It is not at all to be taken for granted that leadership must be in the hands of Western missionaries; leadership has now been vested in Asian Christians who themselves are responsible for carrying the Gospel of Christ out to a thousand million of their fellow men, the continent over.

These are just some of the ways in which Christianity has exercised its influence in India. But the witness of the Scriptures concerning what has taken place once and for all, the message of the cross as the centre and goal of history, is still India's great stumbling-block. There, it is felt that in the noble and beautiful world of religion there must be more exalted realities than the sordid facts of history, records of events that took place more than nineteen centuries ago. This does not however prevent the Indian from holding Christ Himself in deep reverence: modern Indian religiosity regards the epithet "Christlike" as the greatest possible compliment. It is not difficult for Hinduism to fit Christ into its system; and it does so gladly. What, then, is the Church to do? How far is it permissible for the Church to go in order to grasp the opportunity that is now being offered? Is there no alternative to retreat into the shelter of the church building, in which Christians may worship and organize and think and speak as they please? Should such be the case, then a genuine encounter with Hinduism is out of the question. It is, however, clear that that encounter, if and when it takes place, will be the great, the supreme test of mission; here, too, it seems that strength will be fulfilled in weakness. There is hope. Hope because of the great contribution being made by Indian leaders in the Church of today; hope because of their attempt to re-express the changeless Gospel in genuinely Indian terms. Bishop Westcott once said that the world was waiting for the supreme interpretation of the Gospel of John, and that that interpretation would come from India. Here Indian religion, philosophy and mysticism would find the fulfilment of their age-long quest. But not even India can escape the challenge of the Master: "I am the way, and the truth, and the life; no one comes to the Father, but by me."

III. EAST ASIA

The religious and social structures of East Asia is the result of long centuries of slow but sure development; but these ancient edifices have been severely shaken by a few decades of revolution, war, modern ideology and technology. Life was formerly shaped by the rich heritage of myth and ritual. In China the rites of Taoism were closely linked with the precepts of Confucian philosophy. The dialogue of heaven and earth was conceived in terms of a constant striving after harmony and balance, in the interplay of governor and governed, *yang* and *yin* (the principles of male and female, light and darkness, in the universe), between man and his neighbour. This harmony was guaranteed by the worship of the ancestors, and its centre of gravity was to be found in the family and in the fellowship of the local village community. Human existence was threatened by death, but the remembrance of the ancestors, the links within the family, and the great national myths, could be interpreted as expressing the interminable recurrence of all things living, in which death was merely the gateway to a more sublime form of existence.

The religious heritage of Japan consisted primarily of Shinto. The religious historian, Kato Genchi, in Tokyo has said "to be a Japanese and to be a Shintoist are one and the same thing". Shinto embraces the whole of the life of the individual and the community, the life of the country and the life of nature. The family and national ancestor worship—the latter being concerned with the ancestors of the divine emperor—are merely alternative expressions of the same belief. The centre of gravity of Chinese culture was the village community; in Japan all things revolved around the sacred person of the emperor. This cult, whether as State Shinto or Sect Shinto, was the ground of Japanese life, and is still to be found in the most modern contexts.

The Confucianism of China and the Shinto of Japan had something of the same structure; but the differences between them were considerable. Confucius (K'ung Fu-Tzǔ) was a rationalist, a humanist and a moralist; Shinto saw the fulness of life in the beauty of Mount Fujiyama, in cherry-blossom and freshly-fallen snow. In China, religion was a moral code, a system of ethics; in Japan, the experience of beauty, a pattern of aesthetics.

Both Confucianism in China and Shinto in Japan came to terms with Buddhism, that foreign religion which has made such an impact upon the Far East. True, Mahayana Buddhism did not have the same decisive influence on tradition and common life in the Far East as Theravada or Hinayana Buddhism had had in South-East Asia: Ceylon, Burma and Siam. But the noble doctrine of the Bodhisattvas and the message of compassion brought to China and Japan a religious power which the native religions were incapable of generating. Here the meaning of life was revealed as being bound up with *samsara*, the wheel of existence, and Japan learned the basic of doctrine of Asian monism: that of Buddha and the Self are one. The goal of life was fixed: *Satori* (enlightenment).

We have already said that the Christian Churches in the Far East are very much in the minority. Before 1949 Christians comprised rather less than 1 per cent of the

279

population of China, or 4½ millions, of which 3 millions were Roman Catholics and 1½ million Protestants; the total population of China was then 485,000,000. There are no reliable figures available for the present situation. It is, however, certain that the policy of the Communists with regard to religion has led to a decline in the number of Christians, while at the same time the population of the country is increasing by about 200,000,000 every ten years. In Japan, where the population is now at least 90,000,000, there are about 750,000 Christians, of whom 400,000 are Protestants. The minority character of Christianity in Japan becomes clearer if we remember that it is a city religion, whose strongest centres are on the south island of Kyushu and the central island of Honshu. The Church functions in country districts only with the greatest difficulty. An Anglican traveller recently described the Church in Japan as a "microscopic" Church.

In China and Japan the Churches have not resulted from mass movements or group movements, but from individual decisions. In Japan, where almost everyone can read and write, Christianity is the religion of those who look to the West for intellectual stimulation. Another gateway to the Gospel has, since 1945, been the study of the English language by young people.

China. The situation of the Chinese Christian Church must be described in two distinct periods: before and after 1949. Before the Communist revolution the evangelical minority (half a million full members) was thinly spread over the greater part of the country, but four-fifths of the total was to be found in the Yangtse Basin and in the coastal provinces. In most places they were members of small local churches, led by Western missionaries and Chinese pastors and lay leaders. Mission schools had been of great advantage to these Christian groups in public life, but here too there was a great difference between, on the one hand, American-supported churches in Nanking,

Shanghai and other cities, where young people were given the opportunity of proceeding to higher studies, and good jobs, and on the other, revivalist groups of the China Inland Mission type, with street preaching and visits to the villages. Campbell Moody, the American missionary on Taiwan, has investigated the reasons for conversion to Christianity, and has found that the people were first attracted by missionary sermons attacking idolatry. Many were converted in the hope that the new faith would bring them health, prosperity and protection against evil spirits. The ethical principles of the local church were a light in the midst of darkness: here there was no opium, no gambling, and peace at home. The light shone even more brightly from the confession of persecuted Christians: the martyrs of the Boxer rebellion did not shed their blood in vain.

Feng Yü-Hsiang—"the Christian general"—saw a woman missionary offer to give her life in exchange for the lives of condemned Chinese criminals. This he was never able to forget. He became a Christian of the warrior type, observed the strictest discipline and confessed his sins before his soldiers, with the result that thousands of his subordinates followed his example and were baptized. In him we see a characteristic Chinese combination of patriotism and Christianity. Although he was at first deeply influenced by the personality and teachings of John R. Mott, the general soon attempted instead to found a purely Chinese church, free from the control of Western missionaries.

Feng provides an example of the role of the great personalities in the later Christian development of China. Another who was frequently mentioned before 1949 as a Christian ideal, was Chiang Kai-Shek. But the nonchalance of the Soong régime, seen in the light of the scourge of pre-communist China—public and private corruption—has thrown new light on many things, not least on Marshal Chiang Kai-Shek's Christianity. A great deal of the Church history of China before 1949 is to be seen in rather a different light since the Communists' accession to power.

A son of the old established class of *literati* was T. C. Chao, an Anglican theologian and churchman. His earlier position might also be characterized as Liberal Protestant. There were only two ways, in his view, to interpret Christ to China: either as the ideal man, the moral pattern of the perfect Chinese gentleman, or as the second Person of the Holy Trinity—though this was to be understood primarily as a theoretical construction. But he was later to undergo a remarkable process of deepening, as we see from his important contribution to the Tambaram discussions on the authority of faith; here we find Chao stressing the twin themes of the initiative of God and the incarnation of Jesus Christ. After Tambaram, Chao was ordained.

A Christian of the younger generation, educated in the World's Student Christian Federation and the ecumenical movement, was K. H. T'ing, who was appointed Bishop of Nanking in 1952. Throughout the 1950's he was able to retain some measure at least of contact with the outside world—no small achievement for a Chinese church leader in the present situation. The Churches of China have, however, not succeeded in producing independent creative theologians, though the Churches have ever since the 1920's and 1930's stressed the importance of theological education and the training of the ministry.

It has been correctly pointed out that the whole structure and ethos of the Chinese Church was, with few and insignificant exceptions, Western. There were many things —hymn-books, hymn-tunes, church architecture—to bear witness to the connexion with nineteenth-century Basle and twentieth-century Los Angeles. Professor John Foster, who has himself been a missionary in China, has expressed his fears that we have succeeded only in transplanting to the Far East the worst architecture in all Western history, all the pseudo-Gothic ugliness of Victorian church architecture. This was fatal in a land like Japan, which had a noble and refined architectural tradition and taste of its own. The same applied to China, where the Christian church or chapel was usually outstanding simply because it was so Western. There were of course exceptions to this all-but-universal rule, among them Karl Ludvig Reichelt's Tao Fong Shan, designed by a Danish architect, Johannes Prip-Moller.

We may perhaps summarize the situation and vision of the pro-Communist Chinese Church by referring to a programme drawn up by Francis Wei, professor at Wuchang. Some of the questions he raises are of course obsolete by now, but its basic significance is not in any way lessened by that fact. The fundamental unit, according to Wei, is the village, a neighbourhood of between thirty and forty families, held together by common worship and Christian intercourse on the everyday level. It is not absolutely necessary that there should be a church building; it would be preferable in many cases for one of the families in the group to place a large room at the disposal of the group. The church is not merely a place in which services are held, but a place in which Christians can assemble simply in order to be together, a "family church". A congregation of this type would have a paid minister only in exceptional cases, two or three church members normally dividing responsibility among themselves. These are to be educated according to the tradition which the church has chosen as its own. Christian groups in a given area may create another church centre, the task of which is evangelization by means of service. This would be organized as a centre for large-scale education, medical care, school work: in each case in accordance with the needs of the area and the initiative of which the church group is capable within its own area. A third centre would be the responsibility and concern of the whole church: the Christian college, the centre of Christian thought. A fourth centre is the place of pilgrimage. Wei's desire was that hundreds of such pilgrim centres should be established over the whole of China, particularly in the mountain areas outside the towns. Here he wished to see churches or cathedrals built, leaders and saints buried, libraries, guest houses and museums opened. Here an experienced priest would be responsible for holding retreats and courses for church workers, for young people, and for professional groups in the nearby towns. These would serve as centres of pilgrimage and devotion on the occasion of the great Christian festivals and the feasts of the Chinese year.

This was a vision of the future, as it appeared to be in the 1940's, but it fits in remarkably well with the Church's situation in post-revolutionary China. The great emphasis it lays on fellowship and on collective responsibility is not so very different from the tones being heard in present-day China, and ought to ensure a hearing for the Church, if the Church is not to be silenced altogether. Wei's tentative proposals have the further advantage of re-expressing some of the classical attempts which the Christian mission has made to translate the Gospel into Chinese terms. We shall now look at two of the best-known of these instances, one Roman Catholic and the other Lutheran.

Two Translators: Ricci and Reichelt

"O rock, O rock, when wilt thou open?" Alexander Valignano was sent by the Society of Jesus in 1579 to the Portuguese colony of Macao, from whence he was able to look over to the mainland of China. Would China ever be open for the Christian message? His young fellow-Jesuit, the brilliant Matteo Ricci (1552–1610), struck the rock with his staff of knowledge and science, with surprising results.

It was in the capacity of astronomers, cartographers and mathematicians that Ricci and his colleagues Adam Schall and Ferdinand Verbiest were admitted to the imperial court at Peking. But Ricci's most noteworthy achievement was in his attempt to adapt the Christian message to Chinese religion and culture—in a sense the boldest attempt at adaptation which the New Age has seen. It bore fruit. The missionary methods of Ricci and his followers placed the Roman Catholic Church in an extraordinarily favourable position in seventeenth-century China. At the same time, however, criticism of Ricci's methods within the Roman Church aroused a debate which for decades occupied the minds of educated men all over Europe, which re-echoed in the diplomacy of the Catholic states, and which finally proved an effective instrument for the downfall of the Society of Jesus. Ricci was not content merely to dress up like a Confucian mandarin and present himself to China as the wise man from the West. His ambition was much greater: to reach the wise men of the East with the Christian message as he understood it. In 1615 the Jesuits succeeded in getting the Pope to agree to the use of the Chinese language by Chinese priests in the liturgy— a remarkable concession which was, however, fruitless, since there were no Chinese priests at that time (a theological college was opened in Macao, but none of its students was ever ordained). The great problem was one of translation, and in particular the translation of the name of God. Ricci used not only *T'ien Chu* (Lord of Heaven), which term had been used by Taoism, Confucianism and Buddhism, but also *Shang Ti* and *T'ien*, which were both names of the God of Heaven. He also interpreted ancestor-worship in most generous terms, making it possible for Christians to continue practising it. According to Ricci, the honour bestowed upon the ancestors and on Confucius when a person bows to their images and makes sacrifices to their memory is perfectly legitimate for a Christian, since these ceremonies were merely social, and had nothing to do with religion. Similarly, to try and abolish the rites which had been created in honour of Confucius and the ancestors would be tantamount to making an open attack upon the State and the family. Ricci's attitude was developed by his followers. This breadth of vision had the effect of placing the Jesuits in an extremely strong position at the imperial court, and hence in Chinese society generally. In 1675 the Emperor himself visited the Jesuits' church in Peking, where he took a brush and drew two ideograms, *Kiem T'ien*, "Worship heaven."

But the expected reaction was not long in materializing. What was not expected was that it should come from the Roman Catholic Church itself. Its main source was the Dominican order, which had long been opposed to the Jesuits. The most dangerous attack came from a Spaniard, J. B. Morales; it was not less dangerous for being formulated in the commonest of all Christian polemical devices, the ostensibly humble question. The question was asked in a document of seventeen points, sent to Rome in 1631. The Jesuits seemed to be using heathen names for God; was this advisable? They allowed Christians to contribute to pagan sacrifices; was this legitimate? The missionaries regarded it as being a point of Chinese decorum that the priests should not administer Extreme Unction to women; were missionaries really dispensed from administering one of the Church's sacraments? Messengers and messages crossed and recrossed sea and land. The problem for the Pope and his advisers was to estimate the so-called "level of probability" of the views represented by Ricci and his followers. The battle was long, bitter and ultimately fatal to the Jesuits. Benedict XIV's Bull *Ex quo singulari* of 1742 put a papal stop to one of the most dramatic trials of strength in the whole of the history of ideas. The disputed rites were illegitimate, and the missionaries were compelled to swear that they would faithfully and conscientiously adhere to the rules laid down by the Pope. Not for two hundred years would the Roman Catholic Church be prepared to consider the question afresh, but by that time the rock of China was in process of being closed once more.

In more recent years many of Ricci's intentions have been fulfilled by the Lazarist monk, Vincent Lebbe (d. 1940), who has done more than any other in this century to work for the indigenization of the Chinese Church. To propose that the Latin liturgy should be replaced by a Chinese liturgy, and to bring this proposal to completion, required courage and skill in the Roman Catholic Church of this time. But Lebbe was equipped with both of these qualities. He even went so far as to express his regret that the foundations of the Chinese Church had been laid by missionaries using the Latin rite. The soul of China would be reached more easily by an Oriental rite, he felt. A skilled musician himself, he did his best to introduce Chinese settings for the central parts of the Mass. It was thanks to Lebbe that Chinese bishops were appointed at a relatively early stage.

Ricci and Lebbe were not the only Christians whose dearest wish was to reach the wise men of the Far East with the Word of the Gospel. This is, as we have seen, one essential element of the missionary Church in all areas and in all generations. One of those who recognized this central fact was the Norwegian, Karl Ludvig Reichelt (d. 1952). He considered that the Gospel would only be brought to the wise men of the East by representatives of their own class. He therefore attempted to come into contact with Buddhist monks and scholars, to make Christ known to them, and to make these into Christian witnesses. From his earliest days in China he was therefore an energetic student of the scriptures and worship of Confucianism and Buddhism. In his own words, what he wanted was "to see the milieu from the inside". And he succeeded, in hundreds of Buddhist monasteries all over the East. These provided the measure of insight he desired, but they kept him constantly on the move.

We may quote a few lines from Reichelt's biography:

"He enjoyed himself exceedingly on the way up the Yangtse on a fine river-steamer, but he was also happy in an open Chinese boat, or even on a raft. He travelled on horseback or on a donkey. He set out on an overloaded lorry, or sat on the luggage in the last coach of a crowded train. A swaying palanquin or a rickshaw were excellent, but he could manage on a creaking cart. And sometimes he walked, when he had to, but he found it hard to walk long distances, particularly in later years.

Reichelt loved to climb, and when he reached the pilgrims' mountains, he would not be satisfied until he had reached the top. Sometimes he had to be pulled and pushed up steep slopes, but he always got there.

The object of these journeys was first and foremost to bring the Gospel to the world of the monasteries and the monks. When he set out, he was always well-equipped with books, New Testaments, Bible portions and tracts. He was never so happy as when he could place a New Testament in the hands of a monk seeking enlightenment or a wandering lama."[1]

Reichelt's task was that of making known the eternal omnipresent and glorified Christ, the cosmic Christ, to the wise men of the Far East, and to arouse a sense of responsibility for Christian missions among converted Buddhists. Reichelt called his own missionary method "Johannine". The wise men of the East have always been fascinated by the Prologue of the Fourth Gospel, and Reichelt believed that the Logos of the Gospel and the Tao of China were comparable. The Johannine theology had the further important aspect that it stressed the Logos as the light shining everywhere in the world's darkness, in all cultures and in all religions. Rays of the true light have shone here and there, the world over; God has never left Himself without a witness, and everywhere man's longing for fellowship has been aroused.

Eastern religion often uses the symbol of the lotus to represent this longing. Reichelt brought together the symbol of the work of the Logos in arousing and preparing men's hearts and minds, and the Cross, the symbol that the Logos has become man, and has made atonement. "The cross has been planted in the lotus," as a sign that the

[1] N. N. Thelle, *Karl Ludvig Reichelt*, Oslo 1954.

288

Logos—the cosmic Christ—has the final answer to man's quest.

Reichelt was always deeply concerned with the problem of translating the Christian message into terms of Far Eastern symbolism, and it is still a concern of the Buddhist Mission which carries on his work. This is to be seen, for example, in the architecture of Tao Fong Shan ("the mountain from which the wind of Christ blows"), the centre of the Buddhist Mission in Hong Kong, built between 1930 and 1937. A similar centre is active in Japan. It is hoped that the following three lines of activity will form the staple of future work: (i) A study centre, with a pilgrim hall for Buddhist monks and a library for research students. (ii) Intensive agriculture work. (iii) A centre for the training of Western missionaries.

Japan. Evangelical Christianity in Japan has been very much influenced by a few outstanding personalities. The exertions of the gifted first generation of missionaries resulted in the setting up of three centres, in Yokohama, Sapporo and Kumamoto. The converts who made up these three groups were young, intelligent and upright members of Samurai families who came to follow "the Way" as a means of serving their country and people. Their ideal was that of Jesus as the Way to a brighter, more beautiful and richer life. They became outstanding laymen in government and university circles. The Yokohama group, originally Presbyterian, favoured a federal interdenominational approach. The Kumamoto group, influenced by American Congregationalism, gathered around J. H. Nisima and the University of Doshisha. Of the Sapporo group the most outstanding personality was Kanzo Utshimura, who was educated in the United States. During his period there he underwent a second experience of conversion, in which he met Christ as Redeemer and Atoner, but experience of a divinity school in the West turned him away from spiritual professionalism.

He returned to Japan in 1888, where he founded a church of laymen without professional revivalist help. His ecclesiology (such as it was), was traditionally Japanese in its outlook on life. "What is our church, and where is it? It is the universe which God has created. Our church has as its roof the vault of heaven, and green fields as its floor. The true church is the Mukyokai (the non-church). Priests and pastors exist only in this world. In heaven there is neither baptism nor communion. Those who have no church in fact have the best church. Mukyokai will some day be the real church, will build the living church."

Utshimura became the leader of the "non-church", Mukyokai. His theology was fundamentalist, and he wrote a large number of Bible commentaries in Japanese, and expounded his views in frequent contributions to the Christian press. Being Japanese, he was also patriotic. "I love two J's," he said, "one is Jesus, the other is Japan." Mukyokai has grown into a purely Japanese movement, particularly among students and other intellectuals, and is said to have about 50,000 adherents. Mukyokai groups assemble at home and in lecture rooms for Bible study and discussion. Emil Brunner, who spent two years in the 1950's as a professor at a Japanese university, shocked the missions and the churches by saying that he believed Mukyokai to have great possibilities for the future, more so than other branches of Japanese Protestantism.

Mukyokai is interesting primarily as an attempt to create a relevant Japanese form of Christianity. It is imperative that such attempts as these should take place. One of the greatest problems facing Japanese Christendom is precisely this problem of the Western stamp of the churches —a problem which has in no way been lessened by the mass influx of Protestant missionaries from the West during the 1950's. There are now some 150 Protestant missions at work in Japan, and this is probably the main reason why the optimism which was felt in many missionary circles after the end of the Second World War has not been fulfilled. Instead the masses have gone to the new religions, rapidly growing syncretistic movements which promise health, happiness and honour.

We have had occasion to point out that Protestant churches in Japan are to be found in the towns and cities. Many missions, following the example of Kagawa, do valuable social work in the cities, but they also work in the country. As a rule Christian groups are only able to reach a certain sector of the middle class; at the same time the Japanese Christian Council, led by the dynamic figure of Professor Masao Takenaka, has attempted to reach the workers in the increasingly industrialized Japan. This seems to have attracted Christian young people, and the Japanese Church is a young people's church, 60–70 per cent of church members being young people who are often strikingly active in local church work. The Christian Church has been able to make an outstanding contribution by its girls' schools and by its efforts to raise the social and cultural level of women. Church work in the country is nowadays stimulated by village and district institutes.

The level of literacy in Japan is one of the highest in the world, and it is imperative that Christian literature should maintain the highest possible standards. In 1956 the Bible was published in Kogotai (the Japanese vernacular) for the first time, and thereby opening new avenues of evangelization. More than 2,000,000 Bibles and portions of Scripture are distributed annually. Japanese intellectuals are extremely interested in Western theology, and a number of theological journals are published. Modern existentialism has its faithful advocates in Japan; Kierkegaard's writings are translated and discussed, and the theology of Karl Barth is read and debated, both in the original language and in Japanese. It may be that an original Japanese theology will grow out of these encounters. Hitherto, however, Japan's Christ has seemed rather to be a power capable of solving the problem of "principalities and powers", rather than the one who saves from the guilt and power of sin. Japan finds it easier to accept the mystical interpretation of Christ than the moral. Japan may look to the West, but it belongs to Asia.

In Part Two of this present work we mentioned the Kirishitan groups on the south island of Japan, who, with their silent and secret witness, provided eloquent evidence that traditional faith had power to survive in Japan under the most difficult conditions. In recent years, the Roman Catholic missions have spent much time and energy in studying the religion, culture and languages of Japan. The Frenchmen, Aimé Villon and Henri Dumoulin, S. J., have made valuable contributions to the study of Japanese religious history and folklore. A number of Catholic university centres have been built since the Second World War, and the Church has been especially successful in its attempts to make use of the mass media, the Press, radio and films. Modern Roman Catholic architecture attempts to design the liturgical room on a basis of its function as the home of the Christian mysteries, and at the same time in forms that the Japanese regards as natural. In 1958 a new ritual was published in Japanese, which includes a number of special services to be held in connexion with traditional Japanese customs, such as the funeral service.

Korea. The Christian Church often has to fight an uneven battle against the great religions of Asia, a tiny minority in the midst of a mighty population. Korea is the exception. Here for the first time we find a Christian mass movement in the context of one of Asia's higher religions. The mass movement took place in two distinct periods, the first at the beginning of the twentieth century, and the second during and after the Second World War.

A number of the principles formulated in Chinese missions were applied in Korea, where they gave fruitful impulses. In 1885 an American Presbyterian, Dr. John L. Nevius of Shantung, laid down a programme for the foundation and development of missionary churches. In

Seoul on a short visit in 1890, he expounded his plan, and this, the "Nevius plan" came in time to be one of the most important factors in the dynamic development of the Korean Church. It was built on two inter-related principles, systematic study of the Bible and economic independence.

The Korean Church became a great Bible church: John R. Mott once said that if some catastrophe were to result in the destruction of all the Bibles in Christendom, it would still be possible to reconstruct the Bible from the memories of a few Korean Christians. The Presbyterian and Methodist churches which make up the greater part of the Evangelical Christian community of Korea held intensive Bible-study courses. And there was a great demand, a great spiritual longing and hunger. People would walk eighty miles in order to take part in a Bible-study course, and there was no question about their willingness to pay for their food and lodging during the course. Each course included an intensive programme of worship; the study of the Bible; evangelization among the non-Christians of the district; and revival meetings.

Women came to play a prominent part in this pattern. The Bible courses of the Nevius plan were an important factor in securing the emancipation of the Korean woman from her hitherto despised and ignored situation. For example, Dr. Helen Kim, head of the Ehwa college, has played an important role in the ecumenical missionary movement. Lay volunteers were trained as group leaders and Bible women.

In 1917 there were begun correspondence courses in Bible study, in which students extended their knowledge of the Scriptures by means of continuous written examinations, containing between one and two thousand questions. One of the most important goals of ministerial training is to ensure that the future minister is able to lead others in Bible study.

The second principle of the Nevius plan was that of self-support. The Church in Korea practises tithing, a principle which has shown itself capable in all situations of leading to the dynamic development of any church.

The Christian mass movement in South Korea grew during and after the Second World War, and it is now estimated that there are about $2\frac{1}{2}$ million Protestant Christians in Korea. There are two factors, apart from the prominent role of the laity, which may be advanced in explanation of this movement. First, there is the fact that the ancient national culture has disintegrated, and that Koreans are looking for a new and firm ground on which to stand. And secondly, during the period of Japanese occupation, Protestantism became identified with Korean nationalism, which was a great help to its popularity.

The main form of Protestantism in Korea is Presbyterian. All Evangelical Christianity in Korea is influenced by Presbyterianism. The Presbyterian Church in Korea now has about two million members, and there are more Presbyterian churches in Taikyn than in Edinburgh (there are about 100 churches in Seoul and Taikyn).

At the same time it must be pointed out that Protestantism in Korea is at present passing through a period of crisis. Fundamentalism has given rise to tensions and schismatic tendencies, both in the Presbyterian and Methodist churches. The task of integrating Christianity into present-day Korean culture has had to be postponed for the present. However, it is hoped that this essential task will not have to wait too long. Many of the leaders of the church are fully conscious of the exceptional possibilities, and the exceptional risks, of the present situation.

IV. LATIN AMERICA

The situation of the Church in Latin America is a complete missionary problem in its own right, both for the Roman Catholic and Evangelical Churches. Here we can do no more than make some few pertinent observations on this mighty continent, with its twenty countries and its expanding population (200,000,000 in 1960).

Latin America was long considered to be the greatest of the Catholic continents. The influence of Rome on the people of South America was regarded as being so powerful that the international Protestant missionary movement was for many years dubious as to the wisdom and propriety of counting South America as a mission land. This attitude was shared, though for different reasons, by the Roman Catholic Church. But times, and opinions, have changed. An American priest, Father J. J. Considine, has written a book, *Call for Forty Thousand* (1946), which is a call to young people in North America and Europe to come to Latin America as Roman Catholic priests. This book draws attention to the greatest difficulty at present facing the Roman Church in South America, the shortage of priests. The reason for this is to be sought partly in the historical development of South America following the *padroado* decision, which made of it an Iberian province or colony. Spain and Portugal sent their own priests there, but neglected to train native leaders and priests. The fall of the Society of Jesus was a further catastrophe for the Roman Catholic Church in South America—a catastrophe the effects of which were still being felt at the beginning of the present century.

Today the authorities are ready to admit that what was once the greatest of Catholic continents is now Catholic in name only. The Latin American convocation published in 1958 a brutally realistic statistical statement, showing that only 3.5 per cent of the men and 9.5 per cent of the women were practising Catholics. It is now accepted that Latin America is in need of missionary concern, though there is a certain hesitancy in saying so, since Latin American opinion is sensitive on such points. The South American is shocked to learn that European Catholic priests before leaving for the field in Latin America, are given a "missionary cross".

The rapid growth of the Protestant churches has been another difficult problem for the Roman Catholics. Pope Pius XII reckoned Protestantism as one of the four "deadly dangers" threatening Latin America (the three others were secularism, Marxism and spiritualism). It took time for Protestantism to become an effective factor in Latin America; not until recent decades has this in fact happened. The number of Evangelical Christians in the whole of the Latin America, which was no more than a million in 1900, had risen to 8 millions by 1960, while Evangelical Christians in Brazil, who were some 702,000 in number in 1930, had by 1960 grown to 2,500,000. The World Missionary Conference in Edinburgh in 1910 refused to regard this area as a mission-field, and to discuss its problems, but a group of those who were particularly interested held a private consultation immediately after the Edinburgh conference. The first great evangelical conference on Latin America was held in 1916, this work being later incorporated into the International Missionary Council, particularly at and after the Jerusalem conference of 1928. Latin America now occupies an important position in the World Council of Churches.

The most dramatically rapid developments have taken part in Brazil, where the Pentecostal movement plays an important role. The Presbyterians also occupy a strong position. Lutheran emigrant churches have also made a contribution, particularly since the Second World War, and the Lutheran World Federation has shown close interest in developments there.

At present there are about sixty North American and more than twenty European missionary societies at work in Latin America. Some are connected with the Lutheran churches, and many with the Pentecostal movement. And the work has not been fruitless. It is estimated that there are now about half a million Lutherans and about three-quarters of a million Pentecostals in Latin America. Some of the factors in favour of Protestant missions in South

America are the courageous fight put up by the Evangelical Churches in the Catholic milieu, their democratic organization, in which the layman has a voice, the liveliness and sincerity of Protestant worship, prayers and sermons in Spanish and Portuguese, and particularly the theme of personal conversion. Earlier doubt as to whether Latin America was to be regarded as a missionary country has now given place to the realization that the rapidly growing countries of Latin America now provide a missionary challenge of the first order.

CHAPTER 13

PROSELYTISM AND WITNESS

THE CHRISTIAN CHURCH HAS TO BEAR ITS WITNESS IN many and varied milieus. But as the shadow follows the wanderer, so the missionary Church is followed by the problem of proselytism. "Proselytism" is now a term of disparagement and reproach, though in the New Testament it had not come to have its present negative overtones. In the NT "proselyte" meant "newcomer"; now "proselytism" means either persuading a person to become a member of a church or denomination simply in order to have one more name "on the books", or stealing church members from other Christian denominations. Leslie Newbigin's definition is "a promotional programme to get people on to our side". One tends to assume that this is a reprehensible practice carried on by other churches—never one's own; in reality, however, it makes its presence felt in very many areas, and has come to the attention of the World Council of Churches as a separate and distinct problem. A world council numbering some two hundred churches cannot avoid taking a stand on this question. There are two points at issue, or rather two duties, both of which must be fulfilled, and between which there is considerable tension—the duty of bearing witness to the truth and the duty of showing love and consideration for the ecumenical fellowship.

The question came up at an early stage of ecumenical discussion. In 1920, when the Lambeth Conference sent out its "appeal to all Christians"—an offer which was a great stimulus to ecumenical discussion at that time—the

Ecumenical Patriarchate in Constantinople issued an encyclical expressing its readiness to further the cause of ecumenical fellowship, but at the same time urging that all proselytism should cease. It was not by chance that this appeal came from the Orthodox Church. During the "great century" Evangelical missionaries could not help penetrating into Orthodox areas, particularly in the Middle East; we have already pointed out that most of the members of the Evangelical Church in Egypt come, not from Islam, but from the Coptic Church.

We cannot in this context offer to discuss this problem as a whole; but it will help if we consider some examples of this problem in Asia and Africa.

South India: the Syrian Church and the Anglicans

The leaders of the Evangelical revival in England—or such of them as happened to be on the committee of the CMS—were eager that the winds of revival should blow on still more distant shores; but they were also concerned with the situation nearer home. In 1818 they declared that they ought to try and re-awaken and propagate Christianity, both in the Roman Catholic Church in Italy, and in the "rationalist" Churches of Germany, Switzerland and Holland. They also turned their eyes on the Eastern Churches, which ought, they felt, to be instruments of mission among Muslims and pagans, but which had instead come to be "a positive hindrance" to the work of evangelization. However, when the time came to send out the first missionaries to work in these areas, the leaders of the Society issued a warning against proselytism: for instance, should any member of the Syrian Church in South India wish to become a member of the Church of England, they felt that it would be inadvisable to allow it: "The Syrians should be brought back to their own ancient and primitive worship and discipline, rather than be induced to adopt the liturgy and discipline of the English Church; and should any considerations induce them to wish such a measure, it would be highly expedient to dissuade them from adopting it, both for the preservation of their individuality and entireness, and greater consequent weight and usefulness as a Church; and to prevent those jealousies and heart-burnings which would in all probability hereafter arise."

The first of these Evangelical Anglican missionaries for many years celebrated the Eucharist in Syrian churches, trained Indian ministers for the Syrian Church, worked on the translation of the Bible and helped spread Christian literature. Daniel Wilson, Bishop of Calcutta (1832–58), had excellent contacts with the Syrian Metropolitan, particularly with Mar Athanasius, who had studied theology in the Anglican Kottayam College, and was anxious that reforms should take place. But Mar Athanasius was bitterly opposed by his own bishops and laymen. On one occasion, when one of his priests took it upon himself to preach in Malayalam, a language which everyone understood, instead of Syriac, which no one understood, the entire congregation walked out! Athanasius was also opposed by the Jacobite patriarch in Syria.

This was typical of the petrefaction, the self-sufficiency and the fear of reform which characterized the venerable Syrian Church at that time. A new generation of leaders who had encountered Evangelical faith and theology found that their appeals for a programme of evangelization and mission fell upon deaf ears. They soon felt that they no longer had any place in the Church of their fathers. In 1851 six priests of the Syrian tradition were ordained by the Bishop of Madras. By 1875 the Anglican group had grown to 15,000 members, many of whom came from among the outcastes, but whose priests had nearly all come from the Syrian Church. This development was hastened by a powerful revival movement which began in 1875, and culminated in 1879 in the founding of a special Anglican Diocese of Travancore, with a bishop in Kottayam. At the same time a reformed Syrian Church was founded, calling itself the Mar Thoma Church (see above, p. 243).

In the present century Anglican missionaries of the SPG have been in contact with the Syrian Church, while Evangelicals have been closer to the reformed Mar Thoma group. When the Church of South India was founded in 1947, the Anglican bishop, C. K. Jacob, who as his name indicates came of an old Syrian family, was responsible for consecrating the new bishops.

Ethiopia

A situation similar to that in Travancore has arisen in Ethiopia, where the field was shared by two Swedish missions, the Evangelical National Missionary Society (*Evangeliska Fosterlands-Stiftelsen*) and the Bible Friends' Mission (*Bibetrogna Vänner*). The ENMS wanted to reach the pagan Gallas in the south of the country, but first had to work in the port of Massaua, the capital Addis Ababa, and in northern Ethiopia, where relations with the Coptic Church were a perennial problem. The Swedish missionaries tried as far as possible to make contact with the Ethiopians' own Church; vernacular Bible-study and direct evangelistic preaching led in time to the founding of a small Evangelical group; but it also led to bitter opposition and persecution from the side of the Ethiopian priests. One of their number, Heilab, who had joined the Evangelicals, was murdered together with a Swedish missionary, Per Eric Lager, in 1876. A highly educated priest, Tajelenj, was seized and put in prison. To have contacts with the Protestants was held by the Ethiopian Church to be a breach of loyalty; the Copts refused even to bury their own people if they had had such contacts; others were refused marriage in Coptic churches. Finally there was nothing for it but to found an Evangelical Church. In 1959 there was therefore set up an Evangelical Lutheran Church under the name "Mekane Jesus Church"; the first Ethiopian ministers had been ordained in 1952. Two Coptic priests had previously become Evangelical Lutherans, the validity of their ordination being recognized in the Evangelical Church. There have recently been signs of renewal in the Coptic Church, not least in the areas of ministerial training and ecumenical contact, and these are being watched closely by the Evangelical Church.

Uganda

Since the Orthodox Church has found it necessary to protest against alleged Protestant "proselytism", it may be of interest to point out briefly that there has recently taken place in Uganda an interesting encounter, in itself an encouraging instance of increased missionary awareness on the part of the Greek Orthodox Church. Since the early 1880's there have been in Uganda two more or less equally large Churches, the Roman Catholic and the Anglican (Evangelical). Alongside these there has grown up a spontaneous African group, the African Orthodox Church, connected originally with the separatist religious groups in Southern Africa. This movement in Uganda, for a variety of reasons, sought affiliation with the Greek Orthodox Church. Most of the priests whom the latter Church is now educating have been members of the Anglican Church.

But the problem is far from having been exhausted when these and similar instances have been examined. Its commonest form in the twentieth century world of mission is to be seen in the relations between missionary churches in Asia and Africa. The international missionary movement, supported by local Christian councils, had, as we have seen, tried to apply the principle of comity—that is, that each mission was allocated its own territory, within which it was responsible for evangelization, schools, hospitals and the like. This arrangement worked well enough, in Southern Rhodesia for example, so long as the Ndebele kept to their own tribal area, and the Shona tribe to theirs. But what happened was that industrialization and urbanization, together with improved communications, brought about a rapid and extensive migration from the country to a few urban centres. Naturally enough, the mission felt that it ought to follow its people to the mine and the city, whereupon it came and built a church in someone else's territory. The next step came, sometimes gradually, sometimes at once: deliberate fishing in forbidden waters, resulting in defection from one Evangelical church to another. It is not uncommon to meet with examples of energetic proselytism, not least on the part of certain fundamentalist groups. Questions such as the theory and practice of baptism, the keeping of the Sabbath, the sinfulness or otherwise of smoking, the translation of some or other passage of Scripture, become the cause of—or are made the excuse for—annexation in the name of Jesus of individuals and groups.

Should both parties be members of some international organization, such as the World Council of Churches, it is clearly necessary to try and find a way out of the dilemma of conflicting loyalties, to what is felt to be the truth on one hand, and to wider church interests on the other—within the framework of that organization. In 1961 the World Council of Churches made a statement stressing the essential difference between witness and proselytism: "It is the essential task and responsibility of every Christian and every Church to bear witness. The purpose of witness is to persuade people to accept Christ as Lord and to serve Him in the fellowship of His Church." Proselytism is not altogether different from witness; it is a caricature of witness, an expression of individual or group hunger for prestige and power, not an attempt to give glory to the Lord Jesus Christ.

The missionary obligation of the Church means that every denomination must bear its witness, openly and freely, wholly and fearlessly, and do its best to win adherents to the divinely revealed Truth. Witness is an essential part of the office and ministry of the Church.

Witness is not merely something which is directed towards non-Christians; it is equally relevant for those who are no longer in the living fellowship of any Christian church. Should malpractices in a church lead to the distortion or obscuring of central truths of the Gospel, with the result that men's salvation is hazarded, then other churches may feel themselves compelled to intervene, and bear witness to the lost truth. This is an elementary right, which must be maintained. But before a rival church is set up, those concerned must consider deeply, whether there may not be signs of hope in the other church, and whether better results may not be achieved by means of free discussion and co-operation.

Membership of the World Council of Churches compels no Church to suppress, restrict or alter its full confession of the truth, and thereby become crippled. The Council has no wish to have crippled churches as its members, but rather genuine, active churches. At the same time membership of the World Council of Churches implies that one member church has no right to deny another member church the full right to call itself a church.

Our Lord Himself uttered a serious warning to those scribes and Pharisees and hypocrites who "traverse sea and land to make a single proselyte", Matt. 23: 15. Not proselytism but witness! His messengers are sent to bear witness, not to make proselytes. The Risen Lord said, "You shall be my witnesses in Jerusalem and in all Judea and Samaria and to the end of the earth" Acts 1: 8.

EPILOGUE

THE MISSION OF THE CHURCH

WE HAVE CALLED THIS BOOK "THE WORLD OF MIS-
sion". Mission—a dull word, say some; it conjures
up a picture of drawing-room prayer meetings and Vic-
toriana. A challenging word, say others; it reminds us of
imperialism and conversion by force. In fact neither
"mission" nor "missionary" are particularly complimen-
tary terms just now—if they ever have been!

This matters little to the Christian mission. The only
really important thing is the commission which the Lord
of the Church has given, once and for all. That commission was prepared in the Old Testament. It was first given
when Abraham went forth from the land of his fathers.
Since then the people of God have always been on the
march, toward a goal which has been set by Christ the
King. In the New Testament we see mission as the enthronement of Christ the King in the world, until the day
on which He returns in glory to claim His Kingdom. His
Church is sent into the world, to the ends of the earth and
to the end of time, conscious that it is this commission
which, together with her worship, provides her *raison
d'être* in the world. These two elements—worship and embassy; Eucharist and mission—belong together. They are
in fact two aspects of the same thing. The history of salvation which we have seen depicted in the Bible, and which
forms the essence of the biblical doctrine of mission, lies
behind each and every manifestation of the missionary
church in the world—in West and East alike. Missionaries
in Hong Kong, Honduras, Halifax and Houston are all

alike ambassadors, members of the great embassy which has been sent out into the whole world—and which was decreed by God before all worlds.

The study of the Christian mission presses upon us a question: what is the nature of that power which is able so to attract men and women that they are prepared to take the extraordinary step of abandoning the faith of their fathers and the acknowledged religious practices of their people and join the company of the White Christ? It is not something self-evident; nor can it be put down to the pressure of environment; it is least of all natural for a man to leave the known and the familiar and take the step out into the uncertainty of a new faith. It is a surprising, indeed, a paradoxical step to take.

One answer would be to point to the power of mercy— mercy shown to people in sickness, in prison, in loneliness and in distress. The same power is revealed in the new life and the new death: the new life in a fellowship sealed by love and forgiveness; the new way of meeting the terrible reality of death, no longer in fear and sorrow, but in hope and confidence and with singing. It is on this level—the profound level of man's ultimate questions concerning the meaning of life, suffering and distress—that the Word and the Sacraments of the Christian community seem able to awaken a real response.

We are thus bound to take full account of the reasons given by converts themselves as to why this important step was taken. We have touched upon others in the course of our account. But it must be recognized that we cannot give a final and categorical explanation of what it is that has taken place. Above and beyond these factors there is something more: factor X. The Church, remembering what the Scripture says ("No one can come to me unless the Father who sent me draws him," John 6: 44), speaks of "prevenient grace" and "the drawing of the Father". The interpretation of this fact has varied in the history of theology, but the fact itself remains: that the Holy Spirit of

God is at work, preparing the hearts of men, calling them and gathering them out of every nation and tribe and tongue into the Church of Jesus Christ. From that vision and that conviction the Church and the individual derive confidence when they hear the call:

Go from your country and your kindred and your father's house to the land that I will show you. And I will make of you a great nation, and I will bless you; and make your name great, so that you will be a blessing. (Gen. 12: 1–2)

INDEX

Harms, L., 114
von Harnack, A., 22 f.
Harrison, P. W., 225
Hartenstein, K., 54
Hastings, Warren, 111
Hauer, W., 256
Haya Church, 188, 210
Haya people, 184 ff.
Hellenism, 25, 30, 69, 74 f.
Hermannsburg Mission, 115
Herrnhutism, 33
Herzl, T., 33
High gods, 185 f.
Hinduism, 46 ff., 74, 107 f., 111, 124, 162, 203, 234 ff., 262 ff., 277
Hocart, A., 184
Hocking, W. E., 52
Hoffman, B., 140
Hogg, A. G., 252
Hollis, A. M., 273
Holst, M., 227
Holsten, W., 54
Hong Kong, 56, 66, 134, 289
Honolulu, 66
Hooper, J. S. M., 273
Hsianfu Stone, 90
Huddleston, T., 155
Hung Siu-ch'üan, 135 f.
Hurley, J. P., 155
Hyderabad, 257, 263

Ibadan, 229
Ibo people, 169
Ignatius of Antioch, 71
Illyricum, 27 f.
Imperialism, 61, 94 ff., 120 ff., 144, 264
India, 55, 64 f., 74, 99, 106 ff., 120 ff., 123 f., 144, 162, 169, 174, 184, 201 ff., 234 ff.
Indian National Congress, 122
Indigenization, 40 ff., 60 f., 206 ff., 264 ff., 268 ff., 287
Indonesia, 55, 66, 102, 123, 130, 162, 184, 189, 212
Industrialization, 178 f.
Industrial missions, 177 ff.
Initiation rites, 196

Institute for the Study of Religion and Society, 179
Interdenominational societies, 137
International Missionary Council, 33, 43, 56, 168, 173, 177 f., 230, 276, 296
Iran, 66
Irenaeus, 78
Isaiah, 13 ff., 18 f.
Isis, 69
Islam, 46 ff., 75 f., 90, 218 ff.
Israel, 12 f., 14 f., 24 f., 27, 32 ff.

Jacob, C. K., 274, 301
Jacobite Church, 221, 243
Jainism, 242
Japan, 99 f., 120 ff., 130 ff., 141 ff., 278 ff., 289 ff.
Java, 174, 232
Jehovah's Witnesses, 168
Jensen, A. E., 184
Jerusalem, 15, 19, 21, 25 ff., 28 f., 33, 58, 226
Jerusalem Conference 1928, 52, 177, 225, 296
Jerusalem, Council of, 26
Jerusalem, Temple at, 15, 19
Jesuits, 98, 104, 129, 200, 251, 266, 284 ff., 295
Jews, Missions to, 26 f., 32 ff.
Job, G. V., 52
John of Monte Corvino, 91 f.
Johannesburg, 45, 177
Johanon Mar Thoma, 243
Johnson, Lyndon B., 156
Jonah, 12
Jones, E. Stanley, 268
Jubbulpore, 246
Judaism, 32 ff., 49
Judson, A., 201 f.
Julian the Apostate, 78 f.
Justification by Faith Church, 139
Justin Martyr, 76 f.

Kachin people, 204
Kagawa, T., 142, 291
Kähler, M., 22
Karen Church, 66
Karen people, 202, 204

313

316

317

Three Self programme, 41 f., 140 f., 247
Thunberg, Anne-Marie, 175
Tibet, 203
Tien, Cardinal, 140
Tilak, N. W., 254 f., 269
T'ing, K. H., 282
Tiridates, King of Armenia, 73
Tiruchirapalli, 108, 267
Tirunelveli, 123, 264, 271
Tiruputtur Ashram, 256, 267
Togo, 126, 130
Tokyo, 56, 142 f., 278 f.
Tokyo Conference 1907, 141
Tolstoy, L., 240
Toradja people, 193
Torah, 26
Tractarianism, 114
Tranquebar, 105 ff.
Translation, Problems of, 12, 56 ff., 74 f., 134, 169, 171 ff., 191, 284 ff.
Transvaal, 153, 201
Travancore, 74, 100, 123, 251
Tribal culture, 188 ff.
Trimingham, J. S., 229 f.
Troeltsch, E., 52
Tuaregs, 222 ff.
Tucker, A., 198

Uganda, 65, 125, 198, 302
U Kyaw Than, 276
UNESCO, 123, 164, 166
Universities' Mission to Central Africa, 114, 119, 125, 152, 195
Unne, 83
Urbanization, 177, 303
Usambara, 201
Usselinx, W., 102
Utshimura, K., 142, 289 f.

Valignano, A., 284
Vasco da Gama, 94
Venn, H., 41 f., 247
Verbiest, F., 284
Vicedom, G. F., 207, 260
Victoria, Queen, 94
Victor, Bishop of Rome, 76
Villon, A., 292
Vivekananda, Swami, 237 ff.

Ward, W., 111, 172
Warneck, G., 22, 41, 162, 193
Warneck, J., 29
Weber, H. R., 55, 206
Wei, F., 283
Weiss, J., 22
Weizmann, C., 33
von Welz, J., 104
Weman, H., 213 ff.
Wesley, John, 105, 149
West African languages, 169
Westcott, B. F., 49, 278
Westermann, D., 172
Weston, F., 127
Whitby Conference 1947, 38, 43, 139, 145
White Fathers, 125
Whitehead, H., 247 f.
Wilberforce, W., 149
Wilfrid, Archbishop of York, 83
Williams, J., 119
Willingen Conference 1952, 43
Wilson, D., 300
Wilson J., 251
Winslow, J., 256
World Council of Churches, 44, 56, 168, 276, 296, 298, 303 f.
World's Parliament of Religions, Chicago 1893, 238
Wynfrith, 84

Xavier, Francis, 99 ff., 245

Yao people, 196
Yemen, 74
Yen, J., 164
Yokohama, 289
Young Men's Christian Association, 66, 168, 256

Zahn, M., 209
Zanzibar, 127, 152
Zechariah, 16
Ziegenbalg, B., 107
von Zinzendorf, N. L., 105, 109
Zion, D., 34
Zionism, 33
Zion, Mount, 15 f., 19
Zululand, 214
Zwemer, S., 218 f., 226

318